Brand Posi

Strategies for Competitive Advantage

Second Edition

Brand Positioning:

Strategies for Competitive Advantage

Second Edition

Subroto Sengupta (Late)
Former Visiting Faculty
Indian Institute of Management, Calcutta

Tata McGraw-Hill Publishing Company Limited
NEW DELHI

McGraw-Hill Offices
New Delhi New York St Louis San Francisco Auckland Bogotá Caracas
Kuala Lumpur Lisbon London Madrid Mexico City Milan Montreal
San Juan Santiago Singapore Sydney Tokyo Toronto

Tata McGraw-Hill

ISBN-13: 978-0-07-058159-3
ISBN-10: 0-07-058159-2

Published by the Tata McGraw-Hill Publishing Company Limited,
7 West Patel Nagar, New Delhi 110 008, typeset in Garamond at Script Makers, 19, A1-B, DDA Market, Pashchim Vihar, New Delhi 110 063 and text and cover printed at Rashtriya Printers, M-135, Panchsheel Garden, Naveen Shahdara Delhi 110 032

Cover design: Kapil Gupta

To,
Kanika, Bobby, Nandini
Monisha and Maya

From the Publisher's Desk

Among the several large names in the advertising world, Subroto Sengupta's is assuredly of iconic status. His enormously successful and popular book *Brand Positioning* was progressing into its second edition, when the author expired. The Publishers have since taken the book to its conclusion, confident that his active involvement over the greater part of this project validated its publication.

No effort has been spared to ensure that this book is free of errors. To this end, we are grateful for the invaluable aid provided by Mr M.G. Parameswaran, Executive Director, FCB-Ulka Advertising Ltd., in reading the proofs and suggesting corrections. Furthermore, full endeavours have been made to contact the copyright holders of all advertisements and extracts presented here from published literature; any omissions are regretted.

We dedicate this book to the memory of our author Subroto Sengupta in the certainty that our readers will find much to appreciate and value in this posthumously published edition of his work.

Preface to the First Edition

In the early fifties when I began my life in advertising in DJ Keymer, now Oglivy & Mather, the positioning era had not yet dawned. That was the age of 'Art in Industry' when major advertisers like Dunlop and Burmah Shell were more concerned with 'aesthetic creativity' than the compulsions of selling.

Even in the mid-sixties we in India had not heard of positioning. But competition was rearing its head and some of us were groping with ideas like, for instance, 'distancing' Strepsils from Vicks cough drops; of 'placing' it at the more serious end of the 'less serious' to 'more serious' continuum of sore-throat remedies. By 1970 we had seen the light and were boldly positioning Farex for infants of 3 months as "baby's first solid food for all round growth".

Right from those early days and up to 1988 when I played some part in the 'Golden Rendezvous' mission (see Chapter 6), the examples and cases of which I write are those that I have lived with or drawn from the rich experience of fellow professionals.

Many of my lessons in positioning have been learnt in the real world of marketing and advertising action from clients who were fair, very professional and very, very demanding. It was under such result-demanding tension that a highly successful positioning idea for Milkmaid was discovered. Many ideas about positioning emerged from the cut and thrust of debate with my former colleagues in Clarion. Like, for instance, the idea of Cadbury's corporate positioning, expressed in the line—'Making India the cocoa country'. And much of what I write has been learnt from striking campaigns and strategies of other advertising agencies.

How do you enhance the sales of a glycerine soap traditionally used only in winter? By locking it in the consumer's head with the idea of a complexion that never grows old. I am full of admiration when I think of this positioning idea for Pears even though 20 years have gone by. Can anyone take away that position from the cousumer's mind even if he makes a 'better' glycerine soap?

I acknowledge my debt to Al Ries and Jack Trout for their writings on positioning which first stimulated my interest in this new way of looking at consumers, at brands and their advertising. A summer spent in Boston and a rewarding stint at the Baker Library of the Harvard Business School, further whetted my interest and the urge to write on this promising subject, firmly anchored in the realities of Indian marketing and advertising. I warmly acknowledge the contribution of other authors to my ideas, notably Professors Aaker, Wind, Green, Urban, Hauser and Dholakia.

I owe a special word of thanks to Professor Stephen Greyser of the Harvard Business School, who wrote the Foreword to my earlier book, and who took the trouble to offer many valuable suggestions, comments and leads on the outline of this book when I discussed it with him in the summer of 1988. He urged me, for instance, to look up the case of "the happy pickle" to which I refer in Chapter 2 and which provided me with both entertainment and instruction.

Professor Raymond Corey, also of the Harvard Business School and my former teacher, and Professor George S Day of the University of Toronto, as well, offered helpful suggestions and comments. Professor Jaya Sen of Concordia University in Montreal has been an invaluable resource in making a computer search of relevant literature and obtaining references not available in India.

I have been touched by the readiness with which the heads and senior executives of various advertising agencies and former clients have sent me the advertisements that are reproduced in this book. And I am infinitely grateful to those agencies which have contributed, for publication in this book, their views on positioning.

My publishers, Tata McGraw-Hill, have given me a great deal of encouragement and support. Mr Ranjan Kaul, in particular, has played the role of a supportive editor, offering many constructive suggestions. Ms Rama Sudhakar Patnaik has taken much care in making the copy ready for printing.

I need hardly add that all errors, howlers and shortcomings in this book should be attributed solely to me.

Mr Sugata Sengupta and Mr Shyamal Dasgupta of ADAGE were good enough to dedicate a part of their computer facilities to have numerous drafts typed and re-typed. Ms Tapati Das Gupta carried out the endless revisions with unfailing patience and willingness.

Subroto Sengupta

Acknowledgements

The author expresses his grateful thanks to the following organizations and individuals for their cooperation and support.

Ananda Bazar Group
 Mr Aveek Sarkar
 Mr C B Sen
Geoffrey Manners & Co. Ltd
 Mr Manoj Maheshwari
 Mr Sanjeev Goyle
Food Specialities Ltd
 Mr D E Ardeshir
Hawkins Cookers Ltd
 Mr Brahm Vasudeva
 Mr B M Rai
Lipton India Ltd
 Mr Hrishi Bhattacharyya
 Mr P Radhakrishnan
Procter & Gamble India Ltd.
 Mr Gurucharan Das
 Mr Khosla
Reckitt & Coleman of India Ltd
 Mr Shyamal Ghosh
 Mr Kaushik Mazumdar
ITC Ltd.
 Mr J Narayan
 Mr Amit Sarkar
 Mr Kamal Ramnath
 Mr S M Ahmad
 Ms Dickoo Nowroji
 Mr K Dasaratharaman
VST Industries Ltd.
 Mr B P Singh

Clarion Advertising
 Mr Amit Sen Gupta
 Mr B N Chakraborty
 Mr Gour Rudra
 Mr Shib Nath Sen
 Mr Ashis Palchaudhuri
 Mr Kuldip Kawatra
Contract Advertising
 Mr Subhas Ghosal
DaCunha Associates
 Mr Sylvester Da Cunha
Enterprise Advertising
 Mr Mohammed Khan
 Mr M Raghunath
Everest Advertising
 Mr Ahmed Ibrahim
Hindustan Thompson Associates
 Mr M K Khanna
 Mrs Indrani Sen
Interpub
 Mrs Nargis Wadia
Lintas, India
 Mr Alyque Padamsee
 Mr Sumit Roy
 Mr Fazl Ahmed
Marg
 Mr Titoo Ahluwalia
 Dr Meena Kaushik
 Mr Ashok Das

Oglivy & Mather
Mr S R Ayer
Mr Suresh Mullick
Mr Angshu Banerjee
(since retired)

Rediffusion
Dr Ashoke Bijapurkar
Mr Romit Chaterji

Response
Mr Ram Ray

R K Swamy Advertising Associates
Mr R K Swamy
Mr Shekar Swamy

Trikcya Grey
Mr Ravi Gupta

and

Prof. Ashok Pratap Arora, Indian Institute of Management, Calcutta
Prof. Nalin Bhatt, Washington
Prof. Amitabha Chattopadhyaya, McGill University
Prof. Nikhilesh Dholakia, University of Rhode Island
Mr A N Dutta, D P S India
Mr D P Ghosh, formerly of Clarion
Mr Manab Sen Gupta, IIMC
Mrs Ilina Adhiraj Sen
Mrs R Seshadri
Mrs Bharati Shroff

Contents

Chapter 1

The Positioning Concept: Definitions and Illustrations

DIFFERENTIATE OR DIE

There is no greater marketing truth in this era of 'killer competition'; in this era of an insane proliferation of brands; in this era of a shock and awe bombardment of advertisements. Marketers have got into a vicious cycle. To counter this clutter of ads they are creating more clutter. As Seth Godin writes in *Brand Equity* of June 4, 2003:

> *Marketers are doing exactly the wrong thing. They're running more ads, they're putting ads on parking meters, in hotel elevators, in washrooms. Because they think that the answer to clutter is more clutter. That's why there's so much spam in your e-mail box. Because marketers are desperate.*

This desperation is also reflected in a *Harvard Business Review* publication (1999). New products are often line extensions of existing brands:

> *The frequency of line extensions is often a better measure of a company's desperation than of its innovativeness.*

Don't harbour the illusion that this is a problem only of the West. Similar reliable statistics may not be available for India but from a study of ORG data, one can infer that we are fast imitating this crazy, unprofitable drive for more, more, and still more me-too brands. After all, brand managers are often judged by the number of new products they have launched.

If we estimate that for a nationally marketed brand a 4 to 5% market share in a category is the cut-off point for a profitable operation, then here is a summary of eight large FMCG categories which will be similar for most of the FMCGs.

Table 1.1

Category	No. of top brands	M.S. Range from 5% to...	No. of brands with M.S. of 1% or less
Premium Soap	7	5.5% to 9.7%	76
Hair Oil	5	5% to 18%	76
Tooth Powder	3	5% to 48%	38
Talcum Powder	3	8% to 38%	128
Balm	5	12% to 18.6%	66
Skin Creams	3	5.4% to 30%	187
Prickly Heat Powder	4	5.3% to 46%	19
Chyavanprash	3	9.3% to 57%	19

(*Source:* ORG)

Question: How do we overcome this gravitation to the bottom? Are these many hundreds of miniscule brands making money for their owners?

The principal author of the book *Differentiate or Die*, Jack Trout, together with Al Ries, earlier wrote in the landmark marketing classic *Positioning: The Battle for Your Mind*:

> *To succeed, the first step is to position or 'situate' the brand in the target consumer's mind in such a way, that in his or her perception of the brand, it is distinctive and offers a persuasive customer value better than its competitors. This is called competitive advantage.*

Business schools in the USA offer 'Advanced Management Programmes' for senior executives. Why is it that some large corporations in India choose to send their executives to MIT rather than Harvard Business School ? Or to Stanford rather than Carnegie Mellon?

Perhaps the joke which follows will give us a clue and also serve as a practical illustration of positioning.

The story concerns two famous institutions of management education—Harvard and MIT. The Harvard Business School is situated on one bank of the river Charles in Massachusetts. On the opposite bank is the nearly-as-famous Massachusetts Institute of Technology, better known as MIT. The perceptions of the public about these two institutions seem to be quite sharply demarcated. Thus Harvard is considered to be more 'qualitative' in its approach to management education; MIT is said to be more mathematical or number-oriented.

On the MIT side of the river is a supermarket popular with the students and faculty of both institutions. On a Saturday morning, as this story goes, a typical 'Professor', with absent-minded looks, receding forehead and leather patches on the elbows of his jacket, was wheeling his trolley through the supermarket. Having loaded it to capacity, he went to a check-out counter above which a bold sign said: "Express checkout for six packets or less."

Seeing the mountainous load on the trolley, the salesperson at the Express counter clapped her hand to her head and exclaimed:

"My goodness! Are you one of the guys from this side of the river who can't read, or one of the guys from the other side who can't count?"

Business School Positioning

On a more serious note, a study was conducted among MBA students to determine their perceptions of different Business Schools in the USA. In their book entitled, *Perspectives in Consumer Behaviour*, Kassarjian and Robertson describe what the researchers found.[1]

Using a rather complex computer methodology, they were able to create a perceptual map of these Business Schools...Harvard and Stanford were perceived as being quite similar to each other, that is, close in perceptual space. On the other hand, Harvard and MIT were perceived as being quite dissimilar (Figure 1.1).

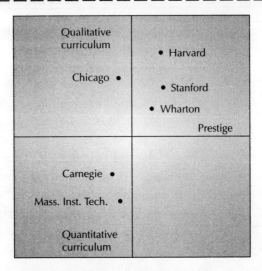

Figure 1.1 *Perceptual map of six Business Schools in the USA (Reproduced with permission from article entitled "Non-Metric Scaling & Methods: An Exposition and Overview" by Profs Paul E Green, Frank J Carmone, and Patrick J Robinson, Wharton Quarterly, Winter–Spring 1968).*

This concept of 'perceptual mapping' and 'perceptual space' is often utilized when seeking to differentiate brands. The advertisement for Sprint soft drink (Exhibit 1.1, Plate 1) very cleverly demarcates this brand from the other more popular flavours of Cola, Lime, and Orange. The layout heightens the perceptual difference by placing Sprint well apart from the others.

It is this concept of perceptual space that forms the theoretical basis for brand positioning. The consumer's mind is regarded as a geometric perceptual space, with product categories and brands occupying different points in that space.

CONSUMER'S PERCEPTUAL SPACE

In marketing terms, there is no such thing as a product or service which exists by itself in space, independent of the consumer. For a product to exist, it must find a place in an individual consumer's perception of the world of products around him or her. And this perception is subjective, governed by the individual consumer's values, beliefs, needs, experience and environment.

> *The cognitive map of the individual is not a photographic representation of the physical world...Every perceiver is, as it were, to some degree a non-representational artist, painting a picture of the world that expresses his individual view of reality.*[2]

This is the core thought behind brand positioning—the idea that each brand (if at all noticed) occupies a particular point or space in the individual consumer's mind, a point which is determined by that consumer's perception of the brand in question and in its relation to other brands.

The spatial distance between the points in that consumer's mind reflects the subject's perception of similarity or dissimilarity between products and brands.

The everyday phrase, 'poles apart', is a simple example of how consumers position products in their mind; for example, an electric shaver versus a cut-throat razor.

In the section entitled 'Product and Brand Positioning' in his book, *Marketing Management*, Prof. Philip Kotler says:

> *Once the core product concept is chosen, it defines the character of the product space in which the new product has to be positioned. An instant breakfast drink means that this product will compete against bacon and eggs, breakfast cereals, coffee and pastry, and other breakfast alternatives...*

Assume that the instant breakfast drink concept is selected. A product positioning map is shown in Figure 1.2 where an instant breakfast drink stands in relation to other breakfast products, using the two dimensions of cost and preparation time. An instant breakfast drink stands in a distinct part of the market...its nearest competitor is cold cereal; its most distant competitor is bacon and eggs.[3]

Similarly, he goes on to say, a brand positioning map can be drawn using the concept of perceptual distance to show the similarity or dissimilarity between several brands of instant breakfast alternatives as perceived by consumers (Figure 1.3).

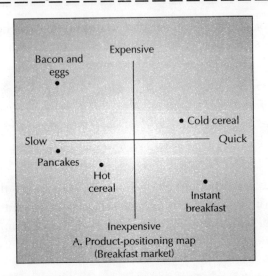

Figure 1.2 *Perceptual map showing the position of an 'instant breakfast' product in relation to other types of breakfast. Reproduced with permission from Marketing Management by Philip Kotler (Prentice-Hall of India, 1983).*

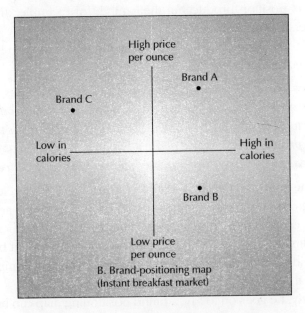

Figure 1.3 *Perceptual map showing the relative position of three instant breakfast brands. Reproduced with permission from Marketing Management by Philip Kotler (Prentice-Hall of India, 1983).*

Only a Few 'Vacancies'

> Positioning, therefore, starts with our understanding or 'mapping' of a prospect consumer's mental perceptions of products.

Figure 1.4 is an artist's impression of a consumer mind. That mind is already cluttered with numerous brand names for various categories. It is as though the consumer has drawn his or her own mental map of his or her various wants and needs and has given different points on that map to different products and brands to satisfy those needs.

A very successful worldwide consumer products company talks of *situating* the brand in the prospect's mind:

> *Today's clutter makes it advisable to give some thought to how best to help the consumer situate the product within her existing frame of reference.*

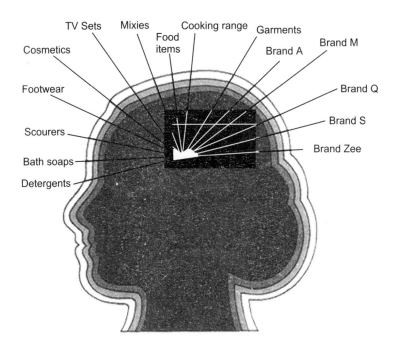

Figure 1.4 *An artist's impression of a consumer mind, its mysterious working represented by the 'black box'. Innumerable products and brands are jostling for a position inside that limited space.*

'Renting' Mind Space

If we carried the analogy of the consumer's mental map further, we can say that the sites or positions on that map are not for outright sale, not even for a 99-year lease! A brand can hope at best to occupy such a position as a tenant, for periods that will vary according to the quality and quantity of marketing efforts behind that brand. Other would-be renters are always putting forth tempting offers to the owner of the site.[4]

Our strategy must therefore be to create a perception for our brand in the prospect's mind so that it stands apart from competing brands and approximates much more closely to what the consumer wants. We must cover that space in the consumer's mind as if we had won a long-term lease and always keep out 'squatters'. We must find a strong position in that mind and sit on it.

FIND A STRONG POSITION AND SIT ON IT

In 1982, when Nestle (then known as Food Specialities Ltd.) considered launching Maggi instant noodles, the company had the option of choosing from several alternative positions. The product could have been launched, for the sake of argument, as a means of cooking tasty Chinese dishes at home, or as a 'TV dinner', or as a 'mini-meal'.

Through consumer research the company felt that the most profitable position would be as a tasty, instant snack, made at home and initially aimed at children. The target market was the in-home segment of the very substantial snack category. This positioning decision automatically determined the competition which included all snack products in general. These would range from ready-to-eat snacks—biscuits, wafers and peanuts—to ready-prepared snacks such as _samosas._ All were bought-out items.

However, such snacks were positioned at some distance from Maggi Noodles; they were not its direct competitors. The position of its direct competition was occupied by snacks prepared at home, such as _papadam,_ fried peanuts, sandwiches, and _pakoras._

Traditional pasta products (Chinese noodles and macaroni) were considered to be near competitors forming a rapidly growing product group. But they were invariably used for meals, requiring a fair amount of cooking time and garnishing was essential.

Maggi Noodles was launched in Delhi in January 1983 and it became an overnight success. The annual target for that market was increased from 50 to 600 tonnes. The Indian market was tipped to become the second largest Nestle market for this product worldwide, next only to Malaysia.

Maggi Noodles, as market results show, found a vacant, strong position and 'sat on it' as 'the good to eat, fast to cook' anytime snack (Exhibit 1.2).

Another brand of instant noodles, called Favvy, entered the market with me-too product features and a me-too position. Its life was brief.

Exhibit 1.2 *Maggi Noodles have found a strong position and sat on it. (Courtesy: Nestle)*

THE 'UN-COLA' IDEA

The very articulate authors of that famous treatise, *The Positioning Era Cometh*, emphasize that

> Positioning is the battle for a place in the consumer's mind.

The authors—Al Ries and Jack Trout—quote the example of that all-time classic in positioning strategy, viz. the announcement of 7-Up as the 'Un-Cola' soft drink.

Originally, 7-Up had a steady volume as a mixer with hard drinks, but this was nothing compared to the potential of the soft drinks category in the USA. To compete in that massive market, 7-Up had to carve out a niche in the consumer's mind, then dominated by the colas—Coke and Pepsi. Using colas as a frame of reference, 7-Up advertising announced itself as the Un-Cola soft drink. It thus related the unfamiliar to the familiar and enabled the consumer to give 7-Up a position in his mind which was at once (i) as a soft drink, (ii) different from colas, and (iii) intriguing ('What's an Un-Cola?').

This new 'Un-Cola' position brought 7-Up a sales increase of 10% in the very first year. It became the third largest selling soft drink after Coke and Pepsi.

As Trout and Ries say:

> *To find a unique position, you must ignore conventional logic. Conventional logic says you find your concept inside yourself or inside the product.*
>
> *Not true. What you must do is look inside the prospect's mind.*
>
> *You won't find an 'uncola' idea inside a 7-Up can. You find it inside the cola drinker's head.*[5]

The spell of 7-Up's positioning has lasted to this day and has spawned innumerable think-alike strategies. For example, Citibank's 'Unfixed' Deposit—once again an attempt to create a perceptual distance between their Fixed Deposit (F.D.) scheme and F.D. schemes of other banks and thus differentiate it (see Exhibit 1.3 and Figure 1.5).

Every bank offers loans against fixed deposits made by its customers. However, there are a few minor formalities. Observing that some customers often need to apply for loans, Citibank hit upon the idea of reducing the formalities to something as simple as signing a cheque. All the other terms remained the same as with other banks.

Exhibit 1.3 *Citibank successfully originated the idea of a fixed deposit that would earn much more than a saving account, while giving the holder a cheque facility to withdraw money; hence the 'Unfixed Deposit'. (Agency: HTA)*

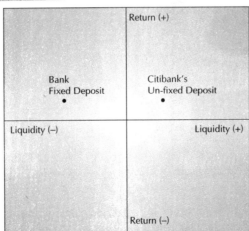

Figure 1.5 *Although governed by the same rules, Citibank has attempted to differentiate its Fixed Deposit from those of other banks.*

The cheque book facility created an immediate perception of easy liquidity, thus reflecting an extremely effective positioning idea—the

Unfixed Deposit. The strength of this idea is borne out by its numerous imitators such as the so-called 'Smart Money Deposit' of the Hongkong and Shanghai Bank.

Positioning strategy, as we said, starts with the prospect consumer's mind: where, in that mind, do we wish to lodge or situate our brand?

The same brand, in the same pack, with the same formulation, can seek different positions in the consumer's mind.

Same Product, Many Positions

A very striking and highly successful positioning and repositioning strategy is that of Milkmaid Condensed Milk. The product and the pack have remained unchanged but we observe four distinct positioning strategies as expressed in its advertising.

Years ago Milkmaid was advertised as a creamer or whitener for tea and coffee (Exhibit 1.4). If you read the fine print you will see that

Exhibit 1.4 *Milkmaid was at one time positioned as a creamer for tea and coffee.*

Exhibit 1.5 *At a time when fresh milk was in short supply, especially in the East, Milkmaid took the position of substituting for milk.*
(Agency: Clarion)

it spans several positions. But of course it is the illustration and headline that really determine the position which the consumer will give the brand in her mind.

Much later, we see yet another position for Milkmaid—product and pack unchanged (Exhibit 1.5). This position is "the tastiest milk made". Notice the jug of milk which comes from the condensed Milkmaid mixed with water. This position was visualized as it had relevance at a time when fresh milk was in short supply in some parts of India.

Once again, we see the portents of yet another position...this time, positioning Milkmaid as a topper (Exhibit 1.6, Plate 1).

And then, through a natural evolution—backed by consumer research and sound marketing judgement—we see Milkmaid's present position: Milkmaid for dessert recipes (Exhibit 1.7, Plate 1). In due course, the pack design was smartened up and changed to reflect the 'recipe' or culinary position; the label depicts a dessert, gives the recipe on the reverse side, and announces a 'Free Recipe Booklet'.

From the time of the dessert recipe positioning (1982), Milkmaid achieved a sales volume increase of 116% by 1988. Sales growth has been relatively steady year after year (an average growth of about 20% annually), suggesting that more households are responding to this position. It is significant that even in traditional milk-shortage areas, Milkmaid usage now is largely in line with the culinary (dessert) positioning. This implies that housewives who may have earlier perceived Milkmaid as a substitute for milk, have now given it a different place in their 'frame of reference'.

Positioning, above all, is a matter of the perception of our brand that we wish to create in the consumer's mind, and its relation to other brands. Essentially,

> Positioning is less what we do to the product and more what we do to the consumer's perception of the product.

PRODUCT POSITION AND POSITION

This is how an article in the *Journal of Advertising Research* defines 'positioning':

> *Product position refers to a brand's objective (functional) attributes in relation to other brands. It is a characteristic of the physical product and its functional features.*
>
> *Position, on the other hand, refers to a brand's subjective (or perceived) attributes in relation to competing products.*
>
> *This perceived image of the brand belongs not to the product but rather is the property of the consumer's mental perceptions and in some instances, could differ widely from a brand's true physical characteristics.*[6]

We will go later to the question of a definition but let us now turn to a very important thought—that the perceived image of the product belongs *not to the product but rather is the property of the consumer's mental perceptions.*

This suggests that the advertiser's main concern should be with that subjective perception of his brand as seen by the target consumer. Creating the desired perception and occupying a particular point or space in the target consumer's mind is the essence of positioning or repositioning strategy as we saw with 7-Up and Milkmaid.

MULTIPLE DEFINITIONS

Can we wrap up what has been said so far with a neat and tidy definition of 'positioning'? This is not entirely easy. Positioning is a comparatively new marketing concept, unlike 'consumer segmentation', for instance, which is an old friend and clearly stands for the same idea to most of us. The debates there are on ever newer criteria for segmentation: demographic; usage volume; loyalty patterns; degree of liking for the brand; brand benefit; social class; life style; attitudes, interests and opinions; personality characteristics; and the like.

In contrast, positioning, to this day, appears to be both a confusing and a confused concept, and there are almost as many definitions as there are writers on the subject. To some, 'positioning' is the 'proposition' or benefit of the product. To others it is its image, or perhaps its status in the market relative to the brand leader. And some equate it with 'brand personality'.

A few, indeed, believe that it is no more than old wine in new bottles; a mere rehash of the ideas of market segmentation and product differentiation. Thus, John P Maggard, 'revisiting' positioning, four years after Trout and Ries proclaimed that the *Positioning Era Cometh*, wrote:

> *The author does not agree with those who would proclaim positioning as something new and revolutionary in marketing strategy. The use of positioning strategy by marketers is as old as the ideas of market segmentation and product differentiation.*[7]

The great Rosser Reeves himself is reported to have written the following definition of positioning:

> *Positioning is the art of selecting, out of a number of unique selling propositions, the one which will get you maximum sales.*[8]

These words are taken from what is described as the 'lost chapter' of *Reality in Advertising*, the famous book written by Reeves, which was reissued but without this 'lost' chapter. "Positioning, because it is imprecise (he went on to write), can be a dangerous buzzword. Too often, it is pseudo-marketing, seeking to seize a segment of the market which exists only in the eye of the beholder".

'Imprecise' perhaps, but a concept so significant that David Ogilvy—no less a prophet than Reeves—says:

> *The most important decision you will ever make about your product is: 'How should I position my product?'*

C Merle Crawford says, "a concept as powerful as positioning can be abused", and gives several cautions. "Positioning is meant to drive the entire (marketing) programme".[9]

Aaker writes:

> *Product Positioning is so central and critical that it should be considered at the level of a mission statement...it comes to represent the essence of a business.*[10]

And Wind believes that product positioning "serves as an integral part of situation analysis as well as cornerstone of the firm's product/ marketing strategy".[11]

This writer regards positioning as the *fountainhead decision*, from which flow all other marketing and advertising decisions.

It is both a fountainhead decision and an integrating concept. It provides the direction and thrust to marketing and advertising planning, and also integrates, that is, binds into a cohesive whole, all the elements of the marketing mix. It becomes the task of the marketing planner and advertising strategist to design and engineer each element of the marketing mix to serve the positioning objective of the brand.

For a start, we need to get out of the jumble of ideas that surround the concept of positioning. We need to arrive at a definition which is clear and comprehensive enough to form the basis for the discussion of numerous real-life brand strategy problems that are taken up in this book.

Whom should Lakme Winter Care Lotion regard as its major competitor? Can one launch a brand of baby talcum powder against Johnson & Johnson with greater success than Glaxo had? What really distinguishes the Yamaha motorcycle from the Hero Honda and the latter from TVS-Suzuki? How do consumers relate in their minds Clinic shampoo to Clinic Special? What can become a strong and abiding basis for differentiating one brand from others like it? All the concepts and strategies involved must start from a sensible and practical definition of *position*.

> The 'position' of a brand is its perception among target consumers.

This perception is based on its functional attributes and benefits ('tasty', 'aromatic', 'sporty', 'roomy', etc.) as well as on the non-functional or emotional associations it has acquired mainly from its advertising ('reliable', 'traditional', 'smart', 'prestigious', 'modern', 'contemporary', 'stodgy', 'lively'). Similarly, because it is a *perception*, it is coloured by the target consumer's own attitudes, beliefs, and experience, thus leading to the fact that different segments may perceive the same brand in different ways.

Another key aspect of a brand's position is the way it is perceived in relation to competitive brands, among which we include similar products in the product line of the same company; for example, Surf, Sunlight, Rin, and Wheel washing powders, all marketed by Hindustan Lever.

Position then, represents the essence of the brand as perceived by the target consumer, in a multi-brand market. In that sense 'position' subsumes the physical or functional characteristics of the brand, sometimes referred to as 'product position' (as in the article from the *Journal of Advertising Research* quoted earlier), and its non-functional or emotional values.

For our purpose, we will not draw any distinction between 'product position' and 'position' and will use the terms interchangeably. Since we are mainly concerned with brands, this text will usually refer to 'brand positioning'. 'Product' and 'brand' for our purpose will also be used interchangeably, except when the context makes it clear that by 'product' we are referring to a product class or category.

And so, to a comprehensive definition.

1. *The position of a brand is the perception it brings about in the mind of a target consumer.*

2. *This perception reflects the essence of the brand in terms of its functional and non-functional benefits in the judgement of that consumer.*

3. *It is relative to the perception, held by that consumer, of competing brands, all of which can be represented as points or positions in his or her perceptual space and together, make up a product class.*

Note that the brand is not passive but active. It *acts* to bring about that perception. Note that *position* represents the *whole* or overall perception of the brand in that consumer's mind and that it is always a *relative* concept.

We conclude this chapter with one important quote on what *positioning* does.

Positioning creates a unique, credible, sustainable and valued place in consumers' minds for the brand.

Brand Asset Management

For the curious reader, the Appendix to this book lists a whole series of definitions and observations from numerous authors and sources. In the next chapter, we will take a closer look at the components of the positioning concept which are embodied in our definition.

THE PITFALLS OF BRAND POSITIONING

Competitive brand positioning is hard work. Many brands falter sooner than they should; some don't even make it out of the gate. Here are five pitfalls to watch out for:

1. Companies sometimes try to build brand awareness before establishing a clear brand position. You have to know who you are before you can convince anyone of it. Many dotcoms know this pitfall well. A number of them spent heavily on expensive television advertising without first being clear about what they were selling.

2. Companies often promote attributes that consumers don't care about. The classic example: for years, companies that sold analgesics claimed their brands were long lasting than others. Eventually, they noticed that consumers wanted faster relief more than sustained relief.

3. Companies sometimes invest too heavily in points of difference that can easily be copied. Positioning needs to keep competitors out, not draw them in. A brand that claims to be the cheapest or the hippest is likely to be leapfrogged.

4. Certain companies become so intent on responding to competition that they walk away from their established positions. General Mills used the insight that consumers viewed honey as more nutritious than sugar to successfully introduce the Honey Nut Cheerios product-line extension. A key competitor, Post, decided to respond by repositioning its Sugar Crisp brand, changing the name to Golden Crisp and dropping the Sugar Bear character as spokesman. But the repositioned brand didn't attract enough new customers, and its market share was severely diminished.

5. Companies may think they can reposition a brand, but this is nearly always difficult and sometimes impossible. Although Pepsi-Cola's fresh, youthful appeal has been a key branding difference in its battle against Coca-Cola, the brand has strayed from this focus several times in the past two decades, perhaps contributing to some of its market share woes. Every attempt to reposition the brand has been followed by a retreat to the former successful positioning. Brand positioning is a tough task. Once you've found one that works, you may need to find a modern way to convey the position, but think hard before you alter it.

(Extract from an article, "Three Questions You Need to Ask About Your Brand", *Harvard Business Review*, September 2002. Readers are urged to study the entire article in the original.)[12]

SUMMING UP

The concept of perceptual space forms the theoretical basis for positioning. The consumer's mind is thought of as geometric space and brands are plotted in that space to represent consumer judgements. This is done with the help of perceptual maps that enable us to see which brands are closer to ours and therefore represent our closest competitors.

The task of the marketer is to mould consumer perceptions so as to occupy the desired position for his brand. Perceptions or brand positions can be changed even if the product is the same; this is known as repositioning of a brand, as in the case of Milkmaid Condensed Milk or 7-Up. Repositioning may also be accompanied by physical changes in the brand.

A significant article in the *Journal of Advertising Research* underlines that positioning is more a matter of the consumers' mental perceptions than of the physical characteristics of the product.

Thus, it is important to find a vacant position in the consumers' perceptual space, occupy that position and defend it. This is well-illustrated by Maggi Noodles which have successfully held on to their unique position against competitors, for many years.

Many definitions of 'positioning' have been offered by different authors. But to suit our purpose, we have given a comprehensive, three-point definition which embraces the key ideas of this concept.

REFERENCES

1. Kassarjian, Harold H and Thomas S Robertson, *Perspective in Consumer Behaviour* (Scott, Foresman & Co., 1981) Chapter entitled 'Perception and Learning'.
2. *Ibid.*
3. Kotler, Philip, *Marketing Management* (Prentice-Hall of India Pvt. Ltd., 1983) pp 322–323.
4. Schultz, Don E and Dennis G Martin, *Strategic Advertising Campaigns* (Crain Books, 1981) pp 70–72.

5. Ries, Al and Jack Trout, *Positioning: The Battle for Your Mind* (Warner Books by arrangement with McGraw-Hill Book Company, 1986) p. 34.

6. Smith, Robert E and Robert F Lusch, "How Advertising Can Position a Brand", *Journal of Advertising Research*, February 1976 pp 37–38.

7. Maggard, John P, "Positioning Revisited", *Journal of Marketing*, January 1976 pp 63–66.

8. Sacco, Joe, "Rosser Reeves' Lost Chapter", *Advertising Age*, October 17, 1986 p. 13.

9. Crawford, Merle C, *New Products Management* (Irwin, 1987) p. 400.

10. Aaker, David A, *Strategic Market Management* (Wiley, 1984) p. 254.

11. Wind, Yoram J, *Product Policy: Concepts, Methods and Strategy* (Addison-Wesley Publishing Co., 1982) p. 166.

12. "Three Questions You Need to Ask About Your Brand", *Harvard Business Review*, September 2002.

Chapter 2

Positioning: Of what stuff is it made?

- Product Class
- Consumer Segmentation
- Perceptual Mapping
- Brand Benefits and Attributes

Positioning, like Virginia Slims, has come a long way from the time when Trout and Ries, all but lonely voices, announced it in 1969 and elaborated on it in 1972. Trout and Ries were advertising practitioners, but the initial interest of some perceptive minds in the academic world had also been aroused about that time. Today, almost every respectable text on marketing and advertising strategy pays, more or less attention to positioning.

Having looked at 'positioning' from a practical and applied perspective in the previous chapter, we can now go further into the key theoretical and conceptual issues that are involved in the three-point definition that we have given.

In what is probably one of the earliest academic references to positioning, as we now understand it, Prof. Volney Stefflre described techniques that could be used to measure consumers' perceptions of judged similarity between brands and products and thus give them a 'position' in a given market.[1] Addressing a symposium on the application of the sciences to marketing in 1966, Stefflre described research which showed that brands and products which were judged to be highly similar—that is, were close in perceptual space—also exhibited a high degree of competition and substitution. His work has been credited as being among the first applications of multidimensional scaling to marketing, a subject which we shall presently discuss.

Stefflre pointed out, in the work referred to earlier, how these techniques could be used to prospect for 'holes' or 'blank spaces' for new products or brands in a product class. They could help a multi-product from firm to develop new products that would

> *...position themselves in the market in a manner that makes them substitutable for and competitive with competitors' brands while not cannibalizing the firm's own related products.*

Shortly afterwards, Norman L Barnett, writing in the *Harvard Business Review* in January–February 1969, talked of the need to go 'beyond market segmentation'; that is, go beyond our understanding of homogeneous consumer groupings and shift the focus to "*consumer's perception of products*" (emphasis ours).

> *Positioning of brands is possible by using consumers' judgements of similarity to calculate how 'close' each brand is to every other brand. Thus brand positions constitute a framework or market structure...*

According to Barnett, new product introduction becomes the search for a position in the market structure for a product which is preferred over the products currently available.

Four Components

The definition that we have given in the previous chapter points to the four basic components of the positioning concept:

1. Product class or the structure of the market in which our brand will compete.
2. Consumer segmentation.
3. Consumer perception of our brand in relation to competitors, which leads to perceptual mapping.
4. The benefits offered by the brand. These benefits may also be expressed as attributes or dimensions along which brands are 'fitted' to represent consumer judgements.

These four components of the positioning concept are so closely interwoven that they must be taken together when we consider the positioning of a brand.

1. PRODUCT CLASS

> A product class or product market can be defined as the set of products and brands which are perceived as substitutes to satisfy some specific consumer need.

The term, product category, is also used interchangeably with product class and product market.

In his seminal work on defining market structures—that is, how to distinguish one product market from another—Stefflre quotes research which tended to show that there were some makes of automobiles (in the USA) whose competition for family dollars came more from home furnishings and vacations than from other automobiles.[2]

This is not as fanciful as it may sound. Research in India has shown that as middle-income and organized sector blue-collar families earn more and move up on the social ladder, they are faced at bonus time with the choice of buying a TV set or a fridge.

Such examples, however, merely point to the fluid nature of product market boundaries; they do not do away with the need to devise some kind of working definition of a market. We cannot put the positioning concept to work unless we get to grips with its very first component—the product class: which other brands must our brand contend with in order to lodge itself in the target consumer's perceptual space? In other words, what is the structure of the market or set of substitutes amongst which our brand is to be positioned?

Consumer judgements of similarity and substitution can form the basis for defining a product market or product category and are likely to be more reliable than categories defined by industry classifications. In India, low-cost detergent powders would undoubtedly be grouped with higher-priced powders in the category of 'washing powders'. There is little doubt, however, that these low-cost powders such as Nirma, Wheel, and Hippolin have *also* been positioned by *consumers* against the traditional (oil-based) laundry soaps and bars and have been perceived by them as substitutes for such laundry soaps (see Figure 2.1).

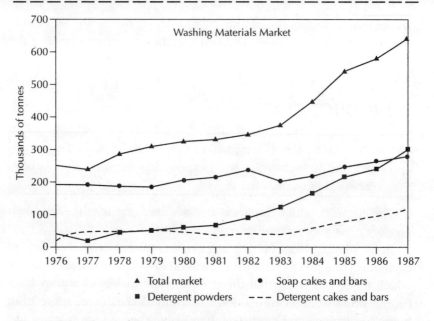

Figure 2.1 *Consumption of detergent washing powders, laundry soap cakes and bars and detergent bars. Detergent powders are evidently growing at the expense of soap cakes and bars. (Source: Operational Research Group)*

It is not difficult to presume that a telegraphic message is, in some ways, positioned against and competes with a long distance telephone call. However, research into consumers' judgements of similarity may show that telegraphic deliveries compete more—that is, are perceived as a closer substitute of—'speedpost' or courier services than of trunk calls.

Today e-mail competes with courier services, and 'voice chats' via computers compete with long distance calls, as will be testified by many senior citizens with children abroad.

If we consider the product class of chocolates, Cadbury's, Nestle, and Amul are clearly positioned against one another. If we consider the 'product class' of festival season gifts, consumers may position a decorative box of chocolates against packaged and branded *halwa* and even, perhaps, a pocket transistor.

Day[3] points out that for some strategic planning purposes, General Electric treats hair dryers, hair setters, and hair brushes as parts of distinct markets, while for other purposes they are part of a 'personal appliance' business since they tend to compete with one another in a 'gift market'.

Giving a tongue-in-cheek example of 'Pearce's Pickles', Stefflre asks how the marketer of the brand should position it in a consuming culture (market) unfamiliar with pickles:

> *Our pickle manufacturer may think he is going into the pickle business but actually, in terms of consumer perceptions, he will be going into the snack business (competitive with candy, fresh berries and certain fruits) with all of his sweet pickles.*[4]

Nearer home, we have the example of Maggi Noodles which we discussed at some length in Chapter 1. In South-East Asia where noodles mean big business, they are consumed as a *meal*. In India, Nestle deliberately chose the product class of home-made *snacks* in which to position Maggi Noodles. In our consumer culture, noodles as a meal would not be readily accepted as a substitute for rice or *roti*. Market growth would need a change in basic and deeply ingrained food habits—a long haul. On the other hand, housewives would be much more willing to experiment with a snack that takes 'two-minutes' to cook.

A brand manager must be ever aware that he may suddenly find himself face-to-face with an infiltrator from across the historical border. For instance, Pond's Cold Cream's comfortable position seems to have been suddenly challenged by a brand from another product class altogether. The first appearance of Lakme's Winter Care Lotion ad (Exhibit 2.1, Plate 2) may well have come as a rude shock—being described as a 'greasy cold cream' by this violator of traditional boundaries which claims, to boot, that it is 'cold cream + moisturiser in one' and is 'so much more than cold cream'.

Toyota's Qualis is not positioned as a Multi Purpose Vehicle (as you would expect from its appearance), but against mid-sized cars such as Lancer and Opel. In the first six months, nearly 50% of Qualis buyers came from the premium car market.

Sandeep Singh, deputy general manager (marketing) at Toyota Kirloskar Motor, says:

> *Indians have large families, and this vehicle is the best to carry them around in comfort. Even traders and such people will find this an ideal vehicle.*

Overholser of Young and Rubicam calls this—the choice of product class—the first 'positioning' decision of the advertising strategist. He has to decide whether to compete broadly within the conventional product class, to compete with only some segment of the conventional product class, or to attract users from some other product class.[5]

In Chapter 4, we will revert to this component of positioning and consider how the brand manager can use his choice of product class to secure competitive advantage for his brand.

2. CONSUMER SEGMENTATION

Most of you would be well versed in the theory and significance of consumer segmentation. What is the profile of the consumers whom our brand will serve and what are their needs?

You would also be familiar with target marketing, that is directing all marketing, promotional, and media efforts for a brand to a chosen, sharply-defined group of consumers.

> Positioning theory marks its departure by placing emphasis on the target consumer's *perceptions* of brands in relation to other brands. But its main focus, like all good marketing theory and practice, is on the target consumer's characteristics, needs, and expectations. Since we are inevitably faced with complex and heterogeneous markets, this means a multitude of consumer segments.

One cannot think of 'positioning' a product or a brand except in relation to a particular target segment. You position a Bank Fixed Deposit for those investors who prize security along with a moderate return. You position an 'Un-fixed Deposit' for similar investors but who, in addition, would prefer easy liquidity for their deposits without undue loss of return (see Chapter 1).

If you wanted to broaden the market for Bank Fixed Deposits by appealing also to those investors who favour high returns and are willing to shoulder risks, your only hope is to position Bank Fixed Deposits in terms of a 'portfolio' of investments in which high-return and high-risk investments are balanced with moderate-return, no-risk investments, plus tax benefits.

In fact, either management judgment or research can lead to defining yet another segment of investors as those who want the best of both

Plate 1

Exhibit 1.1 *One can almost see how Sprint would be plotted on a perceptual map of the category, well apart from the popular flavours. (Agency: Lintas) See p. 4.*

Exhibit 1.6 *Milkmaid as a topper on fruits and puddings. (Agency: Clarion) See p. 13.*

Exhibit 1.7 *Milkmaid now established in a long-run position—for desserts. Note that the product has remained unchanged throughout. (Courtesy: Food Specialities Ltd) See p. 13.*

Plate 2

Exhibit 2.1 *Lakme Winter Care Lotion positioned itself against cold creams as a "cold cream plus moisturiser in one". (Agency: Enterprise) See p. 25.*

See p. 25.

Exhibit 2.7 *This ad in Bengali marks an important step in the 'modernisation' of Margo—with its edges now more rounded and a brighter green wrapper. The headline says Margo was always good for skin and now it looks good too. (Agency: Response) See p. 45.*

See p. 45.

the worlds—a high return with low or 'managed' risk. Unit Trust's 'Mastershare' and Units '64 were positioned for just such a segment followed by State Bank's 'Magnum' shares. Today, there are numerous Mutual Fund instruments offered by, say HDFC, and several other organisations both Indian and foreign such as Templeton.

Have these several Mutual Fund instruments been designed to appeal to different segments of investors or are they scrambling for the same share of the pie? What, you may wish to debate, is the difference in the positioning of these 'brands' of investment? What is the 'distance' between them as perceived by investors? (see Chapter 4).

Exhibit 2.2   *Mastershare, the one share which gives the owner the benefit from many fast growing shares. Issued by Unit Trust of India— hence risk free. (Agency: Interpub)*

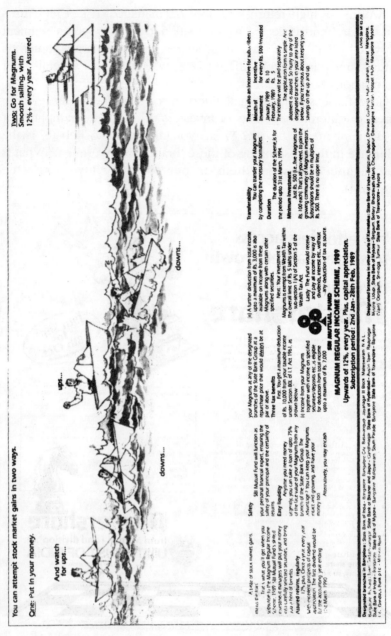

Exhibit 2.3 *State Bank Magnums— 'a taste of stock market gains, minus the risks'—as the ad says. (Agency: Lintas)*

We need not labour the point that leading brands—those with very large market shares—tend to position themselves across several segments; for example, Horlicks, "the great nourisher" (about 45% market share). Other brands are focussed more narrowly like Complan which is the "complete planned food for growing children".

We shall discuss strategies for positioning by segment in greater detail in Chapter 4. What we are considering now is the inseparable relationship between the position of a brand and its target segment.

The closer our product is to a commodity, the lesser the degree of market segmentation and even lesser is the opportunity for sharply defined positioning. We can observe this with regard to the toilet soap market in India, for example.

At the lowest end of the organized sector toilet soap market is the so-called 'economy category'. It has only two major brands: Lifebuoy which dominates the category with about 80–90% market share, trailed far behind by OK.

At a slightly higher rung, the so-called 'popular category', we have at least eight brands with 2% or more market share. This category is led by Lux (34%), followed by Hamam and Rexona (about 20% each).

As we move up to the 'premium category'—which accounts for about a quarter of the total toilet soap tonnage and where margins are generally higher—we find no fewer than 87 brands listed by ORG (Operations Research Group)!

Their market shares vary from about 16% (Liril) to less than 1% for several brands (e.g. Lakme, Johnson's Baby Soap, etc.). The line-up for January–December 1988 can be seen in Table 2.1.

Table 2.1

Brand	Market Share of Premium Segment (%)
Liril	16.3
Cinthol	12.7
Mysore Sandal	8.9
Margo	8.9
Fresca	6.9
Palmolive	6.6
Pears	4.5
Wipro Shikakai	4.2
Dettol	3.75
Swastik Shikakai	3.6
Pond's Dreamflower	2.9
Marvel	2.7
Crowning Glory	2
Moti	2

Lesser brands have not been listed. (*Source:* ORG Retail Audit Data)

You can well imagine the amount of jostling among these brands to gain a loyal segment of users who would be attracted to a particular brand, for its functional benefits and emotional values, and give it a position in their mind, as well as a place in their shopping list.

Positioning is a theory that was born out of the intense competition let loose by a great proliferation of brands. This makes it necessary to understand who our closest competitors are and how we should seek to be unique among the similar. Each brand has to carve out a 'niche' to call its own. In such competitive product markets, only such a brand will survive which has been able to identify the segment that it will serve, the particular benefits to pull that segment and has engineered its position to match most closely with the needs and 'dreams' of that segment.

Thus,

> Positioning a brand and the target segment for which it is designed must be considered together as integrated parts of one strategy.

Integrated, because just as a brand must be positioned to appeal to a target consumer segment, a consumer segment too, would respond to a brand that occupies the position preferred by it.

To quote David W Cravens from the chapter on 'Target Market Strategy' in his book, *Strategic Marketing:*

> *Target market and positioning strategies are like the two sides of a coin. They are inseparable; each depends upon the other.*[6]

Readers wishing to go into market segmentation in the context of positioning may like to read the entire chapter in the book by Cravens.

Matching Segment and Position

We will conclude this section by looking at an example of matching target segment and brand position provided by Paul E Green, probably the best known name in the theory and application of positioning analysis and perceptual mapping. Green says,

> *Brand positioning and market segmentation appear to be the hallmarks of today's marketing research.*

Among several positioning studies described in his book *Research for Marketing Decision*[7] is one that combines positioning and segmentation and is particularly relevant for our discussion. The reader interested in pursuing this question is referred to Chapter 16 in Green's book.

For our purpose we shall summarize some aspects of the study discussed by Green. The study was conducted in a particular region of USA among a sample of male beer drinkers. The data on brand dissimilarities (as judged by the sample) were scaled multidimensionally, resulting in the map seen in Figure 2.2.

The positions of 12 brands of beer are shown as points on the map (indicated by numbers). The various semantic differential (averaged) ratings on different attributes (i.e. 'filling', 'mild taste', etc.) also obtained in the study are then fitted into the map (via multiple regression) to help its interpretation. The horizontal axis appears to

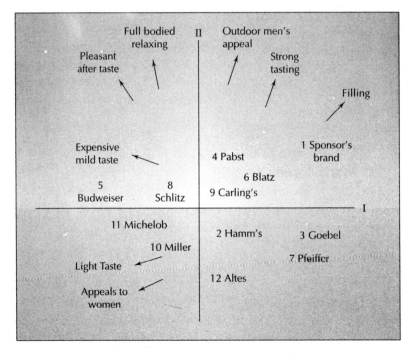

Figure 2.2 *Perceptual vector spaces of brand positioning: a beer example. Reproduced with permission from Research for Marketing Decisions by Paul E Green and Donald S Tull (Prentice-Hall of India, 1986).*

be a premium-popular dimension with the premium brands (like Michelob) on the left. The vertical axis seems to indicate 'strength' with beers perceived as 'stronger' positioned in the top-half. The perceived positions of the brands on various attributes are shown on the 'vectors'. The closer a position is to the head-end of the arrows, the more that brand is credited with having the attribute of that vector (say, 'filling').

We find that the Sponsor's brand (No. 1) is perceived as more 'filling', more 'strong tasting', more for 'outdoors' men than all the others. These appear to be the inherent strengths of the brand.

Information was obtained in the same study on lifestyle and demographic characteristics of the 'Sponsor brand-loyal' segment, 'Other brand-loyal' and 'Switchers'. The Sponsor brand-loyal consumer was found to be:

> *...a heavier beer drinker than average...generally perceives beer drinking as refreshing and rewarding...moderate to conservative politically...low interest in other alcoholic beverages...working class people, for the most part.*

Evidently, there is a good match between this particular segment and the position occupied by the Sponsor's brand. Knowing this we can also evaluate the promotional campaign for the brand which had been running up to that time: "The promotional campaign", writes Green,

> *...was addressed to the more affluent, sophisticated beer drinker and emphasized a folk-rock musical with humorous, clever sales appeals.*

Green concludes that this type of advertising did not seem to be "congruent with either the beer's strong, masculine image or the lifestyle and demorgraphic characteristics of its consumers."

3. PERCEPTUAL MAPPING

When marketers and advertising professionals began to display their interest in the perceptions of target consumer segments, the next natural step was to measure those perceptions. This constituted an open invitation to mathematical psychologists to move in—which they did! Today, you cannot play the positioning game without 'perceptual mapping'.

What perceptual mapping does is to represent consumer perceptions—in (usually) two-dimensional space so that the manager can readily see where his own brand is positioned in the mind of his prospect and in relation to other brands. We had said in Chapter 1 that the concept of the consumer's perceptual space forms the theoretical basis of positioning. It is this concept which distinguishes positioning and sets it apart as a major contribution to marketing theory and practice. Perceptual mapping helps to make this concept operational.

Although the judgements of managers, sales staff or the trade may be used to plotting brand positions in the consumer's perceptual space, it is not advisable to substitute them for consumer judgements, which can only be obtained through field research.

Consumers are asked to rate a set of brands along given attributes or benefits or they may be asked merely to judge, by pairs, how similar or dissimilar the brands are.

The former technique is used for Factor Analysis and the latter technique is used in Multidimensional Scaling (MDS). Both conceptually and operationally, these two techniques are well suited for marketing management's use in perceptual mapping. Developed by mathematical psychologists, the MDS technique provides a representation of consumers' perceptions of brands as points in a geometric space whose axes (attributes/dimensions) can be described as frames of reference along which brands are compared by consumers.

Perceptual mapping techniques identify the underlying dimensions that differentiate consumer perceptions of products and the positions of existing products on the dimensions.[8]

Several examples of perceptual mapping have been given in the preceding pages. Today, the use of such mapping in product positioning analysis and strategy development is observed wherever the concept of positioning plays an important part in the planning of marketing programmes.

Various other techniques are available for such perceptual mapping. Profile charts, for example, are fairly common in India. Further, research organizations offer hierarchical cluster analysis, multiple discriminant analysis and some application has also been reported of conjoint analysis. We will turn to these technical aspects of perceptual mapping in Chapter 11 with examples for the Indian market.

The reader will find an excellent discussion of MDS and other perceptual mapping techniques in Wind;[9] Urban, Hauser and Dholakia;[10] Green;[11] and Aaker and Day.[12] Some lucid illustrations are provided by Wind and these are reproduced in Figures 2.3 and 2.4.

Figure 2.3, for instance, is a two-dimensional configuration of 14 automobile brands. Obviously, the closer any two brands are, the more similar they are thought to be by consumers. Closeness thus denotes a high degree of competition. Note that consumers were merely asked to indicate the extent of similarity or dissimilarity between the brands. Managerial judgement was used to interpret the dimensions—in this case, 'sportiness' and 'economy'.

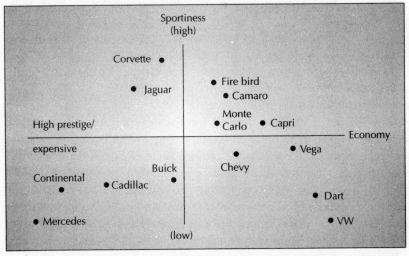

Figure 2.3 *Two-dimensional configuration of brands of automobiles (illustrative output). [Reproduced from Product Policy: Concepts, Methods and Strategy by Yoram J Wind (Addison-Wesley, 1982)].*

A hierarchical cluster analysis was then done to refine this perceived similarity and the results were superimposed on the two-dimensional map (Figure 2.4) giving a much clearer view of similarity and competitiveness among these brands. Figure 2.3 alone could have led to clubbing the Mercedes along with the Cadillac and Continental, but the cluster analysis shows that it is perceived to have a unique position, as also the Corvette and Jaguar.

We have dealt at some length with the application of MDS techniques to marketing in the USA. This is because such applications were first made in that country. Since then, much progress has been made there, both in the development of methodologies and their application.

There is as yet little published literature in India on the application of such techniques for perceptual mapping and product positioning, although there are a few unpublished case studies such as the one written by Dr A Parvatiyar of XLRI, Jamshedpur.[13]

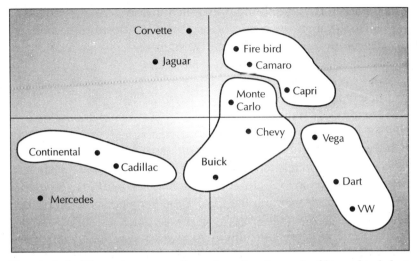

Figure 2.4 *Illustrative output of superimposing the result of hierarchical cluster analysis on two-dimensional configuration of automobiles.*
[Reproduced from Product Policy: Concepts, Methods and Strategy by Yoram J Wind (Addison-Wesley, 1982)].

MARG is one of the few market research organizations in India which has acquired the software and has used MDS techniques to analyse market structures and study positioning opportunities.The author is indebted to Mr Titoo Ahluwalia, Chairman of MARG and Mr Ashok Das, Associate Director, for the following account.

Perceptual Mapping Example from MARG

The role of multidimensional scaling is really to improve one's understanding of the structure of a market from the consumer viewpoint and to understand their needs and need-gaps better. Multidimensional scaling is a series of methods which brings about this understanding through geometrical (spatial) models and helps in assessing the likely consumer response to an offer of a potential or existing product, positioned anywhere in this space.

Essentially, the method involves studying relative positions of different brands in a product field, with the space being defined on coordinates that relate to dimensions or characteristics on which brands are evaluated/chosen by potential buyers. One can readily see the utility of this method in designing product offers for new brands or for modifying those of existing ones. Such methods have been used by MARG for a variety of product fields. One example, using responses from sixty educated, upper-income women on different brands of hair oils available in Kolkata, is presented here.

For an exercise of this nature, the starting point can be broadly with three types of data:

(a) Measures of similarity or dissimilarity between pairs of brands.

(b) Measures of preferences between brands.

(c) Ratings of brands on various attributes.

In the class of models where ratings of brands on various attributes are used, product spaces are constructed, positioning the different brands and also by marking the directions (vectors) for each of the attributes used in the analysis.

In the example given here, this method was used. The eight brands of hair oils and the eleven attributes used are listed in Table 2.2.

Table 2.2

Brands	Attributes
1. Arnica	1. Keeps hair healthy
2. Cantharidine	2. Makes hair greasy/oily
3. Dabur Amla	3. Makes hair glossy
4. Jabakusum	4. Helps hair growth
5. Keo Karpin	5. Prevents hair falling
6. Mahabhringaraj	6. Prevents dandruff
7. Parachute	7. Helps in hair grooming
8. Tata's	8. Has a pleasant perfume
	9. Modern
	10. Meant for people like me
	11. Inexpensive

Table 2.3 *Brand awareness*

Brands	Awareness (%)
1. Arnica	68
2. Cantharidine	75
3. Dabur Amla	80
4. Jabakusum	88
5. Keo Karpin	100
6. Mahabhringaraj	60
7. Parachute	72
8. Tata's	88

Table 2.3 gives the awareness levels of each of these brands. Table 2.4 provides the mean scores on the various attributes.

A study of these tables would indicate that while on an average overall assessment, the brands do not differ very much, there are sharp differences on certain attributes. Keo Karpin is the best known brand, has a high overall rating, is also seen to be modern and respondents identify more closely with this brand than any other. This brand is heavily advertised, specially on TV, with a 'good for hair grooming, non-sticky' theme. Mahabhringaraj, on the other hand, is a traditional oil and does not seem to attract much support nowadays. It is not seen to be 'for me' by the respondent, and is seen to leave hair greasy.

Again, a comparison between the two coconut oils (Tata's and Parachute) reveals that while they are close overall and on many attributes, Parachute, being a new brand, also advertised on TV, is seen to be comparatively more modern.

Table 2.4 *Mean scores obtained on a 1–5 scale*

	Arnica	Canthar-idine	Dabur Amla	Jaba-kusum	Keo Karpin	Mahabh-ringaraj	Para-chute	Tata's
Overall a good brand	3.6	3.6	3.7	3.9	4.0	3.8	4.0	3.9
Keeps hair healthy	3.5	3.4	3.6	3.8	3.7	3.6	3.6	3.7
Makes hair greasy	2.7	2.7	3.5	3.5	2.3	3.7	2.8	2.6
Makes hair glossy	3.3	3.0	3.2	3.2	3.5	3.1	3.2	3.4
Helps hair growth	3.7	3.0	3.4	3.6	3.4	3.5	3.4	3.5
Prevents hair falling	3.5	3.0	3.1	3.3	3.1	3.3	3.0	3.1
Prevents dandruff	2.8	2.3	2.6	2.6	2.7	2.3	2.6	2.6
Pleasant perfume	3.2	3.6	3.3	3.9	4.0	2.3	2.6	3.5
Modern	2.3	1.8	2.3	1.6	4.3	1.7	4.1	2.2
A Brand for me	2.8	2.4	2.7	2.6	3.6	2.2	2.9	2.9
Inexpensive	2.8	2.9	3.0	2.9	3.0	3.0	3.3	3.3

Figure 2.5 is an MDS plot, using all the brands and all the attributes. While Arnica, Cantharidine, Dabur Amla, Jabakusum, and Tata's seem to be closely clustered with no attributes strongly attached to any of them, the other three brands seem to have distinct brand identities. As discussed, Keo Karpin has a large number of positive attributes attached to it, including good hair grooming, modernity, and 'for me'. Parachute is seen to be modern and inexpensive. Mahabhringaraj, while seen to help hair growth, is also considered a greasy oil. Therefore, the brand comparisons which we had obtained by looking at the mean scores earlier (Table 2.4) seem to be closely corroborated in this two-dimensional map.

If we go back to the mean scores (Table 2.4) again, we will notice that out of the 10 attributes (other than 'overall' and 'for me') used, major differences between brands are noticed only on four attributes:

1. Makes hair greasy
2. Helps hair grooming
3. Pleasant perfume
4. Modern

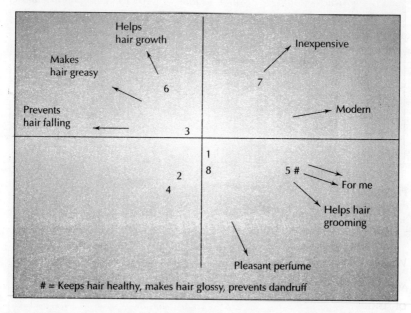

Figure 2.5 *Plot of Stimuli and subjects on dimensions 1 and 2.*

Key: 1 = Arnica, 2 = Cantharidine, 3 = Dabur Amla, 4 = Jabakusum, 5 = Keo Karpin, 6 = Mahabhringaraj, 7 = Parachute, 8 = Tata's

A look at Figure 2.6, which is a brand map using only these four attributes, will reveal that the relative positions of the brands remain roughly unchanged as compared to Figure 2.5.

Thus, the brand positions obtained in the MDS are really dependent on the variables where the brands are seen to be different, i.e. only attributes on which brands are rated differently contribute to the brand map.

A hierarchical cluster analysis (Figure 2.7) closely corroborates the findings from the MDS map, viz which brands are perceived as close to one another and which are distinct.

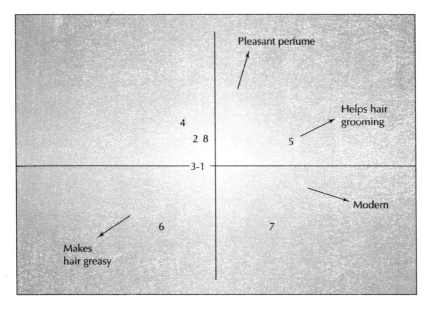

Figure 2.6 *Plot of brands using four key attributes.*

Key: 1 = Arnica, 2 = Cantharidine, 3 = Dabur Amla, 4 = Jabakusum, 5 = Keo Karpin, 6 = Mahabhringaraj, 7 = Parachute, 8 = Tata's

What are the Dimensions?

We may now interpret the horizontal dimensions of Figure 2.6 as one of 'modernity' (to the right) with the attribute (vector) of 'helps hair grooming' being close to it, and the vertical dimensions as relating to 'perfume', the more pleasing perfumes being plotted in the upper half.

The greater clarity of understanding and richness of analysis which such as MDS plot provides the brand manager—as compared to the more traditional tabulation seen in Table 2.4 —will be at once apparent. For example, it is not evident from Table 2.4 that only Keo Karpin, Parachute, and Mahabhringaraj have distinct positions in the perceptual space. Nor can we readily observe the relationships between the brands—their relative closeness to or distance from one another in the consumer's judgement.

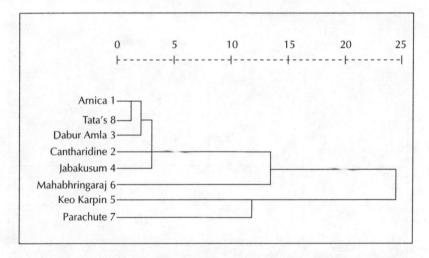

Figure 2.7 *Dendrogram showing clustering of hair oil brands. Arnica (1), Tata's (8) and Dabur Amla (3) form a tight cluster. Keo Karpin, Mahabhringaraj, and Parachute—each has an individual position.*

Table 2.4 may lead the brand manager to observe that Parachute, in comparison to Tata's, is seen to be better on only one count. His attention would still be concentrated on the assumed competitive pressure from Tata's—because both are coconut oils.

Following the MDS plot, the brand manager of Parachute can shake off his preoccupation with Tata's (which is not breathing down his neck) and concentrate, instead, on making Parachute more 'modern'. He may even ask his R&D people to work on making it a less 'sticky' oil so as to associate it with hair grooming and improving its perfume, thus consolidating its distinct position.

By way of caution we should add that the marketing implications from the MDS plot which we noted in the preceding paragraphs— and which have been drawn by this author—should not be regarded as necessarily applicable to, say, hair oil users in Kerala or other demographic segments. Nonetheless, the illustrative value of this example is clear.

4. BRAND ATTRIBUTES AND BENEFITS

> The physical existence of a brand is no assurance that it has a position in the target consumer's mind.

To enter that coveted territory—the consumer's perceptual space— and to secure a 'position' there, the brand must satisfy his question: "What's in it for me?" It must offer a benefit which is of importance to him. This is elementary. So, when we talk of brand attributes, we must remember that these are the manufacturer's views of the brand. The consumer's frame of reference requires that those manufacturer's claims or brand attributes be translated into consumer benefits in order to map consumer perceptions. Thus, when we talk of positioning a brand with reference to an attribute or when we ask a consumer to rate a brand along an attribute, we must reinterpret that attribute as a meaningful consumer benefit.

Blue detergent powders gradually edged out the perceived importance of 'blues' in the Indian washing products market. The comeback of Robin Blue for the modern housewife as Robin Liquid might be linked in the manufacturer's view to the fact that it has features or attributes such as a 'flourescer' and 'ultramarine'. But these attributes can enter the housewife's frame of reference only if she can be persuaded of their benefit to her: Washing powders take away the dirt but Robin Liquid gives clothes that extra 'coat of white'. And in advertising terms this becomes The "whiteness dip" (see Exhibit 2.4).

After washing clothes with powders, give them that dip in Robin Liquid for extra whiteness.

In a sense, Robin Liquid's advertising had to modify the housewife's frame of reference by increasing the 'salience' of extra whiteness of

clothes above and beyond what detergent powders can do—cleaning
clothes but leaving them somewhat off-white (see Figure 2.8).

Exhibit 2.4   *Giving clothes the 'whiteness dip' with Robin Liquid. (Advertiser:
Reckitt & Colman, now Reckitt Benkeiser)*

With this positioning strategy, Robin Liquid achieved a trial rate of
25% among the target segment in Chennai, where it was test launched,
after just 12 exposures over TV. In Kolkata, the percentage of trial
among target households was 14% after the same number exposures.
It may be noted that Chennai consumers were somewhat more familiar
with liquid blues than consumers in Kolkata.

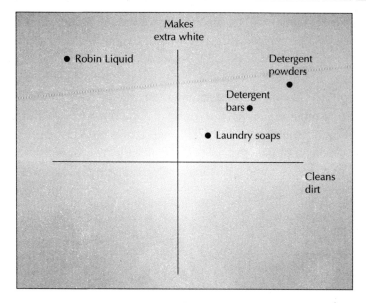

Figure 2.8 *A hypothetical perceptual map showing the benefits offered by different washing products. Robin liquid is attempting to distinguish itself from detergent products on the dimension of 'extra whiteness'.*

Where We Are—Where We Should Be

It is not enough that we plot the existing positions of brands along certain dimensions—brand attributes and benefits. This by itself, is a passive act. It tells us where we are but not where we should be and neither can we judge whether we are where we should be.

For this we need to plot not only consumer perceptions but also the preferences of a given consumer segment in a particular category or product market. Consumers can express such preferences only in terms of benefits: to what degree they are obtaining a specific benefit from existing brands; how important this benefit is to them; whether there is some benefit which they are missing; whether they would prefer to obtain a specific benefit in greater or lesser measure. Such preferences are also termed 'ideal points' when plotted on a perceptual map.

Let us consider the purposes of plotting such preferred or ideal positions. And let us consider by way of example, the premium toilet soap market.

Look at the hypothetical map (Figure 2.9) showing consumer perceptions of some of the prominent brands of premium toilet soaps in India. 'Premium', as defined for retail audit purposes, includes soaps priced in 1988 above Rs 4.50 for 100 g. Lower-priced soaps (like Lux and Hamam) fall into the 'popular' category. The dimensions of the map are based on a market analysis done by Response (see Chapter 7).

Exhibit 2.5 *Margo boldly declares its goodness for skin; so what if its looks are 'ugly'? This is a remarkable positioning which also turns a deficiency into a virtue. (Agency: Response)*

Exhibit 2.6 *Margo as the 'skin-friendly soap'. (Agency: Response). See also Plate 2.*

Preference Mapping

The brand manager for Margo bath soap has a defined consumer segment in mind: a consumer in the middle-income group, who values a bath soap for the good things it does for his skin, much more than its cosmetic properties or fragrance. Such a consumer is also thought to value traditional herbal ingredients which have proven goodness, like Neem (Exhibit 2.5 brings out the essential character of Margo as seen by this consumer—"Pretty ugly? Pretty good."). If the preferred or ideal position 'I' of this segment is superimposed on the map of premium toilet soaps as in Figure 2.9, the brand manager can judge if his marketing efforts have brought the perceived position of Margo closer to the preferred or ideal position of his target segment. In this case, what actions should he consider? How would you evaluate his positioning strategy for Margo as seen in the new campaign he has released, presenting it to the consumer as the 'skin-friendly soap' (Exhibit 2.6), and the face-lift he has given to his product with rounded edges and a brighter green wrapper (Exhibit 2.7, Plate 2)?

You can see how valuable an action guideline such an exercise can be. This is the first purpose of 'preference mapping'—to measure the gap, if any, between the position of the brand as actually perceived and the preferred or ideal position of its target segment.

Looking for 'Holes'

The second purpose for which we track such preferred positions is to discover 'holes' or vacant positions in the market structure because they represent opportunities for new products. To illustrate this we will use an excellent example from the book by Urban et al., with reference to the analgesic market in the USA.[14]

Figure 2.10 shows a perceptual map of pain relievers which represents where the existing brands were positioned by consumers at that point of time. Even visually, certain gaps are apparent, e.g. in the upper-right quadrant. Through consumer probing, the relative importance of 'gentleness' and 'effectiveness' can be obtained from users of the product category and the output might indicate that there is indeed, a vacant position which represents the preferred weights given by some consumers to 'gentleness' vis-a-vis 'effectiveness'.

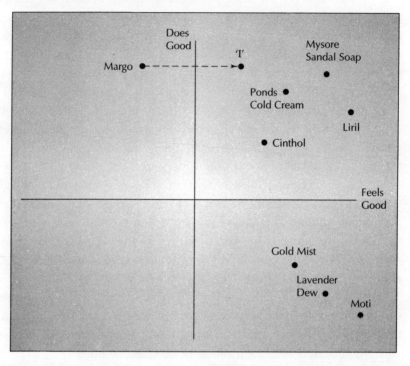

Figure 2.9 *This illustrative map shows the positions of selected premium toilet soap brands along the dimensions of 'Feels Good' and 'Does Good' which are considered critical by Response advertising agency (see Chapter 7). 'I' is taken to represent the preferred position or 'ideal point' of many Margo users.*

The 'preferred' or 'ideal' position of a single consumer would appear as a particular point on the map. If several consumers have a similar preferred position, they would form a cluster. And if we continue the process, we may discover more than one cluster, each gravitating around a preferred position, which represents the respective weights or degree of importance attached to the two benefits by that group or segment of consumers.

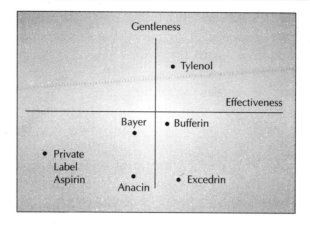

Figure 2.10 *Perceptual map for pain relievers.*

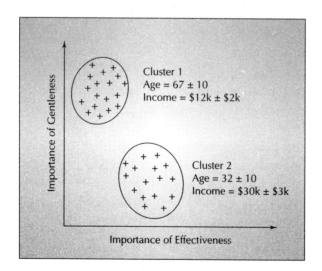

Figure 2.11 *Illustrative clusters of consumers for pain relievers.*

Figures 2.10 and 2.11 have been reproduced with permission from Essentials of New Product Management by Glen L Urban, John R Hauser, and Nikhilesh Dholakia (Prentice-Hall, New Jersey, 1987).

This can be portrayed on a map which also indicates the characteristics of each cluster or segment. The illustration from Urban *et al.*, is reproduced in Figure 2.11.

It is evident that Cluster (segment) 1 places more importance on 'gentleness' and Cluster (segment) 2 on 'effectiveness'. If these two segments can provide adequate sales volume and profit, we have two new product opportunities: one brand would be very gentle but less effective, and the other, very effective but not so gentle.

You will note that such techniques of preference mapping can also superimpose on the map various consumer characteristics.

It is possible through such analysis to identify the 'gaps' which new or repositioned products can hope to fill by offering that combination of benefits which existing products do not have.

Enough of pain-relievers! Let us look at the fascinating case of the 'happy pickle'. Having regaled us with an account of how Pearce's Pickles found themselves in a pickle, Stefflre unfolds for us the adventures of the happy pickle in quest of a 'preferred position'.

The context is entirely business-like: attempting to build new products to match preferred descriptions. It is this basic methodology which has been improved and developed to provide preference maps such as we saw earlier. Let us follow his somewhat fanciful but entirely relevant example.

Suppose that a survey among pickle users shows a sizeable response to a description such as 'the happy tasting pickle'. We might then ask the respondents to list the 'happiest tasting things' they could remember and a predominant answer may be 'a birthday cake'. So we tackle the problem of making a pickle that is perceived as more similar to birthday cakes than any other pickle. We take our 'happy pickle 1' to consumers to taste and ask them to rate it versus other pickles on the scale of 'very happy' to 'not at all happy'. If some competitor's pickle is 'happier', we examine how it is different from our own 'sadder' pickle. By the time we have tested 'happy pickle 7', consumers would have discovered the happiest tasting pickle of all!

Strategy Decisions

The strategy decisions which follow such preference mapping are the following:

(a) When we know the 'ideal point' or preferred position of our target segment, as revealed through such mapping, we can judge whether the perceived position of our brand needs to be brought closer to that ideal point. This may involve some change in its advertising to create a revised perception of the brand more in line with the ideal point. It may also involve some corresponding changes in the physical features of the brand (the easiest to change is the pack design).

(b) On the other hand, we may decide to change the preferred position or ideal point of our target segment and bring that ideal point closer to the perceived position of our brand. This is admittedly more difficult. In the lower-priced transistor radio category it was found, at one time, that consumers preferred models which offered high volume of sound. The marketer in question decided to change the preference of this target segment through advertising to increase the salience of tonal quality over mere volume and thus get a closer match with the existing position of his brand which was perceived to have a lower volume of sound.

(c) Thirdly, as we have seen, we may decide to launch a new brand altogether—or perhaps, reposition an existing brand—to get a closer fit with a preferred position which represents a consumer need unfulfilled by existing brands.

SUMMING UP

Positioning has come a long way from the late sixties when it first caught the attention of practitioners and academics. The concept itself has become somewhat better understood and more widely accepted for its theoretical as well as practical value.

Positioning has four components.

The first component is the product class or product category in which the brand is to operate. To give a specific name to such a category is not always easy since the boundaries are fluid, e.g. a moisturising lotion may decide to position itself in the cold cream market.

The second component is consumer segmentation. It is impossible to think of a position for a brand without, at the same time, considering the segment for which it offers benefits that other brands do not. Positioning and segmentation are like two sides of a coin, inseparable and integrated.

The third component is perceptual mapping, an essential tool to measure where brands are located in the perceptual space of the target consumer. Multidimensional scaling is a widely used method for such mapping, but there are others.

Brand benefits and attributes make up the fourth component of positioning. A consumer can allot a position in her mind only to a brand whose benefits are meaningful to her. She compares and places brands in relation to these desirable benefits.

Similarly, the search for vacant positions in the market must be conducted with reference to the preferred benefits and the preferred importance of such benefits. These preferences can also be portrayed in the form of preference maps.

The strategy decisions which follow are:

(a) When we know the ideal point or preferred position of our target segment, we can judge whether our brand needs to be brought closer to the ideal point.

(b) Alternatively, we may decide to change our target consumer's perceptions of such an ideal point and bring it closer to the position of our brand.

(c) Third, we may decide to launch a new brand to match that preferred position or ideal point.

The Strategy Leap of Miller Lite

No discussion of positioning is complete without a reference to Miller Lite beer, hailed as "the most successful new beer introduced in the United States since 1900". The following account is based on a video cassette produced by the Centre for Advertising Services of the Interpublic Group in the USA (*Courtesy:* Mr Charles A Mittelstadt).

Miller Lite was not the first light beer in the USA. Two earlier attempts to introduce a light beer had been made. In 1968, Gablinger was introduced as a 'diet beer' but failed. In 1970, Meister Brau Lite was also introduced as a diet beer and met the same fate.

When Miller decided to launch a light beer, they first analysed, with the help of the Interpublic Group's research organization, why the other light beers had failed. The ads of those brands seemed to be aimed at women and some, in fact, showed a slim woman drinking the beer.

Mr. Van Bortel of the Interpublic Group found a very significant fact. Despite the 'sissy' looking advertising, Gablinger light beer had high initial trial among 'real' beer drinkers, the 30% who consumed 80% of the beer. For any beer to succeed it had to appeal to the heavy user; that was the only way to attain enough volumes to win shelf space and earn profit.

The heavy beer drinker was not a weight watcher, he was not interested in the low-calorie appeal—so why did he try Gablinger in such large numbers? What was he looking for?

The consumer insight obtained through research was that the heavy beer drinker does not say:

'One third less calories, therefore less fattening'.

He says:

'One third less calories? That means three beers instead of two'!

This showed the marketing opportunity, provided the taste of such a light beer was improved, unlike Gablinger which had a poor taste.

Thus came the positioning strategy for Miller Lite when it was launched in 1975:

(a) *It was to be positioned for the heavy beer drinker with a strong masculine image;*
(b) *The heavy drinker likes his beer; therefore, Miller Lite must be positioned as the 'less filling' beer so that he can drink more of it.*

This strategy leap from 'less fattening' to 'less filling' and the targeting of the heavy drinker with a masculine appeal made the all-important difference.

REFERENCES

1. Stefflre, Volney, "Market Structure Studies: New Products for Old Markets and New Markets (Foreign) for Old Products" *Applications of the Sciences in Marketing Management,* (John Wiley & Sons, 1968) pp 251–268.
2. Stefflre, op. cit.
3. Day, George S., Allan D. Shocker, and Rajendra K. Srivastava, "Customer Oriented Approaches to Identifying Product-Markets" *Journal of Marketing,* (Fall, 1979) pp 8–9.
4. Stefflre, op. cit.
5. Overholser, Charles E. and Kline, John M., "Advertising Strategy from Consumer Research" *Journal of Advertising Research,* (October, 1971) pp 3–9.
6. Cravens, David W., *Strategic Marketing* (Richard D Irwin, 1982).
7. Green, Paul E. and Donald S. Tull, "Brand Positioning and Market-Segmentation" *Research for Marketing Decisions,* (Prentice-Hall of India Pvt. Ltd., 1986) Chapter 16.
8. Urban, Glen L., John L. Hauser, and Nikhilesh Dholakia, *Essentials of New Product Management,* (Prentice-Hall, New Jersey, 1987) Chapters 6 and 7.
9. Wind, Yoram J., *Product Policy: Concepts, Methods and Strategy,* (Addison-Wesley, 1982) Chapter 4.
10. Urban *et al.*, op. cit.
11. Green, op. cit.
12. Aaker, David A. and George S. Day, *Marketing Research,* (John Wiley and Sons, 1980).
13. Parvatiyar, A., "Gold Cup Tea", (unpublished case material of XLRI, Jamshedpur).
14. Urban *et al.*, op. cit.

Chapter 3

Positioning is Rooted in Product Features—Or is it?

OPTIONS FOR THE BRAND MANAGER

The problem that we will further pursue in this chapter is the extent to which the physical attributes of a brand influence its perception by the target consumer. Must the physical or functional features of the brand dictate its position? Or, can the brand manager override these physical features and achieve the position he desires, through crafting other elements of the marketing mix, notably packaging and advertising?

Recall the discussion on positioning in the *Journal of Advertising Research* from which we quoted in Chapter 1:

Position...refers to a brand's subjective (or perceived) attributes...

This perceived image of the brand belongs not to the product but rather is the property of the consumer's mental perceptions and in some instances, could differ widely from a brand's true physical characteristics.

We have earlier seen situations (Milkmaid, 7-Up), where the physical characteristics of the product were unchanged, but a substantial change in its perception was created through advertising. To what extent does the brand manager have flexibility in targeting a position for his brand 'which may differ widely from its true physical characteristics'?

A Slippery Problem

Let us return to the premium toilet soap market in India. Suppose research has discovered an emerging cluster of consumers—young, modern, well-to-do—who believe that a bath soap should have good-for-skin qualities, who even think well of traditional herbs like Neem, but would accept it only with much more pronounced cosmetic benefits in terms of perfume, lather, colour, shape, and packaging. Recall our discussion on Margo in the previous chapter.

Is it possible for a 'dressed-up' Margo to aim for that new position? Can Margo make the jump from where it is (that is, the way it is perceived now) so as to occupy the preferred position of this new cluster? Would the present physical characteristics of Margo—dark-green colour, strong Neem perfume, squat shape—permit the brand to match the ideal point of this new cluster merely on the basis of some superficial feature-changes like new packaging and brilliant advertising?

And if the brand manager were to make the gamble of trying to position Margo—with some physical changes—both for his present target segment and the new one, how successful would he be? On the other hand, suppose he decides to make radical changes to Margo, so as to greatly enhance its cosmetic values, how would that affect his present loyal segment of users?

Should he pause and recall that old saying—"Beware of greed and grow fat"? Would it be better to consider a new product altogether? A product whose physical features are specifically designed to fit the new position, and whose concept can be stated as:

> *A highly emollient soap. Floral perfume with topnote of Neem: 'The Creamy Neem'. The benefit of pure, age-old neem goodness without the drab looks of average neem soaps.*

This is the type of real-life question that will confront the brand manager, when he considers the relationship between his brand's physical features and the position he would like it to occupy.

At this point let us deliberately recapitulate our observations on how brand positions are formed.

Sizing up a Brand

What we call 'positioning' is really the consumer's shorthand for 'sizing up' a brand, its physical and emotional benefits, and where it fits into her framework of needs and wants. As we said earlier,

> Positions are the consumer's perception of brands in a product category and their perceived distance from one another.

If that perception of our brand has stimulated her interest, she tucks it away in a corner of her mind. She gives it a position.

And she relates our brand to competitive brands which may also have earned positions in her mind.

She is creating an imprint on her mind, as it were, for each of these fortunate brands which have aroused some degree of interest.

It is our job to capture those imprints on her mind. We do this through research (which is preferable) or judgement. And we portray those imprints in the form of a perceptual or positioning map of the product category. Can those imprints or perceptions be formed independent of the product's attributes?

We will now look at this question afresh in another context—the toothpaste market in India.

Colgate and Forhan's

A consumer can allot a position in her mind only if she can form a picture of a given brand. And this is based on its functional attributes, performance and emotional values through advertising.

Thus, Colgate has a dominant claim on the position of an 'anti-tooth decay' and 'fresh breath' toothpaste. This strong positioning is supported by suitable product features (minty taste, foaminess) and consistent advertising (Exhibit 3.1).

Forhan's Regular (in the orange pack) has a dominant hold on the 'Good for Gums' position (Exhibit 3.2). Its taste is disliked. It does not foam well, but it does have an astringent which is good for the gums (it could be that it is difficult to combine this astringent, which is highly beneficial for gums, with high foaming properties). This

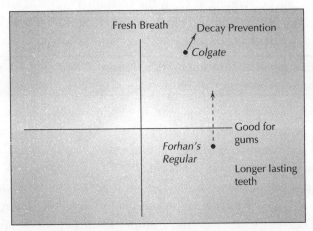

Figure 3.1 *Initially the company strengthened the 'Good for Gums' position of Forhan's Regular by explaining how healthy gums led to longer lasting teeth. Later, the company chose to link healthy gums with fresh breath. (See also Exhibit 3.6)*

Exhibit 3.1 *For decades, Colgate has dominated the position representing the dual benefits of fresh breath and decay prevention.*

functional attribute has been backed by strong advertising to create the Forhan's Regular position in the consumer mind.

Forhan's Regular has strengthened its 'Good for Gums' position by pointing out how the astringent, by tightening the gums, keeps teeth in place longer (see Figure 3.1).

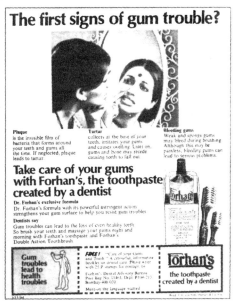

Exhibit 3.2 *Forhan's Regular singlemindedly pre-empted the position of gum care with ads like these. (Agency: Clarion)*

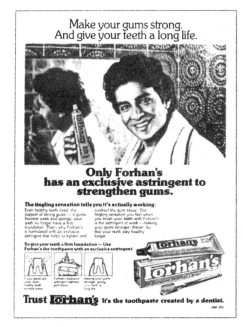

Exhibit 3.3 *This ad represents a major strengthening of the Forhan's Regular position. The astringent property is linked to tightening the gums and giving teeth a firmer foundation. (Agency: Clarion)*

Thus, the Forhan's position was reinforced to become (Exhibit 3.3):

- Good for Gums
- Longer-lasting Teeth

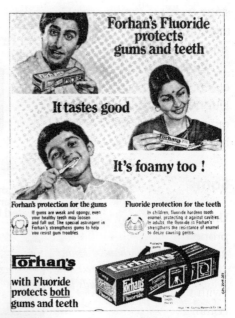

Exhibit 3.4 *Forhan's Fluoride was initially advertised with a two-in-one benefit.*

Exhibit 3.5 *At a later stage, Forhan's Fluoride took the stance of a 'super cavity fighter'. The gum care message was implied.*

We see then that a brand's position must be supported by the brand's attributes. But a brand's attributes may be communicated to the consumer in a variety of ways. And the consumer can be persuaded to perceive the same, unchanged product in different ways. At some stage we may decide to secure another, more profitable position in the comsumer's mind without doing anything to the product, or its attributes, and merely changing the way it is perceived.

We can do this by emphasizing one attribute of a brand and de-emphasizing another. By way of example, let us take Forhan's Fluoride, which was launched in 1978 as an extension of the Forhan's range of dental-care products. At that time, marketing management had three major positioning options.

Same Features, Three Options

Unlike Forhan's Regular, Forhan's Fluoride has far greater foaming properties (lack of foam is one of the perceived negatives of Forhan's Regular and has caused many users to switch). Thus, Forhan's Fluoride could have been positioned as "Foaming Forhan's", that is, a toothpaste "with the goodness of Forhan's plus foam". Indeed, one of the early commercials for the brand had a line, *Yeh Jhagwala hai*, meaning this is the foaming variety of Forhan's. Such a positioning would have placed the brand very close to Forhan's Regular in the consumer's perceptions, increasing the dangers of 'cannibalization'.

> Cannibalization can be thought of as a perceptual map in which like products of the same company (say, toothpastes) are positioned very close to one another and compete more with one another than with brands of other companies.

A second option was to seek a mid-way position in which both attributes were more or less equally emphasized, and to hope that this would reduce cannibalization while attracting users of other fluoride brands.

The third positioning option was to emphasize the fluoride content of Forhan's Fluoride (the super cavity fighter), bringing it, in the consumer's eyes, close to other fluoride brands such as Binaca.

In fact, the company exercised both the second and third options at different points of time (see Exhibits 3.4 and 3.5).

While the brand manager has some flexibility, a brand cannot hope to attain a desired position if its physical attributes and performance are felt by the consumer to be strongly at variance with that position. On the simplest plane, a brand wishing to be seen as an expensive man's soap, cannot have a 'feminine' perfume or a cheap pack (see the case on Aramusk soap in Chapter 7).

A toothpaste with poor foaming properties cannot seek a *Jhagwala* position.

To return to our toothpaste example, later ads for Forhan's Regular have attempted to broaden its market by embracing the fresh breath position as well, without changing the product attributes (Exhibit 3.6). Also notice that what used to be Forhan's Fluoride is now positioned as "Foaming Forhan's". This seems to take us back to the first option!

The question is: what new imprints on her mind, for Forhan's Regular, would the consumer accept? And what is the relationship of that imprint (or perceived position as a 'fresh breath' toothpaste) to the functional attributes of Forhan's Regular? You may like to deliberate upon this.

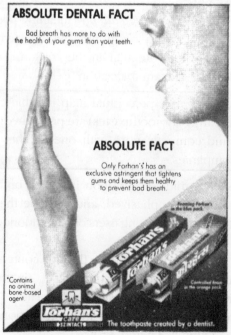

Exhibit 3.6 *Forhan's has now adopted the position of a fresh breath toothpaste. The astringent feature tightens gums and prevents bad breath, says the ad. (Agency: Contract)*

Brand Benefit Options

The brand manager also has flexibility in positioning decisions, in terms of which particular benefits he will emphasize, when a brand offers more than one benefit, which is true of many brands. Complan, for instance, is a many-splendoured brand and offers several benefits.

Because it has "23 vital foods which your body needs every day" it can be positioned as the complete planned food for convalescents and others who cannot take their normal diet. Likewise, it can be positioned as the busy executive's mid-day nourishment (the Complan break), since workaholics often miss their meals. And, of course, it can be positioned for the reassurance of the concerned mother, as the health-drink for growing children (for a more detailed account of Complan's positioning, see Chapter 6).

But notice again that each of these positioning options is strongly supported by the functional properties of Complan. In fact, in such situations, it is not the lack of positioning flexibility that should bother the brand manager, but the problem of greed.

And finally, we can attempt to change the perception of an attribute—a more difficult task. For example, we may try to make a filter cigarette appear to be manly and not 'sissy' as we shall see with Marlboro, one of the early filter brands in the USA.

'Campaign of the Century'

We cannot cover the subject of how product attributes relate to positioning, without a thoughtful look at the 'Campaign of the Century'—as it has been called—the campaign for Marlboro cigarettes.

Way back in 1954 in the USA, there were only six filter cigarettes and together, they added up to only 10% of the market. Lung cancer because of smoking had not yet hit the headlines and filters were regarded on the 'sissy' side. Marlboro was known as a "woman's cigarette"—it even had a red tip to mask lipstick smears! And its market share was barely one-quarter of one per cent—a near-demise state of affairs.

Philip Morris, who had bought the brand, commissioned a research study to find out if filters had a future and drew their own conclusions.

The legendary Leo Burnett, head of the Advertising Agency which bore his name and which was given the Marlboro business at the time, said:

> We had this huddle with our top creative people and we thought, if filters were regarded on the sissy side, and Marlboro was regarded on the sissy side, the natural thing was to look for a masculine image. I asked around what was a masculine image and four or five people, all said a cowboy...
>
> We wanted to talk about flavour, too. What would a cowboy say about flavour? 'Delivers the goods on flavour.'

This was a spectacular change for Marlboro—from the perceived position of a 'woman's cigarette' to the virile and masculine position represented by the 'cowboy'. See the Marlboro ad which heralded this positioning change (Exhibit 3.7) in 1955.

Exhibit 3.7 *The ad that launched the world's most successful cigarette. Created by Leo Burnett Agency. Reproduced from The New Advertising by Robert Glatzer (Citadel Press).*

To match this positioning change, the cigarette itself was given a more aromatic blend of tobacco. And the pack design was modified. To quote Burnett:

> *The package they were using looked pink because of the stripes and it had an effcte look. Why not make it red? Take the damm stripes out of here. Well, we came to New York (to present to the client) with one ad: the Cowboy. They bought what we said, ripped the old package off the machines, and went with the ad.*

Robert Glatzer, from whose book *The New Advertising* the above account of Marlboro has been taken, says of the later campaign for the brand ("Come to where the flavour is, Come to Marlboro Country") which is still running, that this is "one of the most beautifully photographed series of television commercials and print ads ever done in this country".[1]

Through all this it should be noted that the product feature of *Marlboro* was unmistakably that of a filter cigarette. But the campaign altered forever the *position* of Marlboro in smokers' minds. As the 'Cowboy' ads said: "You get a lot to like in Marlboro—Filter, Flavour, Flip-top box"; not to mention the rugged masculinity which the ads projected. Today it is the largest-selling cigarette in the world.

Prof. Kotler has described this exercise as managing the "most successful cigarette brand in history".[2]

The Marlboro example illustrates a situation where it was not right to change a key physical attribute of the existing product, its filter tip, and therefore the brand's position or perception in smokers' minds had to be changed. The given 'attribute' had to be communicated in such a way that its perception by the consumer was radically altered. In the rugged, virile hand of the cowboy, Marlboro filter lost its sissy image.

To make this task easier, we must ask, can other attributes be changed? In this case, it was possible to improve the flavour and pack of Marlboro in the desired direction.

By way of comic relief see Exhibit 3.8 which has been facetiously described as an ad for 'Marlboro bidis'!

Exhibit 3.8 *'Governor Bidis' reads the Tamil legend on this hoarding seen near Madras airport. A wag has named it 'Marlboro bidis'! (Photograph—Courtesy: Mrs. Mala Mukherjee.)*

Wills Filter

Is there scope for a variety of communication strategies through which the perception of a specific attribute can be changed? For example, were all marketers of filter-tipped cigarettes condemned to the route of masculinity when positioning their brands in the early years of the filter? Not at all, as we see from the classic Indian illustration in a somewhat similar context, that of Wills Filter Tipped cigarettes.

This brand was launched in 1963 when regular smokers thought that filter-tipped cigarettes had a *phika* or insipid taste. At that time, plain cigarettes made up an overwhelming share of the market in India.

ITC and its agency, J. Walter Thompson (then HTA), had a similar problem as Leo Burnett. They too had to change the perception of the filter cigarette in the minds of regular smokers; they too had to convince the smoker that the newly launched Wills Filter offered a highly satisfying smoke which was smooth as well.

The physical features of the brand gave the inspiration to the creative advertising person. ITC blenders had taken great care to see that the quality and the blend of tobacco effectively matched the filter to create a satisfying smoke. It was not just a case of slapping on a filter on the top of a stick of tobacco. This gave rise to the memorable line:

Filter and tobacco perfectly matched—made for each other.

One of the early ads of Wills Filter is seen in Exhibit 3.9, a very different route from that of Marlboro, to accomplish a somewhat similar positioning task.

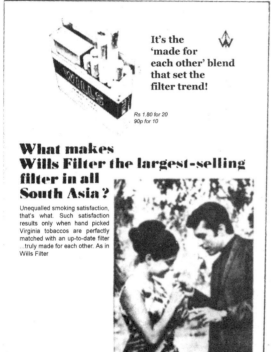

It's the 'made for each other' blend that set the filter trend!

Rs 1.80 for 20
90p for 10

What makes Wills Filter the largest-selling filter in all South Asia?

Unequalled smoking satisfaction, that's what. Such satisfaction results only when hand picked Virginia tobaccos are perfectly matched with an up-to-date filter ...truly made for each other. As in Wills Filter

Exhibit 3.9 *An ad from the historic campaign of Wills Filter, making it the most successful filter brand in India—the 'made for each other' blend. (Agency: HTA)*

The creators of the campaign discovered an added emotional value as well which blended beautifully with the functional attribute of the brand: a young couple who looked as though they were made for each other and this has remained the constant backdrop in ads for Wills Filter. The rest, as the saying goes, is history. Today, filter-tipped cigarettes account for 50% of the market in India. Wills Filter is indeed "the made for each other blend which set the filter trend".

In positioning terms, what Wills Filter marketing and advertising did was to push the brand along the dimension of satisfying taste in smoker's minds, much closer to the perceived best-tasting plain (non-filter) brands of the day—Gold Flake and Capstan—while adding a new dimension: smoothness.

The Marlboro and Wills Filter cases bring into focus the truth that brands are composite entities which comprise functional or physical attributes as well as non-functional, subjective attributes and values. The latter values—referred to as

> The added values of the brand—are created not on the factory floor but by the strategist and the creative person in the advertising agency.

Beyond Functional Values

You are, no doubt, familiar with the phenomenon of blind tests in which physically identical brands are given more or less equal ratings by consumers when their identities are masked, but widely different ratings when their brand names are made known. This is especially true of products like detergents, beverages, biscuits, soft drinks, cigarettes, textiles, apparel and many others.

Beverage companies in India have made more than one attempt to compete with Nescafe by producing a virtually identical blend of instant coffee, using similar coffee beans and a similar manufacturing process. When served in cups without any distinguishing label, the two coffees were rated about equal by the consumer. When served to the same consumer, or a matched sample of consumers, as 'Nescafe' and in the name of the other brand, Nescafe's rating immediately shot up. When actually marketed, the other brand fared poorly in comparison with Nescafe.

Food Specialities (Nestle) have apparently consolidated the position of Nescafe over the years, through careful attention to its physical attributes and by enriching the brand with strong, non-functional values which add up to its reputation and image. When this happens, there is a rub-off on the consumers' perceptions of the brand's physical attributes themselves. Even though blind tests prove otherwise, consumers begin to feel that the brand is superior in terms of its physical performance—it has better 'aroma', 'it tastes better', 'it washes whiter', 'it gives a smoother smoke', 'it relieves headache faster', and so on.

It will thus be seen that there is an integral connection between the position of the brand as perceived by the target consumer and at least some of the brand's functional and non-functional attributes. Knowing this, the brand manager will want to bring about a close cohesion between these two sets of attributes and the desired position for his brand. The ideal condition in which to do so is for a new brand.

Positioning a New Magazine

We turn now to a situation where a marketer has discovered a 'hole' or vacant position in the market and is planning a new product to fill that position. He is not constrained as in the case of the existing product.

What is the relationship to that vacant position of the physical and other attributes of the product-to-be? Let us take the example of a magazine, in this case, launched by the Ananda Bazar Group.

A magazine is also a product, and like any other product, as the *Journal of Marketing* writes, "the success of a journal depends to a large extent on establishing a unique position for it in the market place".[3]

Positioning calls for mind-reading and the marketing team of the Ananda Bazar Group and its agency, Clarion, began by studying the minds of the readers of Bengali magazines and came up with this positioning hypothesis.

> *There is high female readership of Bengali magazines but there is only one magazine devoted to women—Sukanya (as of 1986). There is scope for a new Bengali magazine for educated, younger, middle and upper middle class women; it has to be modern and contemporary and it must be smarter and more elegant than magazines currently available.*

The client and agency team then had to spell out in greater detail the attributes that would be needed by the new magazine, to fill that vacant position.

This is true consumer-oriented thinking. Positioning strategy came first: looking at the world of Bengali magazines through the consumer's eyes and locating a promising vacant position in the minds of a certain segment. Product attributes came next. They were determined by that position. And a very successful Bengali magazine was born: *Sananda*.

The original target of circulation was 30,000 copies, but the orders from agents were much higher. In fact, the first issue dated July 31, 1986, sold 75,000 copies. It was a sell-out within three hours of appearing on the news stands.

Brand Personality

The following paragraphs (see Box on pp. 68–69) laid down the tangible, visible attributes of *Sananda*, in order to claim the desired position in the target reader's mind.

The authors of the strategy were emphatic that *Sananda* should also be endowed with the more subtle emotional values that would really 'lock' the journal to that coveted position in the psyche of the Bengali woman magazine reader.

To do this, they went through an illuminating exercise in verbalising the 'personality' that was to be projected for the magazine through its advertising and in the design and contents of the 'product' itself.

Why 'personality'? What is meant by 'personality of a brand'?

The functional features of a brand should draw the consumer response: "That is the benefit I am looking for". This response is on a rational plane.

(Continued on p. 72)

Sanada Projects Herself

On a Sensory Level

I would like to be thought of as a trim, well-dressed, bright and attractive person. Someone who brings colour and polish to individual expression and can carry off smart clothes, cosmetics and accessories on her person with elan. A woman with style and a cut above the rest.

On a Rational Level

I would like to be seen as an intelligent and outgoing person who is easy to make friends with. My ability to entertain, inform and empathise should make me welcome. My kind of language, views and style should identify me as independent, sophisticated and contemporary.

My contemporariness and independence are reflected in my responses to a changing world, in my life style and also in my balance of inherited values and my own discovered values. These are apparent in the way I decorate my home, in my name, my originality in cooking; my more self-assured attitude towards the opposite sex; my attitude towards social taboos and the discovery of individual ways to enjoy leisure.

On an Emotional Level

I would like to feel wanted and loved as a person close to the heart of my friends. Warm, intimate, charming and understanding...these are the impressions I would like to project about myself. I am unlikely to forget a birthday and will send flowers to a loved one. When I visit a friend, I am likely to be greeted with a big smile.

এই হল আমার জমজমাট সংসার

Exhibit 3.10

I am Sananda
Meet my 'impossible' family. While Sananda's *horizons are larger than the home and the kitchen, she certainly enjoys all her traditional roles: mother, wife, daughter-in-law. The mundane also offers a lot of fun. The values of sharing love, affection and care are what come from a family. These are also facets that reflect* Sananda. *The photograph depicts the simple pleasures inherent in* Sananda's *everyday life.*

আমি স্বামীর সঙ্গে কাঁধ মিলিয়ে রোজগার করি

Exhibit 3.11

I am Sananda
I work shoulder to shoulder with my husband to care for our family.
Sananda *shares the attitudes and beliefs of the target consumer. The values of sexual emancipation are fundamental to the personality of* Sananda. *The photograph shows her completely at home in her office.* Sananda *is projected as a woman who, while believing in the equality of the sexes, also likes to stand by her husband.*

Exhibit 3.12

I am Sananda
If I can't look after myself how can I look after my home?

Sananda's *personality is also inward-looking. Hence this advertisement projects her as one who is conscious and attentive to her health and physique. But her interests do not prompt her to seek glamour. She believes in being fit...fit to do her job and fulfil her self-appointed role well.*

নিজের শরীরের খেয়াল না রাখলে সংসারের খেয়াল রাখব কেমন করে?

Sananda Positioning Note[4]

Target Segment
- Women 25–40 years; with education of SSC level/higher; household income Rs 1,500 plus per month, living in towns of 5 lakh and over.
- Attitudinally, they are modern, somewhat contemporary but they also respect some traditional values. 'Upwardly mobile'.

Competition
- Directly positioned against *Sukanya.*
- Indirect competition from other magazines with high women's readership.

Proposed Positioning
- A magazine primarily for women—also friendly to men.
- Modern and contemporary.
- Reflects the taste of sophisticated readers.
- Serious in its coverage of issues, yet offers entertainment and relaxed reading.
- Contents similar to competition but more smart and elegant in presentation.

Sananda *is a Modern Woman's Magazine*

Product Specifics
- Choice of editor was a critical part of the positioning decision. She had to be someone who would reflect the tastes and aspirations of this 'modern and contemporary' Bengali woman. Better still, she should be someone whom the target audience would recognize and readily accept such as a symbol. Who else but Aparna Sen, the noted actress-turned-film director of *36 Chowringhee Lane* fame?
- The price was fixed at Rs 5 a copy compared to Rs 3.50 of *Sukanya.*
- A fortnightly.
- Better editorial environment and presentation.
- More literary content than competition.
- Smart and elegant design.
- Bright printing on better quality paper.

The non-functional features should draw the response: "I have a good feeling about this product". This is a response on the emotional plane. One way in which such emotional values are added to a brand—although not the only way—is to give the brand a 'personality'. That is, to breathe life into the brand and make it appear as a 'person'. The objective is to create a feeling of warmth for the brand, a feeling of 'friendship', to draw from the prospect the response: "It's my kind of product".

But remember that

> As with a human being the totality of a brand is a composite of physical and psychological features.

In parenthesis and by way of an amusing digression, guess the 'personality' of the well-known analgesic in the USA—'Excedrin'. In a study of brand personalities conducted there, "Excedrin was linked most often with Richard Nixon!"[5]

The authors of *Sananda*'s strategy prefaced the search for its personality by starting at the right place. What response from the target consumer should the magazine's 'personality' arouse? They phrased this response, which they called the consumer positioning statement, as: "I love *Sananda*'s sparkling style and her warm, bright personality".

Together with their agency, the client went through a process of 'making of the brand come alive' so as to sharply define the intended 'personality' and to stimulate the right advertising creativity.

A series of six press ads (in Bengali) and TV commercials on the same theme and projecting the same personality were used to launch the magazine.

Some of these ads are reproduced here (Exhibits 3.10 to 3.12). We give an English rendering of the headlines and a synopsis of the message.

SUMMING UP

> The position that we seek in a consumer's mind is based upon the knowledge of the consumer's perceptions of a product category.

What is the imprint of various brands in that consumer's mind? Is there a vacant position? Of what stuff is it made? The answers lead us to a product concept—a configuration showing its functional attributes and benefits, and the emotional or psychological values which it must offer.

This is the practical as well as conceptual relationship between position, product attributes and product proposition or consumer benefit. The positioning decision comes first. The other decisions follow. They are integrated to the position sought and help to reinforce it in the prospect's mind.

The position which a brand seeks in the target prospect's mind is influenced by its functional features or attributes. The attribute must be such as to make the position credible. Thus, the position of a children's toothpaste requires a likeable taste, with foaming properties.

The brand manager, however, is not completely constrained by such attributes. He has the flexibility to emphasize some attributes, which is more in line with a desired position and de-emphasize some other attribute, which does not reinforce that position. He can also change the consumer's perception of an attribute—although this is a more difficult task—as in the case of the early filter-tipped cigarettes. In a like manner he may create or modify the position of a brand by emphasizing a particular benefit to the exclusion of another.

The position of a brand is also influenced by its non-functional features because a brand is a composite entity, comprising functional as well as emotional or psychological values.

One important way in which such emotional values are added is by creating a personality for the brand, a subject we will examine further in Chapter 5.

In Chapter 5 we will look at the various positioning strategies which the brand manager has at his command.

REFERENCES

1. Glatzer, Robert, *The New Advertising* (The Citadel Press, New York) pp 121–135. The reader is referred to another account of 'The Marlboro Story' in the chapter on "Image & Competitive Position" in the book on *Advertising Management* by David A. Aaker and John G. Myers (Prentice- Hall of India Pvt. Ltd., 1977).
2. Kotler, Philip, *Principles of Marketing* (Prentice-Hall of India Pvt. Ltd., 1983) Chapter 2 on "The Marketing Management Process".
3. "Repositioning the Journal of Marketing" *Journal of Marketing*, (Spring 1970).
4. *Sananda* Campaign Presentation Note (Courtesy: Ananda Bazar Group and Clarion Advertising).
5. Alsop, Ronald and Bill Abrams, "Hitchhiking on Proven Brand Names" *Wall Street Journal on Marketing* (Dow Jones-Irwin, 1982) pp 41–49.

Chapter 4

The Pursuit of Differential Advantage: Strategies for Competitive Advantage

CORNERSTONES OF POSITIONING STRATEGY

Positioning is the pursuit of differential advantage.

Brands can create franchises of loyal consumers only when they are seen to be different in some way which is persuasive for the target segment. Recall that famous article by Prof. Levitt, "Marketing Success through Differentiation—of Anything".[1] There is no such thing as a commodity, he argues. All goods and services are differentiable.

We know that as brands tend to become physically similar—as the better mousetrap is followed by a dozen 'me-too' mousetraps more or less equal in performance—the brand manager falls back more and more on non-functional factors to distinguish his brand. Persuasive differentiation becomes an increasingly difficult task.

One of the major contributions of positioning theory to marketing strategy has been to bring out the concept of 'distance' and dissimilarity between brands in the 'perceptual space' of the prospect and to uncover the many opportunities for such perceived differentiation based upon the capabilities of the product and its antecedents.

Positioning puts in the hands of the brand manager an entire array of differentiating strategies. He must judge which of these strategies can help him locate a niche in the market where his brand may be perceived by his target segment as unique and where it will hold a competitive advantage.

These strategies revolve around different aspects of the brand which can be expressed as four questions posed on its behalf.

The four strategic questions are:

1. Who am I ?
2. What am I ?
3. For Whom am I ?
4. Why Me ?

The answers to these would determine the brand's position in the prospect's mind. Let's take a closer look at the four questions.

1. WHO AM I?

This question concerns the corporate credentials of the brand. The prospect is urged to think of the brand in terms of its origins, its family tree, the 'stable' from which it comes; the idea being that this can give the brand a competitive advantage.

Positioning by Corporate Identity

We see this most often with durables when a tried and trusted corporate identity or source—which has become a household name for some products like Philips for radios and lamps—is used to imply the competitive superiority of newer products bearing that name: Philips Mixies; Philips Electric Irons; Philips Refrigerators.

This can be such a strong positioning element that companies who market each brand under a different name, e.g. Hindustan Lever (Surf, Sunlight and Wheel detergent powders; Lifebuoy, Pears, Lux, Rexona, Liril bath soaps) nevertheless introduce the corporate credential as a byline:

A quality product of Hindustan Lever

The Tata Oil Mills Company Ltd. (TOMCO) endorses its brands (e.g. Hamam, Jai, OK, Revel, 501) with the words, "A TATA Product". So does the Godrej Company.

Positioning by Brand Endorsement

When a brand has proved very successful the marketer can exploit the strength of that name for entering another product category. After the phenomenal success of Nirma Washing Powder (see Chapter 6) it seemed logical to give the next entry—a detergent bar—the same brand name. The third entry of this company—a toilet soap (presently in test markets)—also bears the same brand name. The popular toilet soap market in India is very competitive with strongly entrenched brands like Lux, Rexona, Hamam. Nirma bath soap enters this market with a credible, competitive answer to the consumer's query, "Who are you? Do I know you?" C. Merle Crawford refers to this positioning strategy as 'parentage'.

> *Parentage...because of where it comes from, who makes it, who sells it, who performs it, etc. The three ways of parentage positioning are brand (Cadillac or Citizen printer), company (the Data General/One or Kodak diskette), and person.*[2]

Some of the practical questions that arise are: "How much of parentage?" "How much of offspring?" When Vazir Sultan Company, owners of the Charminar brand of cigarettes, decided to diversify and launch new cigarettes they had to find answers to this difficult question. Charminar at one time was considered among the world brands in terms of its sales volume. At that time it was by far the largest selling brand in India. The brand was priced at the lower end of the market, but its smokers cut across various strata.

With new brands on the drawing board, the Company had to decide whether the well-known Charminar name should be used to position its new entrants. If so, with what degree of emphasis? It should be noted that Vazir Sultan, the Company, was relatively unknown. It was often referred to as 'the Charminar Company'. Hence 'parentage' was embodied in the name 'Charminar'.

The first major new brand from the Charminar 'stable' was a filter called 'Charminar Gold'. The company had a two-fold objective. First, it wanted to establish a distinct identity for 'Gold' with its promise of "smoothness and satisfaction—only Gold has both". Second, it wished to give the new brand a good start with the trade and consumers alike by referring to its origins. The pack designs of the mother brand, Charminar and of Charminar Gold (Exhibits 4.1 and 4.2) and the press ad for the new brand (Exhibit 4.3) show how this dual purpose was tackled. Note the varying emphasis on 'Charminar' and 'Gold'.

You will find a completely different emphasis in another filter brand of this company: 'Charminar Filter' (Exhibit 4.4).

A major landmark for this company was the decision to enter the upper reaches of the cigarette market in India with a Virginia type king-sized filter. If you are too young to remember, your older friends will recall that the vastly popular Charminar was affectionately nick-named 'Charms' by many of its up-market loyalists.

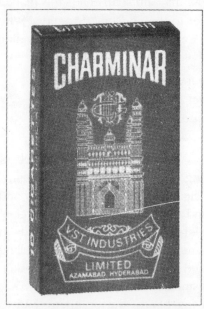

Exhibit 4.1   **Exhibit 4.2**

Note the differing emphasis on 'Charminar', the parent brand and its offshoot, 'Charminar Gold'. The colours of the packs are also different.

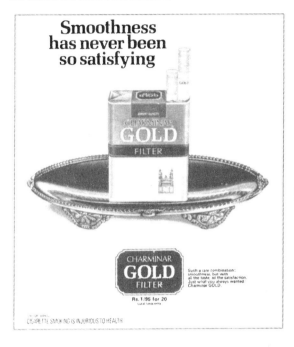

Exhibit 4.3 *The 'satisfaction' associated with well-known Charminar and the 'smoothness' created by the filter are brought together to create a new identity. (Agency: Clarion)*

Exhibit 4.4 *This pack design makes it clear that the cigarette is Charminar in its filter version.*

In 1981, a spectacularly successful king-sized Virginia filter cigarette entered the market with the brand name of 'Charms', clothed in a handsome denim-like packet and bearing a tantalizing message:

Charms is the spirit of freedom;

Charms is the way you are.

In such situations, marketing management has to find the right balance. How much of parentage positioning will give the new brand a good start against competition? How much will swamp its identity and prevent the prospect from recognizing a new and different offering? Do you think the right balance was struck as seen in the Charms ad (Exhibit 4.5 Plate 3)?

This can be quite a thorny dilemma as you will find from this account of a new toothpaste brand launched in 1984 as an extension of the Forhan's range.

For some time, Geoffrey Manners (who make and market the Forhan's range) had noted with concern that their flagship brand— Forhan's Regular—was attracting fewer and fewer of younger, urban consumers with modern tastes. At one time this was the No. 2 brand in India after Colgate. With the launch of Forhan's Fluoride (see Chapter 3) the total market share of the Company had increased but they still felt the absence of a brand which would carve out a niche within the broad spectrum favouring Colgate (about 50% market share).

The positioning concept of the new brand was expressed as follows:

A high quality foaming toothpaste for modern, young people;
it has a pleasing minty taste and also gives the reassurance
of care of the gums.

From this positioning concept arose the name: 'Forhan's Freshmint'. Getting down to brass tacks, the Company had to decide "How much of Forhan's? How much of Freshmint?" Freshmint is what differentiated the brand from its 'parent'.

The parentage positioning dilemma was this. Had the name 'Forhan's', over the years, acquired a highly therapeutic and 'stodgy' image which would detract from the modernity and taste appeal of the new brand? Yet, how could the brand position itself, not as a pimply little me-too to Colgate, but as a strong contender for those young urban men and women who would opt for a brand that tasted as good as Colgate, appealed to their sense of modernity, and also promised them a meaningful difference compared to Colgate?

The name 'Forhan's' was already well-known and had a widely accepted association with gum care. If the power of this name did not back the new brand, would it be easy to challenge Colgate with a brand which was totally unknown? Should 'Forhan's' be played up? Played down?

The first testing ground to resolve this dilemma was the pack design. Eventually, after many designs, it was felt that the pack seen in Exhibit 4.6 (Plate 3) represented the optimal answer to the question: "Who am I?" The ad which launched Forhan's Freshmint is seen in the same exhibit. Such strategies touch upon 'line extensions' and 'brand extensions' which we will discuss further in Chapter 10.

The reader will find a good discussion of this delicate balance between a familiar corporate or umbrella brand name and the identity of the brand struggling to be born, in John Diefenbach's *The Corporate Identity as the Brand.*[3]

2. WHAT AM I?

The positioning strategies around this question relate to the product's functional capabilities. They offer the brand manager considerable scope for perceived brand differentiation.

'What am I?' differentiating strategies can be grouped under:
(a) Category-related positioning
(b) Benefit-related positioning
(c) Positioning by usage occasion and time
(d) Price–Quality positioning

Category-Related Positioning

An important differentiating strategy when an existing product category is too crowded is to take the same basic product and position it in another category, provided the attributes of the product can match consumer expectations from that category. Your brand will then be perceived by prospects in a different light. This is referred to in the jargon as 'macro-positioning' or 'inter-set positioning'.[4]

If you are marketing a skimmed milk powder, for instance, the same basic product can be positioned as:

(i) *reconstituted milk* as we see in the hypothetical 'Akul Home Dairy' concept ad (Exhibit 4.7).

If this position is already occupied you can position your brand as:

(ii) *a whitener for tea and coffee* as in the 'Akul Special' ad (Exhibit 4.8).

Considering the growing interest in physical fitness you can position it as:

(iii) 'Akul Weight-Watcher', the health-giving, low-calorie *milk for the diet conscious* (Exhibit 4.9).

Again, following international trends you might decide to enter the *breakfast foods* category and position your milk powder as:

(iv) 'Akul Instant Breakfast'—see the product concept in Exhibit 4.10.

Remember we are talking of the same physical product in four different incarnations. What are the implications of such category-related positioning or repositioning?

Once you have chosen the category in which to slot your brand, you should be prepared for suitable modifications in the product and other elements of the marketing mix. If a milk powder has to be positioned as a 'whitener' for tea or coffee you will take great care over its instant solubility. You may also introduce a creamier variety. For the 'Home Dairy' position, it should be readily soluble in hot and cold water without leaving lumps. As an 'instant breakfast' you may need to add vitamins and other nutrients and possibly, flavours. It must also offer good taste.

Thus, once the category positioning decision is taken, the smart marketer will try to modify the functional features of his existing brand to mesh more closely with that position. If it is a new brand he will design it from scratch so as to make it a perfect match (see Chapter 3).

The packaging form for 'Home Dairy' may be a metal can. For the 'whitener' it may be serving-size sachets. For 'instant breakfast' it may be a glass jar.

Plate 3

Exhibit 4.5 *This brand's link with Charminar is deliberately tenuous and expressed only through the symbol of the famous monument on the pack and the abbreviation, 'Charms'. (Agency: Enterprise) See p. 80.*

Exhibit 4.6 *How much of 'parentage'? How much of 'offspring'? An experiment in marrying the reputation of Forhan's to the taste and modernity demanded by the younger generation. (Agency: Clarion) See p. 81.*

Plate 4

DOES YOUR TOOTHPASTE GIVE YOU DENTAL INSURANCE?

Get free dental insurance worth Rs. 1000/- with every Pepsodent pack.

"FILL UP THE PROPOSAL FORM AS THE INSTRUCTIONS PROVIDED HERE AND GET 1 YEAR DENTAL INSURANCE POLICY FROM NEW INDIA ASSURANCE WORTH RUPEES 1000, FREE OF COST**"

INSTRUCTIONS FOR APPLICATION

• USE A BALL POINT PEN WITH BLACK OR BLUE INK AND WRITE IN CAPITAL LETTERS. WHILE WRITING DO NOT TOUCH THE BORDER OF THE BOXES IN WHICH YOU ARE WRITING.
• Proposals must be in ENGLISH ONLY. Proposals will not be accepted in any other language.
• All Addresses must be accompanied with PINCODE. Applications without PINCODE will not be processed.
• After filling up the Proposal form completely, read the DECLARATION and sign it at the bottom mentioning the Date as token of acceptance of the terms & conditions of the Policy.
• Send the completed Proposal Form along with one empty carton of Pepsodent Superior.
• Cut the Proposal Form along the lines indicated, insert it in an envelope along with one empty carton of Pepsodent Superior, fix RS. 5/- Stamp on the envelope and post it to:
PEPSODENT SPECIAL CONTINGENCY INSURANCE, POST BOX NO. 4335, KALKAJI, NEW DELHI 110019

** Note
• Conditions apply as per Prospectus printed below.
• Postage for application & claims to be borne by the applicant.
• Hindustan Lever Limited is not responsible for Proposals or Policy certificates lost in transit.

PROPOSAL FORM (Print Advertisement)

PLEASE FILL THE FORM WITH BALL POINT PEN IN CAPITAL LETTERS USING BLACK OR BLUE INK. DO NOT TOUCH THE BORDER OF THE BOXES WHILE WRITING. APPLICATION FOR MINOR WILL HAVE TO BE SIGNED BY THE GUARDIAN. ONE PROPOSAL FORM IS FOR ONE INDIVIDUAL ONLY. KINDLY ATTACH ONE EMPTY CARTON OF PEPSODENT SUPERIOR ALONG WITH THIS PROPOSAL FORM.

Name of Beneficiary — First Name / Middle Name / Last Name / Family Name / Surname

Date of Birth: DD MM YY — Sex (tick✓) Male Female

Address: House No. / Street / Area / City / State / Pin Code / Telephone (if any)

Signature / Date

Put this form along with 1 empty carton of Pepsodent inside an envelope, affix Rs. 5/- stamp and send it to: "Pepsodent Special Contingency Insurance" Post Box No. 4335, Post Office Kalkaji, New Delhi 110 019

Notice: Filling up this Proposal Form does not entitle any person to be insured under the Policy. M/s. Hindustan Lever Limited reserves the right to reject any person from being covered under this Policy. The details provided by the intended beneficiary may be verified by Hindustan Lever Limited and failure on part of the beneficiary to provide documents certifying the details will result in rejection or cancellation of the cover ab initio. Incomplete Proposal Forms shall not be accepted for coverage under this Policy. Beneficiary Certificate along with Unique Beneficiary ID shall be sent to the Applicant within 30 days from the day the Application is received. M/s. Hindustan Lever Limited is not responsible for Proposals or Insurance Certificates lost in transit. **Last date for receiving completed Proposal Form is 30th April 2003.**

DECLARATION

I hereby declare and warrant that the above statements are true and complete. I consent and authorize the insurers to seek information from any hospital/dental Surgeon who has at any time attended or may attend concerning any dental disorder which affects me. I agree that this proposal shall form the basis of the contract should the insurance be effected. If after the insurance is effected, it is found that the statements answer or particulars stated in the proposal form are incorrect or untrue in any aspect, neither Hindustan Lever Limited nor The New India Assurance Company Limited shall incur any liability under this insurance.

I have read extract of the prospectus and am willing to accept the coverage subject to the terms, conditions and exceptions prescribed by the Insurance Company therein.

Signature: _____ Date: _____

(Contd)

Exhibit 4.12 *(Courtesy: Lowe)*

Plate 5

PEPSODENT SPECIAL CONTINGENCY INSURANCE - PROSPECTUS

SALIENT FEATURES OF THE POLICY (This is an extract from the complete Prospectus of the Policy. The complete Prospectus is available for Public reading at the Registered Office of Hindustan Lever Limited, 165-166, Backbay Reclamation, Mumbai 400 020 and at all the branch offices).

DEFINITIONS

CLINIC: Clinic shall mean any registered institute or establishment under the supervision of a qualified Dental Surgeon.

PERIOD OF INSURANCE: Coverage period commences from the first day of the month that follows expiry of 6 months from the day of issue of Beneficiary Certificate and ends after 1 year from the date of commencement. Both these days are shown in the Beneficiary Certificate. The last date of receiving completed proposal forms is 30th April 2003.

COVERED EXPENSES: Expenses shall mean and include the following:

1. Expenses for the extraction of a permanent tooth or teeth due to severe caries including cost of medication in relation thereto
2. Expenses for treatment of Periodontitis resulting into loss of tooth including cost of medication in relation thereto.

But does not include the expenses whatsoever incurred by any Beneficiary in connection with or in respect of:

1. All dental conditions requiring orthodontics, crown and bridge-work, aesthetic dental work, dentures, implants, precision attachments or prosthesis for any cause whatsoever, expenses for fillings or root canal treatment and expenses for extraction of tooth or teeth due to any other cause other than severe caries.
2. All systemic underlying disease causing and/or leading to tooth or teeth extraction e.g : AIDS, Diabetes, mellitus, congenital Periodontal diseases, tumors both benign and malignant and oral pre-cancerous conditions, and treatment of tobacco related disorders.
3. Any disorder that happens to the BENEFICIARY outside the Period of Insurance as shown in the Beneficiary Certificate.
4. Any disorder that happens to or leads to extraction of milk teeth.
5. Any disorder that happens to beneficiaries not within the age limit specified in the prospectus.
6. Impacted wisdom tooth.

REIMBURSEMENT

The policy covers reimbursement of medical/surgical treatment for the covered expenses at a dental clinic/hospital as detailed below. In the event of any Beneficiary incurring medical/surgical expenses at a dental clinic/hospital for treatment of disorders listed under **COVERED EXPENSES**, the company will reimburse the Beneficiary the amount of such expenses as per the following limits:

- Dental Surgeon's Consultation Fee up to Rs. 150
- Cost of dental procedure under Local Anesthesia up to Rs 400
- Cost of related medication up to Rs 250
- Cost of extraction of tooth due to severe caries up to Rs 100
- Cost of x-ray up to Rs 100
- (Rs 200 in Delhi, Mumbai, Chennai, Kolkata, Bangalore & Hyderabad)

Provided the total amount for all the expenses incurred on the above heads do not exceed the insured amount of Rs. 1000 (Rs. 1100 in case of named 6 cities).

AGE LIMIT: This insurance is available to users of Pepsodent in respect of permanent tooth or teeth, provided the age of the beneficiary does not exceed 50 years as on the date of Application for Enrollment.

CLAIM PROCEDURES

Final Claim along with particulars relating to I. Unique Certificate ID Number, II. Name of the Beneficiary, III. Nature of Disorder, IV. Name and Address of the Dental Clinic, V. Receipted Bills/Cash Memo, VI. Claim Form, and, list of documents as listed in claim form should be sent to 'Pepsodent Special Contingency Insurance' Post Box no. 4335, Kalkaji, New Delhi 110019 within 30 days of completion of treatment. Every claim should be accompanied with 3 empty cartons of Pepsodent Superior of any size as proof of continued use of Pepsodent Toothpaste during the period of Insurance.

PAYMENT OF CLAIM

Payments for admissible claims will be made in Indian Currency and through A/C Payee Cheque/Pay Order/Demand Draft after due processing and on receipt of duly signed Discharge Voucher from the Beneficiary. Such payment will be made within 30 days from the date of receiving the signed Discharge Voucher from the Beneficiary.

OTHER TERMS

- This Policy is available to citizens of India.
- All medical/surgical treatments under this policy shall have to be taken in India.
- This Policy shall benefit only those who fill up the Proposal Form as per the INSTRUCTIONS provided.
- M/s. Hindustan Lever Limited reserves the right to reject any person from being covered under this Policy without assigning any reason.
- The details provided by the intended Beneficiary may be verified by Hindustan Lever Limited and failure on part of the Beneficiary to provide documents certifying the details will result in rejection of claim and or cancellation of the Beneficiary Certificate ab initio.

IN ASSOCIATION WITH THE NEW INDIA ASSURANCE CO. LTD.

GET PEPSODENT. GET FREE DENTAL INSURANCE.

A quality product from Hindustan Lever Ltd.

LOWE PEP 1 404

Exhibit 4.12 *This is a good example of how a competetive advantage can be created by adding a service value to an FMCG brand.*
(Courtesy: Lowe) See p. 86.

Plate 6

Exhibit 4.25 *"Power Jogger is all about fitness", says this ad. See p. 112.*

Exhibit 4.26 *Power Ultimo—positioned for the tennis enthusiast. See p. 112.*

Notice how the three Power brands have been positioned for different lifestyle segments. (Agency: Clarion).

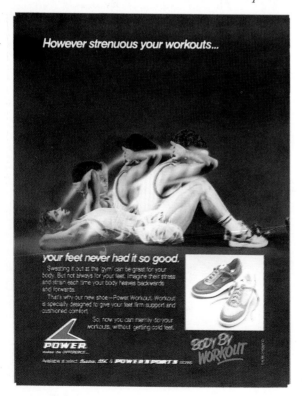

Exhibit 4.27 *Power workout. See p. 112.*

Exhibit 4.7 *Skimmed milk powder positioned as reconstituted milk (with apologies to Amul).*

Exhibit 4.8 *The same generic product now positioned as an instant whitener for tea and coffee.*

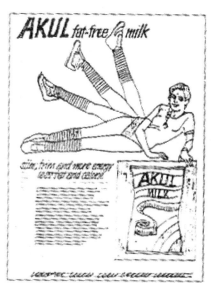

Exhibit 4.9 *The hypothetical product now seen as fat-free milk.*

Exhibit 4.10 *Yet another incarnation of 'Akul'—an instant breakfast full of nourishment.*

Distribution modifications may be needed as well. The 'weight-watcher' product may also fit on chemists' shelves for example, and certainly in the emerging health-food outlets.

The category-related positioning decision determines the product market in which you will operate. It defines your competition. You will wish to choose a category where there are no strong competitors making your brand a 'me-too'. You may choose to enter a long haul category because you believe it has a future, like 'instant breakfast' or a food for the diet conscious.

In an ad for a capital issue which appeared in November 1988, a new Company, the Amrit Protein Foods Ltd., announced as its object:

> *A complete line of fitness foods: Health and fitness are making big headlines these days. And to meet the growing demand for new generation fitness foods, Amrit Protein will manufacture a wide range of products: Soya Milk, Soya Milk Beverages, Soya Dessert, and High Quality Soya Paneer.*

Somebody evidently believes that there is a long-term future for beverages and foods positioned in the category of 'fitness foods'.

With this positioning decision you are really making your bed and you must be prepared to lie on it. Repositioning is indeed possible and may sometimes be unavoidable. But it is better to make a long-term decision in the first place.

The Maruti Van was initially positioned and advertised as a van. It was to compete against Bajaj and Standard Vans. Later it was renamed 'Omni' and repositioned as the most spacious car on the Indian road. Its competition was with the other cars like Ambassador and Fiat and indeed, the Maruti car itself. As a matter of fact, many consumers had already placed the Maruti Van in this position in their minds as shown by their attitudes to it and the way they used it. Maruti Udyog was recognizing this fact in their new advertising (Exhibit 4.11).

Benefit-Related Positioning

A well made product would usually offer more than one benefit. Promises of multiple benefits, however, tend to get lost because they leave in the consumer's mind a vague and diffused imprint. Successful

Exhibit 4.11 *The Maruti 'Van' (as it was initially positioned) was repositioned as the most spacious car on the road. (Agency): HTA)*

consumer products promise one or at the most two benefits and brand franchises are created around those specific benefits. Thus we have the opportunity for differentiation of similar products based on benefit positions which have not yet been occupied.

Consumers, who are similar in important ways, tend to cluster around the same benefit. Other consumers would cluster around other benefits. This enables differentiation in a product market and has been well documented as 'Benefit Segmentation'.[5]

Russel J. Haley conducted research among toothpaste users in the USA (1963) and divided them into segments, each desiring a specific benefit from their brand of toothpaste. He uncovered four such benefit segments and their respective brand choices:

Economy : those who were looking for low price.

Cosmetic : those who wanted white, bright teeth.

Taste : those to whom taste mattered the most.

Medicinal : those who were concerned about prevention of decay.

Each benefit-seeking group or segment had certain common characteristics—demographic, psychographic, and also behaviouristic.

There is no published account of similar research on the toothpaste market in India. Judged by their advertising, the benefit positions occupied or sought by major brands would be approximately as follows:

Benefit Position	Brand
Cosmetic: White, bright teeth	Close-Up
Fresh breath	Colgate, Close-Up, Forhan's Regular
Taste	Colgate
Decay prevention	Colgate, Colgate Fluorigard, Binaca Fluoride, Signal
Gum care and other therapeutic	Forhan's Regular, Promise, Neem
Decay prevention and tartar control	Crest

As you can see, Colgate, the market leader by far, is positioned across a broad band of benefits. Others are positioned by more specific benefits.

A new differentiated positioning opportunity can be sought by offering a unique combination of benefits. This was the thinking behind Forhan's Freshmint which offered the gum-care benefit of Forhan's plus the minty taste associated with Colgate.

The introduction of 'Crest' in the above table is pure speculation at this time (1989) on the part of the author. But since Procter & Gamble are now formally in India, one may well expect this gifted brand to surface here.

Features or Benefits?

In some texts, the phrase 'positioning by features and attributes' is also used and is referred to separately from 'benefits'. For example, Wind in his book on Product Policy says:

> *Positioning on specific product features:*
>
> *Positioning a product by its performance on specific product attributes is among the most common approaches to positioning, especially for industrial products...product feature positioning can range from specific tangible benefits (such as Chevette as the economy car or VW's 'Think Small' to more abstract features such as Avis' 'We Try Harder').*
>
> *Positioning on benefits, problem solutions or needs:*
>
> *Strongly linked to product feature positioning is benefit positioning, which is generally more effective than positioning which describes product features without their benefit to the consumer.*[6]

It is clear from the above that even when positioning is based on a specific feature of a product, the objective is or should be to position it in terms of the benefit flowing from that feature or attribute. There is no contraction between the two because consumers buy benefits not features. Even industrial product purchasers buy solutions to problems and not attributes *per se*. Features become important to the consumer only when they lead to that special benefit which the consumer seeks.

The importance of a brand's physical features or attributes in the context of positioning lies more in offering a convincing 'reason-why' the brand will indeed deliver the promised benefit. We will, therefore, look at 'Positioning by Product Features' with regard to the brand's question, 'Why choose me?' later in this chapter.

In some cases the tangible, functional differences between brands would be substantial and these are situations where the marketer has the inestimable advantage of a USP (Unique Selling Proposition) enabling him to promise a benefit which others do not or cannot. This would be true of Forhan's Regular or Close-Up toothpaste for instance.

But even when the physical characteristics or attributes of brands are similar, benefit-related positioning enables the brand manager to create a perceived differentiation between basically like products.

Let us take the example of a hypothetical chocolate malt-based beverage and let us christen it 'Brown-Vita'. At least four strong positions can be created around the basic formulation or physical characteristics of the product. For the sake of our example, we will use the same brand name throughout this example but each of these positions can be filled by a distinct brand commanding its own loyal segment. Thus, our brand, Brown-Vita, can be positioned in the health beverage category as a chocolate-based drink which has a lot of good taste.

The health drink that's full of Taste

Or we can position Brown-Vita as the energy drink emphasizing its carbohydrate contents.

The health drink packed with Energy

Or Brown-Vita can be positioned for its natural goodness. We would make much of its ingredients—malt, milk, cocoa—and stress the absence of artificial ingredients. It would be:

The health drink full of Natural Goodness

And finally, we might highlight the non-fattening properties of Brown-Vita as well as its proteins and vitamins to promise the benefit of low calories plus nourishment value:

The health drink high in Nourishment and low in Calories

There are four major brands belonging to this category of cocoa and malt-based health beverages which are presently marketed in India:

Bournvita

Maltova

Boost

Nutramul

Look at the ads for these brands reproduced here and judge how they have differentiated themselves through benefit-related positioning (Exhibits 4.13, 4.14, 4.15 and 4.16).

Emotional Benefits

When we talk of benefit-related positioning, we must remember that a brand is a composite entity and the position which the consumer gives it in her mind represents her perception of the brand in terms of its tangible or functional benefits and also its non-functional or emotional benefits.

How do we handle the concept of emotional or non-functional benefit in the practical task of creating a distinct and persuasive position for the brand?

Although the concept is now well accepted by marketing and advertising practitioners, applying the concept to create a persuasive difference between functionally similar brands is a more complex task. We will look into this in Chapter 5.

Exhibit 4.13 *An ad for Bournvita.* **Exhibit 4.14** *A Maltova ad. (Agency:*
(Agency: O&M)   *Frank Simoes Associates)*

Exhibit 4.15 *The base line says that Boost is the vitaminized energy fuel. (Agency: HTA)*

Exhibit 4.16 *An ad for nutramul. (Agency: Da Cunha Associates)*

Exhibit 4.17 *Cadbury's drinking chocolate's earlier positioning. (Agency: O&M)*

Exhibit 4.18 *Later positioning of the same brand. (Agency: O&M)*

Positioning by Usage Occasion and Time of Use

Positioning by usage occasion or application is another strong differentiating strategy within the ambit of the question, 'What am I?'. If a brand employs this strategy well, it can virtually pre-empt that particular usage. Find a strong usage position and sit on it...for instance, the condensed milk brand, Milkmaid (see Chapter 1), has come to dominate the dessert usage position so strongly that it cannot be easily dislodged by a competitor.

Cadbury's Drinking Chocolate experimented with two usage positions (Exhibits 4.17 and 4.18):

(i) *The relaxing way to end your day: The Good Night Cup,* and shortly afterwards,

(ii) *Now is the time to sit back and put up your feet...make this the happiest time of your day with Cadbury's Drinking Chocolate.*

As you see, usage occasion and time of use, or when to use, are often combined.

The reason for abandoning the Goodnight Cup position is not known. Can it be that this position was not given a proper trial? In these days of stress, tension, high pressures of work and competition, this represents in our view a potentially valuable usage position for a product with suitable features. At this moment it remains a vacant position in the branded beverage market in India.

An exceptionally single-minded usage positioning strategy, linked also to the time of use, is the positioning of Vicks VapoRub to be applied for a child's cold, at night. Many have tried to breach this position and failed. Vicks VapoRub has made this usage position virtually unassailable. We shall look at this striking example in greater depth in Chapter 6.

Burnol antiseptic ointment is for burns and strongly entrenched for that usage. Dettol antiseptic is for nicks and cuts, insect bites and other minor infections. Each of these brands has sat on its usage position for decades without any serious challenger. If you have found a good usage position for your brand, sit on it, make it your domain.

Interestingly, Dettol soap, re-launched in 1984, has made headway in the crowded premium toilet soap market by adopting a strategy of creating and dominating a specific usage occasion. This is the occasion when you feel particularly sticky or dirty or grimy and would respond to the idea of a '100% bath' (see Exhibit 4.19).

Exhibit 4.19 *A delightful way of communicating the position of Dettol soap. (Agency: Karishma)*

This makes Dettol more like a soap for a middle of the morning bath after a gruelling visit to the bazaar or the after-work bath at the end of a long hard day (no doubt, many consumers also use it at the start of the day). This is a courageous decision—having the boldness to dominate a specific usage position rather than peck ineffectively at a broad usage market—'A high quality soap for a bath'—or aim for an extremely narrow usage, 'the antiseptic bath soap'.

With this positioning, Dettol soap has climbed from 1.7% market share before its relaunch in 1984 to 3.7% share in 1988. This compares with 4.5% market share of a well-established, long-time brand like Pears. A selective usage position may turn out to be quite profitable after all, if it attracts an adequate number of consumers and you dominate the position.

Differentiate Similar Products

How do you draw upon positioning-by-usage to distinguish two physically identical products? Take a simple illustration—two brands of processed peanuts which serve as snacks.

'Cheers' Peanuts may be positioned as the tasty, crunchy snack to go with drinks.

'Champion' Peanuts, virtually identical in the laboratory, can be positioned as the nourishing after-a-game snack.

Mother Dairy in Kolkata has launched what is probably the first branded yoghurt in India in the internationally used polystyrene container. It is called '*Mishti Doi*' (literally, Sweet Curds) and its usage is as a dessert.

A competitor may launch his own very similar youghurt (unsweetened) as 'Chef's *Dahi*' to be used as a cooking aid by the housewife to create favourite dishes for family and guests such as *Dahi-bada* or delicacies such as '*Dahi* Fish Curry', etc.

For both the actually branded youghurt, '*Mishti Doi*', and the hypothetical one, 'Chef's *Dahi*', the main competition is of course with the unbranded *dahi* which is available from the sweetmeat shop around the corner in sweetened and unsweetened versions. Judging by international trends, branded youghurt may well be a growth category.

The Milkfood Company has launched Milkfood Yogurt with multi-usage positioning.

> *Eat it for breakfast. Or as a mid-morning snack. With a sandwich for lunch. Or even instead of tea. It's great as a dessert too.*

A competitor with a similar product may decide to dominate one or two of these positions or open up new usage positions such as in the school lunch box or as the *fitness snack* after a workout.

Product Line Positioning by Usage

To minimize cannibalization, as we said in Chapter 3, marketers adopt different positions for their brands in the same product category. Differentiation by usage occasion is one such strategy.

Union Carbide's Eveready (dry cell) batteries provide a good example.[7] Till the seventies, over 95% of the total battery demand came from torch and transistor usage. However, since the eighties, there has been a boom in the population of cassette tape recorders, two-in-ones, cameras using photoflash guns, battery-operated toys, calculators and other sophisticated equipment like TV remote controls, hearing aids, etc. These equipments are normally high drain devices and they consume more electrical energy per unit of time compared to equipment like torches and transistors. In addition, since these equipments are high value products, the need is more pronounced for a battery which is 'safe', i.e. less prone to leakages.

To meet this demand, Union Carbide developed a battery in 1985 using zinc chloride technology. Pricing for the product was fixed at a 20% higher level than Red Eveready, the company's premium brand in the standard range (see Exhibit 4.20). The pricing was arrived at after considering value to the consumer and price-elasticity. The following comparative table highlights the price-performance benefits of this product in relation to the best 'standard' battery available.

Exhibit 4.20 *A hoarding design for Red Eveready. The batteries are painted in red. (Agency: Rediffusion)*

AA Size	Performance Indices				
	Price Index	Torch	Transistor	Photoflash Guns	Toys
New Battery	120	125	120	200	200
Red Eveready	100	100	100	100	100

The company and its agency, Rediffusion, then considered the following positioning options.

1. *The Most Leakproof Battery Available in India*
To carry conviction one would have to compare it to standard batteries including Red Eveready. Also, 100% leakproof performance could not be guaranteed.

2. *The Superior Modern Technology Position*
Valid, but again this would have involved a comparison with Red Eveready. Besides, the competitive edge would be diminished when other brands like Novino and Nippo followed suit.

3. *Performance Positioning*
This could be a legitimate and strong positioning, but more than any of the other alternatives, this position would hurt Union Carbide more than its competitors. It would have implied the inferiority of the Eveready Standard range (Red, Blue and White) which comprised 45% of the total battery market.

4. *End-Use Based Positioning*
Market research studies conducted for batteries had clearly indicated that consumers have a definite hierarchical perception of quality relative to the end-use for the battery. For example, a transistor is perceived to be a higher order equipment than a torch and hence if a battery is said to be designed specially for transistor usage, it is superior to a battery made for torches.

Research data had also indicated that in the hierarchy of equipments, photoflash equipment was at the top, followed by cassette tape recorders (CTRs) and other motorized gadgets. Transistors came next, with torches at the bottom of the rung.

Positioning this battery as a product for 'modern machines', i.e. CTRs, photoflash equipment and other motorized equipment would have allowed consumer beliefs regarding the equipment hierarchy to rub off on to the new product and would definitely help to position the product as a top-of-the-line battery, without endangering Eveready's standard-line volumes/market share.

However, a focus on end-use equipment to prove performance superiority could only be effective if the consumer were given a 'reason-why' to believe the claim. The substantiation of this product claim lay in its zinc chloride technology. The technology linkage provided not only the 'reason-why' but also created a premium image by clearly establishing the battery in 'a class of its own' because of its modern, exclusive technology. It also allowed Union Carbide to exploit the technology leadership factor inherent in the zinc chloride process, without worrying about the impending competitive product launch.

Accordingly, this positioning statement for the new product, 'Eveready Super', was finally developed (see Exhibit 4.21):

> *No other battery can deliver such exceptionally high power and life for your power-hungry, high-drain devices because it is made with the breakthrough, first-time-in-India zinc chloride technology.*

Exhibit 4.21 *An ad for Union Carbide's top-of-the line battery: Eveready Super. (Agency: Rediffusion)*

Positioning by Usage to Broaden Market

A positioning-by-usage strategy is also adopted when a brand wishes to expand its market by creating and occupying other usage positions. This happens more often with mature brands where the existing market by usage has reached near-saturation as with Dettol antiseptic in urban markets in India.

Dettol antiseptic liquid, having dominated the cuts and wounds usage of the household market, went on to position itself for use in the shaving mug and for washing baby's nappies. Of late, Dettol ads have been recommending its use during illness to ward off infection (Exhibit 4.22). When a good product is formulated, its properties often lend themselves to multiple usage of the brand. These many usage positions are visualized when the label itself is written up.

Take a bottle of Dettol antiseptic and you will read about the following uses on its label apart from 'Cuts and Wounds'.

Personal Uses

As mouthwash and gargle
As dandruff shampoo
When shaving
For baby's nappies

(How-to-use instructions are given for each application).

The instructions on the label, if thoughtfully drawn up, thus give a general indication of the potential of the brand to broaden its usage. In retrospect, one can speculate whether ICI's Savlon antiseptic liquid would have had an easier passage if it had opted for a 'flanking' positioning strategy instead of taking Dettol head-on.

In the laboratory, Savlon was proved more effective against germs than Dettol. This was one of the reasons why Savlon commanded a good share of the institutional market like hospitals. Drawing inspiration from this, Savlon was advertised to the household market in India, in direct confrontation with powerful Dettol, with the message:

The other antiseptic (meaning Dettol) kills only the gram-positive germs. Savlon kills both gram-positive and gram-negative germs.

Exhibit 4.22 *An example of how Dettol is broadening its usage position. Other ads in the series urge its use on all baby's things—nappies, toys, etc. (Agency: Lintas)*

It is not surprising that the brand did not make much headway with the housewife who usually makes the buying decision for such a product.

Suppose, on the other hand, Savlon liquid was positioned as the antiseptic to be used like a shampoo against dandruff. Savlon's parentage—ICI—would have given it competitive credibility for such usage. The dandruff sufferer may have proved more receptive than the housewife to the semi-clinical message of Savlon's efficiency against multiple germs.

Other product features may have aided this usage position. Savlon does not sting. It lathers well. It does not discolour (as Dettol does) when mixed with water. It does not have Dettol's obtrusive smell. If it succeeded in this usage, Savlon antiseptic could have later broadened its market by nibbling away at Dettol's 'nicks and cuts' usage position.

As a footnote, we are tempted to make a comment based on Burnol's label. One would think that the brand name itself determines what Burnol's principal usage position would be.

The label, however, lists 'Burns' last in its catalogue of applications.

> *Burnol antiseptic*
> *soothing for treatment of wounds,*
> *abrasions,*
> *simple suppurating or*
> *topical sores,*
> *infective skin conditions, and*
> *Burns.*

If Burnol wished to broaden its position by usage, which way should it go?

Technology's Impact on Positioning by Usage

In course of a discussion at the Harvard Business School in summer 1988, Prof. Stephen Greyser gave this writer examples of how technology was causing firms to reconsider their positioning-by-usage strategies.

He referred to facsimile technology and its effect on overnight mail services. This impact of technology on positioning strategies can be visualized in India in the same context. Several large post offices and private firms are offering facsimile or fax services for immediate transmission of mail and documents. Air carrier services for overnight delivery of mail and packages, called 'courier' services, have mushroomed in India. If the Postal Department or privately owned fax services follow a 'penetration' pricing policy and attend to other consumer requirements, the courier services will have to reposition themselves for use as overnight package delivery services, and not for mail or documents.

The growth of fax services in India is also causing teleprinter manufacturers to defend and differentiate their usage. An ad of Hindustan Teleprinters (*The Statesman*, October 2, 1989) makes a comparison with PC-based telex and fax and positions the teleprinter as the only communications system suitable for 'tamper-proof', answer-back facility and the telex message as a legal document.

Research for Usage Positioning

Positioning by usage offers so many possibilities for new brand introduction and perceptual brand differentiation that the brand manager may wish to know about a research technique specially suitable for this purpose called 'item-by-use mapping'.

Take a product like potato chips as an example. By questioning respondents we may find that they think of it as a mid-afternoon snack. We then ask the respondent, "What else would you consider for this use?" The answer may be "Pretzels". We ask again, "Is there anything else you might eat as a mid-afternoon snack?" And the answer may be "a piece of cake". Other items mentioned may be "bar of chocolate", "toast and jam". When the respondent has no more ideas we ask him, "When else might you eat potato chips?" And the answer: "When friends drop in for a beer or a drink". The next question is, "What other items might you use when offering drinks?" The answer: "Cheese and crackers, peanuts, olives".

The interview continues until he can think of no more uses of potato chips. The interviewer takes up another item like peanuts which has been mentioned by the respondent and continues the questioning. The interviewer will also ask about the attributes of the products which the consumer has named for a particular use like the mid-afternoon snack or when friends drop in for a drink.

We have described only the start of this research process called 'item-by-use mapping'; which was developed by Alan Frost and has been applied by McCann-Erickson worldwide. Already, the brand manager would have seen how many possibilities for new product ideas and product positioning this technique opens up.

Concentration or Litany?

We can round off our discussion on positioning-by-usage with the thought that there is more to be gained by concentrating on those one or two usages which have the greatest realistic sales potential for the brand and also represent distinct positions served by it.

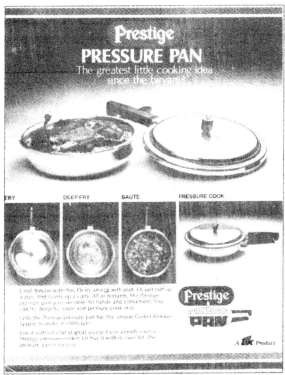

Exhibit 4.23 *An example of positioning by versatility of usage. (Agency: Marketing & Advertising Associates— MAA).*

A catalogue of usage positions can find a place on the label but the positioning statement of the brand and its advertising should not be burdened with a litany of uses.

An exception would be a product designed specifically to give the benefit of versatile usage to the consumer, as in the case of the Prestige Pressure Pan (see Exhibit 4.23).

Price-Quality Positioning

This is a simple concept but a powerful one in a developing economy like that of India. The consumer looks at the products in a category, at different levels of price, offering different standards of quality, and decides which price-cum-quality level is most suitable for a given need. The importance of the concept is that consumers in such a heterogeneous market as ours, have different expectations of quality, are at different levels of social mobility, and offer the opportunity for greater price–quality stratification and positioning than in any other third world country.

Even a cursory glance at outlets or at advertisements will indicate that far-reaching changes are taking place in the Indian consumer market. Probably the two most powerful forces driving this change and making it possible for a thousand price–quality positions to bloom are the 'demonstrations effect' and the process of economic development.

Economic development in India has been uneven and has taken a zig-zag course, but by 1988, it had put disposable incomes in the hands of around 250 million consumers. Each of these consumers, after meeting basic needs, and each according to the level of his income and social and cultural status, is avidly looking for things to buy—things put into his head by the 'demonstration effect'.

The more fortunate, some six million or so in 1988 alone, visited foreign lands and returned with suitcases full of goods for their neighbours to envy. Those who have stayed behind are affected by the same styles and fashions which they see when visiting the cinema hall (about 45 million adult audiences in 1988); or watching TV (well over 50 million adult viewers); or when leafing through the pages of magazines (about 46 million adult readers); or on the persons and in the homes of their better-placed fellow citizens and in glittering shop windows.

For every pair of Levi's or Calvin Klein jeans purchased abroad there are a hundred other homemade jeans at varying price levels giving their wearers the sense of being 'with it'. Adidas and Nike designs are quickly copied and flood the stalls put up by pavement vendors. The array of products in the shops of Hongkong, Singapore and Dubai have spurred numerous imitations available in India at price levels to suit different strata.

Listen to a copywriter quoted by *India Today*:

> *'Bombay worships exclusive labels', says Christopher d'Rozario, advertising copy writer. He points out the row of shoesellers at Churchgate Station which has become a veritable shoe bazaar. Every self-respecting shoe there wants to be called Nike or Reebok even if its pedigree is questionable. 'But even lower middle class guys will pick up these and feel they are getting value for money.'*

What inspires these marketing activities is the belief that in India varying levels of price–quality for such coveted products will attract different segments of consumers. Not many of these entrepreneurs or brands have yet made it big. The most outstanding example of a brand that has made a fortune for its owner through a bold price–quality positioning strategy is Nirma detergent powder. The owner of the brand is Karsonbhai Patel, a one-time modestly paid government chemist in Gujarat, whose business venture has been described as "the most sensational success story of the decade".[8]

Many years ago, Patel realized that every advertisement for Surf, Magic or Det (the high-priced detergent powders available in the sixties and early seventies) was having a powerful demonstration effect. Millions of housewives wished to reduce the toil and drudgery of the everyday household wash—rubbing and scrubbing with a laundry bar—but could not afford these washing powders.

In 1975, Patel gave them the product they were waiting for—a detergent powder which was not of the same quality as Surf or Det but which lathered well and cleaned well, was widely available and cost less than one-third the price of Surf or Det. In 1988, the total volume sold of Nirma washing powder was 176,000 tonnes compared to the premium powder Surf's 24,000 tonnes. This is a price–quality position for washing powders that does not exist in developed markets like the UK and USA. Patel then launched Nirma detergent tablet in 1986 at a much lower price than the market leader Rin, and by 1988, had achieved a market share of 33.40% compared to 23.5% of Rin.

The magazine *India Today* described Patel's marketing philosophy in these words:

> *Give quality at the right price and whatever you make will sell on its own.*

We will look at Nirma's positioning strategy in more detail in Chapter 6.

The packaged goods companies of the organized sector in India appear to have given their attention to higher price and higher quality market positioning:

> *The corporate consumer goods sector in India is still (with rare exceptions) a highly restricted kind of activity which has not yet acquired a broad social purpose in terms of providing consumer satisfactions to the many...*

> *The 'barefoot' concept applied to Indian marketing is simply that in order to reach basic products and services to millions of people one must reduce the cost to the barest minimum...Just as we have a view about 'intermediate technology'. I am pleading for a view on 'intermediate consumption goods'.*

A Multinational's View

It is worth quoting at this juncture, from the 'Positioning Strategy' document of a very successful worldwide packaged goods company:

> *In developed markets today there no longer exists such a thing as a bad product... The notion of cheapness is therefore not synonymous with poor quality but. on the contrary, implies 'value for money'.*

> *When the average housewife is more than ever conscious of the need to buy wisely, marketing men would be well advised to underdesign—rather than overdesign—their packages for daily consumption goods.*

What is true of developed markets is even more true of ours.

Price–Quality Positions at the Top

It is notable that new price–quality positions are opening up in India not only at the lower and middle levels of the spectrum but also in the upper ranges.

Take the home construction industry as an example. What has been most visible in the seventies and eighties is the construction of high-rise blocks offering apartments for sale at varying prices to middle and upper middle class families. Such construction continues to flourish. In 1987, an ad appeared in the newspapers announcing:

> *Now is the moment for the widely travelled who have seen gracious living everywhere. A world famous architect styles exclusive designer homes...*
>
> *Welcome to the finest concept of the world's latest living styles. An internationally acclaimed architect, Ramesh Khosla, expertly styles designer homes that combine city comforts with the tranquillity of the countryside. At Garden Estate— India's first ever condominium.*

Here is the headline of another ad seen in 1988:

> *Only a few very expensive homes in Kodalkanal...*
> *MILHAVEN*
> *Exclusive. Extravagant. Expensive.*

The Problem of Image Upgrading

The manager for a brand positioned at the lower end of the price–quality spectrum is constantly tempted to upgrade the image of his brand. The pressure mounts when the price of his brand goes up— due to cost increases but without change in quality. It seems that the only way to reward the consumer and motivate him to pay the higher price for the old quality is through a 'more pricey' image which is most readily attempted through advertising and packaging changes. The trouble is, the consumer may not buy this image; there may be a credibility gap.

This was the experience with the medium-priced Berkeley cigarettes. Many years ago its commercials featured top stars of the Indian screen smoking the brand. It was projected as 'Filmland's Favourite'. Smokers did not quite believe this and in due course the campaign was changed.

However, when a consumer is satisfied with the value-for-money brand which he has purchased, he is likely to feel reinforced in his decision when the advertising for that brand creates an image that places it above its perceived rung on the price–quality ladder. A dual purpose is being served here. The tangible product gives the target consumer value for money and satisfies him. The added, subjective values of the brand created through advertising and packaging echo his aspirations which are usually pitched higher than actuality and make him feel doubly good about his brand choice.

This is what appears to have happened with Nirma Washing Powder. The commercial, which has been running unchanged for years, gives the brand a lively, modern, up-market image, and it is this commercial which has been associated with Nirma's phenomenal growth in penetration, volume and market share. Quite deliberately perhaps, the pack has not been changed and does not match that up-market image. This plain unadorned plastic pack distinctly conveys 'value for money'.

Perhaps we can argue that the image for a 'value' brand can be pitched upward to the level where it reinforces the user's purchase decision but not to the point where it stretches her credibility. And the only sure way to determine where this fine balance lies is through research or market testing.

3. FOR WHOM AM I?

We have looked at strategies for positioning brands in terms of corporate identity or as extensions of familiar brand names ('Who am

I?'), and also positioning them according to the brand's capabilities and benefits ('What am I?'). We will now turn to the third aspect, viz. positioning the brand by target segment ('For whom am I?').

In Chapter 2 we examined the concept of the target segment for a brand and its position as being inseparably linked, like the two sides of the same coin. In this section, we will look at the target segment decision as another means of giving our brand a distinct position and identity.

A segment is made up of consumers with more or less similar needs and expectations from a product and who have some important similar characteristics. Their responses to product and brand offerings are also likely to be similar. The factors which bind such consumers together into a market segment are:

(a) *Demographic* : Age, income, sex, occupation, education and sometimes, geographic location, and/or

(b) *Behavioural* : For instance in terms of usage volume: heavy, medium, light users, and/or

(c) *Benefits or satisfactions desired*: We have already studied this factor, viz. segmentation by benefits sought, and/or

(d) *Psychographic* : Personality, life style, social class.

As with other aspects of a brand's capabilities, the brand manager has flexibility in determining the target segment for which he will position his brand. His obvious choice will be that segment for which his brand seems to be just right and will be better preferred to any competing brand. Through the process of becoming strongly identified with that segment, his brand will acquire a distinct identity. Let us look at some examples.

Demographic Fit

Farex, the easy-to-digest cereal food was initially positioned for infants and also geriatrics and this was reflected in the pack design at that time. Later in 1967–68, the brand was very specifically repositioned as the weaning food for infants from the age of three months to one year. This was reflected in the new pack design (Exhibit 4.24).

Exhibit 4.24 *Positioning Farex by the age of target user is reflected clearly in its pack design.*

The ads said:

> *3 months onwards, milk alone is not enough. For all-round growth, your baby needs Farex, the first step to solid food.*

The clear-cut concentration on the age of the user, accompanied with the strong idea of milk being not enough at that age, gave the brand a very distinct identity and led to a dramatic sales increase. After this repositioning decision, the sales volume doubled within the first three years alone. Later, the brand was overtaken by Cerelac (Nestle) because the product features and benefits of Cerelac were considered by mothers to be superior.

Take another product category—Ayurvedic tonics like Chyavanprash. Dabur's brand is for all ages—grandfather and grandchild alike. Zandu Special Chyavanprash, which is more expensive, is explicitly positioned for families with small children with the reasoning that the housewife would be more willing to spend that much extra if she believed that Zandu Special really built up the resistance of her children to coughs and colds.

On the other hand there may be demographic segments for which no brand has been suitably designed or positioned. This can well happen in a changing society like ours. The far-sighted marketer tries to track emerging demographic changes which may influence his brand positioning decisions. The Clarion Urban Housewife study, for instance, throws some light on an emerging occupational segment—the white collar or middle-class working housewife—which is growing in numbers and purchasing power. As yet, few brands are positioned directly for this high-potential segment. The study observes:

> *One key insight from the study is that the working housewife feels guilty about not having enough time for her husband and children. This can be a strong motivator to bring into her home products that can help her to 'look after,' home and children in a more rewarding way despite the demands of her job. Cooking is affected—there is less variety, say many husbands of working wives. Marketers of instant/fast foods please note.*
>
> *Stretching one's imagination a little, why can't private enterprise—which already runs schools and hospitals—also get into the business of Day-Care Centres for the children of working housewives? Housewives did evince a good measure of interest for this service as well as for a Domestic Servant Agency.*[10]

Behavioural Fit

You are no doubt familiar with the concept of heavy, medium and light users. There is that phrase about the 'heavy half', meaning that a small fraction of consumers (of a product type or brand) account for a proportionately much higher percentage of its sales (with beer, for example, about 30% drinkers would account for about 80% of sales).

It makes good sense, therefore, to study the heavy-user segment and to position for them brands that best satisfy their high volume consumption.

In the USA, Johnson & Johnson did this with great success. They found that the heavy user of shampoo, one who shampoos often, prefers a mild product. The company saw market share move up from 3 to 14% when they broadened the positioning of their shampoo from one used for babies to one that is also best suited for those who wash their hair frequently and therefore need the kind of mildness in their shampoo which they can be sure of.

You may have also heard of:

> *Schaefer, the one beer to have when you are having more than one.*

Can you think of an Indian example where a brand has been developed and is positioned and advertised for the heavy user in a product category?

We certainly do observe marketers adopting other elements of the mix to target the heavy user: larger packings which work out to lower unit prices for the heavy user; promotional offers which give special incentives to those using a product or service frequently.

Satisfaction Fit

The marketer seeks to identify consumer segments that are linked together by the benefit or satisfaction which they demand from a product type. He develops or modifies his brand and positions it to be just right for that particular benefit seeking segment.

The Complan and Horlicks user households have fairly similar demographic profiles. At one stage in the history of Complan, it was though that the benefits consumers sough were also identical and Complan was positioned accordingly. It became a slugging match between 'the great nourisher' (Horlicks) and 'the greatest nourisher' (Complan).

The strategy was changed later to pick out those housewives and mothers (the decision maker) who were looking for a different benefit from their health beverage—the benefit of *complete* nourishment for members of her family in specific situations, especially her growing children. Complan had found its niche (see Chapter 6).

We have seen that well-made products are versatile and give the brand manager flexibility in his positioning decisions. The target segment decision itself can be a differentiating strategy for similar products. One protein-rich biscuit can be positioned for school children as part of their noon-day meal. Another similar product can be positioned for convalescents.

A Farex-like product with a different brand name can be positioned for the elderly. We have looked at other examples while discussing benefit-related positioning earlier in this chapter.

Psychographic Fit

Positioning a brand to match the psychographic characteristics of a segment takes us into a more esoteric area. Nevertheless such matching of brand and segment is often the key to differentiate products such as cigarettes, textile fabrics, beauty and fashion products like cosmetics and apparel and even footwear.

Cigarettes: Gold Flake Filter Kings and Classic are so close to one another in price and physical characteristics that it would be virtually impossible to differentiate them in terms of demographic segments or benefits. Both are ITC brands. The only effective strategy of differentiation is to position them for segments which are demarcated one from the other by psychographic characteristics (see Chapter 6).

Soft drinks: Campa Cola and Thums-Up, as cola drinks, are understandably positioned for the same demographic segments by income and age. One would have expected them to demarcate their respective segments in terms of personality and life style. Judging from their commercials, they appear to be positioned for identical segments in terms of such characteristics as well.

Footwear: By contrast, Bata has positioned its several brands of 'athileisure' and sports footwear for four segments which are visibly distinct in their life styles.

North Star is positioned for the younger generation which favours a more relaxed, easy going and informal life style, "the shoes for easy living". Power Jogger was announced in its first commercial with the words, "the birth of the fitness cult". It was positioned for those people, young and not so young, who had been caught up in the 'fitness fever' (see for example, the report in a cover story of the magazine, *India Today*).[11]

Then came a much more advanced sports footwear in the Power range, technically named the PU Shoe. The task was to position this shoe for another segment with the least cannibalization from the Power Jogger. Bata decided to brand one version as Power Ultimo and position it uncompromisingly as the specialist tennis shoe for the tennis enthusiast.

The other version, slightly modified and less costly, was branded as Power Workout and positioned for athletes who take their workouts seriously and for whom physical training is a must. They were regarded as the primary segment.

To achieve sales volume targets, the secondary segment was defined as those who also go in for physical training because "keeping their body in shape" is a serious goal. This segment also embraced the many tens of thousands of starry-eyed 'emulators', who idolize sports stars and identify themselves with an athletic life style. See the ads for the three versions of Power (Exhibits 4.25, 4.26 and 4.27, Plate 6).

Concentration

As with other elements of positioning, specificity in choosing the target segment for a brand generally pays a higher dividend. Even a large-share market leaders is vulnerable to competitive brands, strongly positioned to wean away segments of the leader's market through strategies that hold greater appeal for those specific groups. "First place will go to a brand that carefully nurtures a particular target."[12]

The Consumer as a Whole Person

We have discussed the main bases on which brands are matched with segments and how they can be differentiated by segment. In terms of concept as well as practical action, a positioning statement regarding the target group will invariably describe the consumer as a whole person and not in a piecemeal manner. As an example, study this definition of the 'core prospect group' for Harpic, the new specialized toilet cleaner from Reckitt & Colman:

Decision maker :	Housewife
Demographics :	Age group 22–45 years
	• Monthly household income: Rs 2,000 plus. Residing in selected launch towns with population over 1 lakh
Behavioural :	• User of 'traditional' toilet cleaners or Sanifresh or Flush Kleen for the purpose of toilet cleaning
	• In most cases, where 'traditional' products are used, she employs a sweeper for getting the toilet clean
Psychographics :	• Modern
	• 'House-proud' and meticulous in matters of homecare
	• Regards the appearance of her house including the toilet an important way of projecting her personality

4. WHY ME?

We began this chapter by describing positioning as the pursuit of differential advantage.

Throughout this chapter we have looked at the various ways to achieve this differential advantage for our brand. At the end of the day, we would have identified our particular target segment; isolated the usage occasion for which our brand fits the bill; selected the benefit which will make our brand more suitable than others for that target segment, for that usage; and found a price–quality equation that strengthens our competitive standing. "The buyer's mind", says C. Merle Crawford, "is a memory blank with slots or positions for each competing alternative".[13]

By now we should have crafted and 'machined' our brand, so to speak, so that it fits a particular slot in that buyer's mind more snugly than any other alternative. By now we should have given him or her the answer to the question: "Why me?", the reason why he or she should select our brand in preference to any other.

Do we need anything else? Do we need a 'clincher', one last clinching argument to make the cash register ring?

Positioning by Unique Attribute

There are some companies (Procter & Gamble, Hindustan Lever, Nestle, Nirma) who will not market a product unless they have endowed it with some unique feature or benefit that makes it superior to competition. This unique feature becomes the clinching reason why— the 'support', as it is called—to claim the consumer's preference.

This is the relevance of positioning a brand by its features or attributes: giving the brand a differential advantage because of some unique or exclusive feature or attribute that translates into a benefit for the consumer. See the ad for Avanti Nova Moped (Exhibit 4.28) and Lipton's Lal Kila 'pouch tea' where the differentiating feature is the packaging which helps to reduce price (Exhibit 4.29).

Positioning by Competitor

Marketing has been likened to warfare. 'Positioning by competitor' is an offensive strategy to deal with the questions: "Why me?"

A special kind of clinching argument as to why our brand should be preferred is through direct comparison with the competitor we wish to dislodge.

The most widely quoted example is that of Avis, the car-rental service in the USA, which positioned itself vis-a-vis the market leader, Hertz. Avis gave a powerful promise to its prospect:

We try harder because we are No. 2.

This positioning strategy succeeded, say Trout and Ries, because "it related No. 2 Avis to No. 1 Hertz on the product ladder in the prospect's mind; it also capitalized on the natural sympathy people have for the underdog".[14]

Exhibit 4.29 *Pouch packaging is the distinctive feature of Lipton Lal Kila tea, enabling its price to be "attractively low!" (Agency: Lintas)*

Exhibit 4.28 *The Avanti Moped, claims this ad, has features which make it a vehicle "designed with your family in mind". (Agency: Trikaya Grey)*

Exhibit 4.30 *Lipton Anikspray ad in Assamese. There is a direct comparison with another brand (not named) showing how it leaves lumps of undissolved milk powder in the strainer test, which Anikspray does not. (Agency: Lintas)*

Aaker and Shansby also quote this example:

> *In most positioning strategies, an explicit or implicit frame of reference is the competition...perhaps the most famous positioning strategy of this type was (that of) Avis...The strategy was to position Avis with reference to Hertz as a major car rental agency, and away from National, which at the time was a close third to Avis.*[15]

Another form of positioning with respect to a competitor is through the use of comparison advertising of which we see a growing amount in India. Here, the competitor is explicitly named or shown in a masked form which everybody can recognize, and the respective attributes are compared to prove that 'our' brand is superior.

See, for example, the ad for Anikspray milk powder (Exhibit 4.30) and Lakme Winter Care Lotion (Exhibit 2.1, Plate 2).

Strategy is 'Holistic'

In practice, the step-by-step positioning decisions should end up by presenting a whole picture of the brand. The consumer should be able to comprehend it as a complete entity.

She should be able to perceive the type of product it is: Is it meant to be a snack or a fast-to-cook mini meal (Category)?

For what usage is it most suitable—as an antiseptic for burns or nicks and cuts (Usage)?

What is the particular benefit which distinguishes it from alternatives? Is it a cold cream plus moisturiser in one (Benefit)?

Is it a good value-for-money product or a top quality premium offering? What is its rung on the price–quality ladder?

She should be able to identify with it as a product meant for her. Having formed her perception or impression of the brand as a whole, including any unique features and how it compares with alternatives, she should be able to give it a place or position in her mental map of products. She should be able to decide whether to put it on her shopping list.

In his search for differentiation, the brand manager would probably find that the unique perception of his brand can be created through a particular combination of the positioning factors that we have discussed.

Thus, Vicks VapoRub was distinguished from its major competitor, Amrutanjan, through a combination of usage, target, benefit and time of use positioning. In Chapter 6 we will discuss in some detail Vicks VapoRub and three other cases which illustrate this 'holistic' approach to brand positioning.

SUMMING UP

In this chapter we considered the various strategies available to the brand manager for differentiating his brand from its competitors. We considered explicitly the situation when brands are functionally similar and how they can be differentiated.

These strategies revolve around four aspects of the brand which we expressed as four questions.

1. Who am I?

This question deals with the origins of the brand, its parentage. We can position the brand with reference to its corporate identity or as an extension of a well established brand.

2. What am I?

This question relates to the capabilities of the brand and can be further broken up:

(a) *Category-Related Positioning:* By choosing the product category in which to position our brand we are defining its competition. Similar brands can be differentiated by positioning them in different categories. Old brands can also be repositioned to advantage.

(b) *Benefit-Related Positioning:* We select that particular benefit which will give our brand the greatest competitive advantage. We have flexibility in differentiating a functionally similar product by emphasizing a benefit which the competitor has not exploited.

(c) *Positioning by Usage Occasion:* This strategy enables us to dominate a particular usage. It also enables us to distinguish similar products by identifying our brand with one or two usages that competition has neglected.

(d) *Price-Quality Positioning:* There are many marketing opportunities opening up in our country which can be turned to advantage by this strategy. Nirma products are outstanding examples.

3. For Whom am I?

This is the strategy of positioning a brand for a carefully chosen target segment where it is the best fit and has competitive advantage. Again, functionally similar products can be differentiated through positioning by different segments. Such positioning can be by demographic, behavioural (usage pattern), benefit seeking and psychographic segments.

4. Why Me?

All the above strategies should enable us to create a distinct and persuasive perception of our brand. Aggressive marketing companies try to add to their brand a clinching advantage through some unique feature. Positioning by competitor, that is through comparison with the main competitors, is another way to demonstrate a brand's superiority and answer the question "Why me?".

Brand positioning strategy should end up by presenting to the prospect a picture of the brand as a whole.

CURRENT EXAMPLES

Mr Madhukar Sabnavis, Planning Director, O&M, has made the following observations on the Positioning Strategies of well-known brands as seen in 2003.

A. Titan watches: In a market dominated by HMT, mechanicals and watches as time keeping devices—Titan decided to ride the wave of growing grooming consciousness in the late 1980s and positioned itself on style and class with its all quartz range. Basic positioning: Titan enhances the status of its wearer and gifter. This was later successfully translated into a full-fledged gifting campaign (What am I?—Benefit related positioning).

B. Asian Paints: In an attempt to get consumers to become more involved in the painting process which is naturally a low involvement, distasteful process, Asian Paints focussed on the post painting joy rather than pre-painting fears.
Positioning: Asian Paints gives you the true joy of a freshly painted house.
From this arose the long lasting 'Celebrate with Asian Paints' campaign that ran through the decade of 1990 (What am I? Benefit related positioning—Emotional benefit).

C. Cadbury Dairy Milk: In 1993–94, it did its now famous repositioning of moving from targeting children to targeting the child in every human being. And the rest as they say, is history (For whom am I?).

D. Allen Solly: In 1993, riding the wave of changing corporate culture and using its unique product features (bright colours, all cottons and looser fits) to create a new category of 'Informal Formals' and thus emerged the 'Friday dressing' campaign which has run through the 1990s into this century! It was positioned for those who bend rules, not break them—the immaculate maverick! (For whom am I?).

E. Amaron batteries: In a category that has very little advertising and with a product that has a distinct product that has a distinct product advantage, Amaron batteries look up the promise and has successfully owned "lasts long, really long". Something the brand consistently positioned itself on since its launch in 1999 (Why me? Unique attribute).

F. Perk: Perk was launched in the mid-90s as a light snack that can be had anytime, anywhere. From here emerged the famous *'thodi si pet puja'* campaign (What am I? by usage and time of use).

G. Brooke Bond A1 Tea: Launched in 1995 to get conversions from loose tea into branded tea. Positioned on the basic platform of strength and priced at almost the same as loose tea in all markets (price was benchmarked market wise). The advertising platform of 'strong tea for strong hearted people' emerged from this position. In 3 years hit 20000 tonnes (What am I? price/quality).

H. Bru Instant Coffee: From the eighties was built up on the basic platform of 'closest in taste to filter coffee' using the friendly deception creative idea. Built up a market leader position based on this proposition (What am I? Category related positioning).

I. 100 Pipers Premium Whisky: Launched in the mid-90s on the positioning of 'premium whisky from Scotland' building on the associations of the pipers. 'Can you hear the pipers play?' was the TV campaign developed on this position. However last year in an endeavour to broaden the base, the brand weighed two options—go the connoisseur route and build the Scotland heritage. However it was felt that it would make the brand old. An alternative was to build on the status value of the brand. This was pursued from which emerged the recent Who is who and Who is He campaign (For whom am I).

J. Dove: An international brand that was brought into India fairly successfully for its segment and niche with the position—Dove is not a soap, it does not dry skin like other soaps because it contains 1/4 moisturiser (Why me—unique attribute).

These are 10 examples based on brands that Ogilvy has built from fairly early days. And which been based on the position for several years and whose advertising has been created based on this position over the period.

Mr Rohit Srivastava, Planning Director, Contract Advertising (Part of the GWT group), contributes the following thoughtful examples of Positioning Strategies as practised currently (2003).

I. Who am I?

(1) Positioning by corporate identity

The obvious ones here would be the durables, automotive and white goods companies like Toyota, Sony, BPL, Kinetic, etc. These follow the norm of signing off all communication with a common logo and baseline. Bajaj attempts an interesting, even if incremental variation in driving a core corporate value through a line created for that purpose, which appears along with the corporate logo; I am referring to the legend 'Value for money for years' that appears on the top right in all communication. The Tatas have taken it a step forward by actually asking the group companies to pay a royalty for use of the Tata name in their company.

In services most financial services companies like LIC, ICICI Bank follow this approach; not surprising given that the higher the stakes, the more critical is the trust factor, which is where the company origin and credentials become key drivers of a customer relationship. Besides these, the Taj Group of hotels is another example, where their luxury, business, leisure and budget chains all carry the Taj identity. Even the Times Group could be an example, driving brands like the Times School of Marketing, Times Foundation, Times Music apart of course from TOI and ET.

The interesting trend since the earlier edition of this book has been the entry of FMCG in this arena. While Godrej and Dabur have done it historically as an endorsement, Britannia made a bold move to drive itself as a master brand across all its products with the design and launch of the 'Eat healthy. Think better' campaign. Interestingly, companies like Nestle have started to sign off all their communication with the Nestle logo. Cadbury too is working towards consolidating a lot of its products under the Cadbury master brand.

(2) Positioning by brand endorsement

A lot more of the FMCG here with examples like Lakme (colours, moisturizers, creams), Ponds (talcum, soap, creams, lotions), Biotique, Maggi (sauces, soups, noodles), Annapurna (*atta*, salt) and Himalaya (chyavanprash, herbs, skin care products like moisturizers, healthcare products like digestive capsules and cough syrups).

Interestingly again, the Unilever Group worldwide is now developing Lipton and Brooke Bond along similar lines after years of building individual product brands like 3 Roses, Taaza and many more. These are now being merged to sell under a single umbrella. The Lipton exercise has been finalized worldwide while the Brooke Bond one is underway. ITC too has undertaken a similar exercise in the last few years in trying to consolidate various brands under the endorsement of Wills.

Looking beyond FMCG, there are examples of Nike (footwear and apparel), Tractor (distemper and emulsions). What makes the last one radical is that emulsions are premium (in pricing and imagery) while the Tractor was known for distempers; conventional wisdom would have suggested that this could be a baggage for the launch of emulsions. However, the equity of Tractor was found strong and robust enough and in fact a source of credibility for the new launch.

II. What am I?

(1) Category Related Positioning

- Tanishq....watches sold as jewellery
- Vaseline...petroleum jelly sold as lip salve and moisturizer
- Waterbury's Compound...iron supplement being sold as protection against cold and cough

Another interesting example is Sugar Free. This is a sugar free sweetener, historically sold to diabetics through chemist outlets, now being sold as weight control device, targeted at the figure conscious, being sold through supermarkets.

At a category level, seemingly functional products like sports shoes, sunglasses, wrist watches and bags are now being sold and bought as fashion accessories.

Plate 7

Brighter Coloureds, Whiter Whites

Because Sunlight is harsh only on dirt, not your clothes.

A washing powder should only remove dirt, not the brightness of your clothes. That's why Sunlight Detergent Powder has been specially formulated to harm neither your hands nor your clothes. Wash after wash, your whites and coloureds remain Sunlight bright.

A quality product from Hindustan Lever

SUNLIGHT DETERGENT POWDER *For a brighter wash*

Exhibit 4.31 *As opposed to Surf and Rin, Sunlight powder has been positioned for brightness rather than whiteness. (Agency: O & M)*

"It's the feeling, it's the caring, it's the giving, sweet feeling of joy..."

Bring home these moments

Sometimes, Cadbury's can say it better than words

Exhibit 4.32 *Part of an umbrella campaign for a range of Cadbury's Chocolates, this ad shows the power of positioning with an emotional benefit. Following this campaign, says Mr Suresh Mullick, Creative Director of O & M, "there was a dramatic rise in sales". (Agency: O & M)*

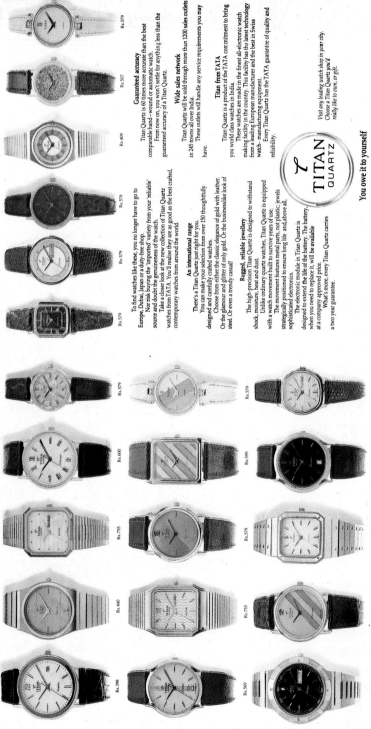

Plate 8

Titan Quartz, the international watch you can pay for in rupees.

Now keep your dollars, pounds and dirhams in your pocket.

To find watches like these, you no longer have to go to Europe, Dubai, Japan or a duty-free shop.

Nor risk buying the 'imported' variety from your 'reliable' source and doubt the genuineness of the watch.

Take a closer look at the new collection of Titan Quartz watches from TATA. You'll realise they are as good as the best crafted, contemporary watches from around the world.

An international range

There's a Titan Quartz just right for you.

You can make your selection from over 150 thoughtfully designed and carefully crafted watches.

Choose from either the classic elegance of gold with leather. Or the glamour and glitter of only gold. Or the businesslike look of steel. Or even a trendy casual!

Rugged, reliable jewellery

The high-precision Titan Quartz is designed to withstand shock, moisture, heat and dust.

Unlike ordinary quartz watches, Titan Quartz is equipped with a watch movement built to survive years of use.

The movement features metal parts, not plastic; jewels strategically positioned to ensure long life and, above all, sophisticated electronics.

The electronic module in Titan Quartz is designed to extend the life of the battery. The battery, when you need to replace it, will be available at a company approved price.

What's more, every Titan Quartz carries a two year guarantee.

Guaranteed accuracy

Titan Quartz is 60 times more accurate than the best comparable hand - wound or automatic watch.

From now on, you won't settle for anything less than the guaranteed accuracy of a Titan Quartz.

Wide sales network

Titan Quartz will be sold through more than 1200 sales outlets in 245 towns all over India.

These outlets will handle any service requirements you may have.

Titan from TATA

Titan Quartz is a product of the TATA commitment to bring you world class watches in India

These watches are made in the finest all-electronic watch making facility in the country. This facility has the latest technology from a leading European manufacturer and the best in Swiss watch- manufacturing equipment.

Every Titan Quartz has the TATA guarantee of quality and reliability.

TITAN QUARTZ

You owe it to yourself

Visit any leading watch shop in your city. Choose a Titan Quartz you'd really like to own, or gift.

Rs.579 Rs.507 Rs.409 Rs.579 Rs.579 Rs.579

Rs.579 Rs.579 Rs.579 Rs.600 Rs.595 Rs.569

Rs.755 Rs.579 Rs.512 Rs.640 Rs.755 Rs.579

Rs.398 Rs.569 Rs.600

Exhibit 4.33 *Titan was singlemindedly positioned as a quartz watch comparable only with international brands.*

(Agency: O & M) See p. 201

(2) Benefit Related Positioning

(a) *Functional* Erickson (surprisingly small), Lifebuoy (kills the germs you cannot see), Apex Exterior Paint from Asian Paints (time proof beauty), Dabur Chyavanprash (immunity against infections), M-Seal (seals all leaks), Pepsodent (12 hour protection against germs), Fevicol (*jod jo tootega nahin*).

An interesting category in this respect is shampoos with various functional positions being used to build a portfolio. For instance Pantene offers Lively Clean (for bounce), Volumizing (for volume), Long Black, Anti-dandruff, Smooth and Silky.

(b) *Emotional* The way I see this, it's all about how that brand makes you 'feel'. Some examples of that would be:

- Close-Up (confident)
- J&J (caring)
- Franklin Templeton Blue Chip Fund (secure)
- Axe (irresistible)
- JK Tyres (in control)
- LG (invincible...*mujhe kuch nahin ho sakta*)
- NIIT (inspired...*Life begins at NIIT*)
- Liril (fresh)

(3) Positioning by Usage Occasion and Time of Use

- Kwality Walls...(post dinner treat...10 o'clock)
- Listerine (Night time rinse...Get fresh tonight)
- Babool (perfect way to start the day...*subah Babool ki to din tumhara*)
- Clorets (after drinking, smoking, eating...After Anything)
- Nescafe (great start to the morning)
- Brittania's *Chai Biscoot* (for tea times)
- Domino's (when families are having fun, e.g. watching TV or playing scrabble)

Examples of usage being cued to expand market could include Boroplus which showed occasions like shaving, nick and cuts, chapped lips, winter dryness, nappy rash to suggest expanded uses for the antiseptic cream. Cadbury Celebrations was launched to leverage the adult gifting segment. Research showed that two of the largest occasions for gifting in India were Raksha Bandhan and Diwali. Cadbury now has special pack and advertising that present

Celebrations as the perfect gift for these two festivals, in order to exploit this market. Maggi could have presented its noodles as, well, noodles. Instead it chose to position them for the evening time when kids come back from play and announce that they are hungry. The results of this of course are well known.

(4) Price–Quality Positioning by Usage Occasion and Time of Use

The biggest innovators here were probably brands like Akai and Aiwa which redefined pricing across the consumer electronics category with their aggressive price–quality platforms.

Peter England (The honest shirt) and Westside (surprisingly affordable) have done it in the clothes and accessories segment. The Apex fares of Indian Airlines and the Steal-a-seat auction offer from Sahara could also be considered cases in point.

From the image upgrading perspective, the Tractor example I have quoted earlier is an interesting one.

III. For Whom am I?

(1) Demographic Fit

- Elle 18 (for teens)
- Colgate Kids
- Kid-e-bank from ICICI
- Benetton 012 (for under twelve year olds)
- MTV
- Lee Kids
- Femina Girl
- Cartoon Network
- Citibank's Women Card

(2) Behavioural Fit

Lays (No one can eat just one) exploits the typical behaviour of the heavy eaters of potato wafers. Gelusil too targets the compulsive eaters (who are typically the largest sufferers from acidity) through their ads. Perhaps *'Thanda matlab Coca Cola'* also leverages a behavioural insight about the TG, i.e. they tend to ask for a chilled carbonated beverage with the phraseology *'ek thanda dena'*, now made memorable by Coke and Aamir Khan.

(3) Satisfaction Fit

Such examples abound in satisfaction led categories like cigarettes and alcohol. Depending on what is a particular TG's source of satisfaction, the drink for instance could be positioned on smoothness (McDowell's No. 1), taste (Blender's Pride), good cheer and high spirits (Bagpiper), strength (Haywards). This category of course has a strong overlap with the benefit positioning described earlier.

(4) Psychographic Fit

The way I see it, this could be to do with my self image, or sometimes to do with "what am I seen as" when I use this brand, the latter being referred to as a self-expressive benefit by some authors. Examples here would include Pepsi (youthful), Van Huesen (corporate...Power Dressing), Bajaj Pulsar (masculine....Definitely Male), Hitachi (perfectionists), Thums Up (macho...Have you grown up to Thums Up yet?). One of my personal favourites here is an international press ad for Chivas Regal that actually does not mention the brand name at all!!! The reader who gets it feels discerning and those who don't, feel left out. It's a dramatization of the discerning nature of the Chivas drinker.

(5) The Consumer as a Whole Person

The Whirlpool housemaker, the J&J mom, the Saffola wife and even the Surf housewife (*Surf Excel hai na*) are good examples of this.

IV. Why Me?

(1) Positioning by unique attribute
- Center Shock (sour center)
- Moov (special ingredient for backache)
- Dove (1/4 moisturising cream, not a soap)
- Amaron batteries (silver)
- Dermi Cool (prickly heat powder that cools)
- Blue Pepsi

(2) Positioning by Competitor

Captain Cook (free flow vs. Tata Salt)

Time Pass (safe & healthy vs. pan masalas)

Savlon (does not sting vs. Dettol)

Borosoft (non-greasy vs. Boroplus and Boroline)

Annapurna salt (iodine that stays active post cooking vs. Tata Salt)

REFERENCES

1. Levitt, Theodore, "Marketing Success through Differentiation—of Anything" *Harvard Business Review*, January–Febuary, 1980 pp 83–91.
2. Crawford, Merle C., *New Products Management* (Irwin Series in Marketing, Irwin 1987).
3. Diefenbach, John, "The Corporate Identity as the Brand" *Branding—A Key Marketing Tool*, Ed. John M. Murphy, (McGraw-Hill Book Company, 1987) pp 156–164.
4. Sarel, Dan, "Product Positioning—A Reassessment" *Theoretical Developments in Marketing*, (American Marketing Association, 1980).
5. Haley, Russell J., "Benefit Segmentation: A Decision Oriented Research Tool" *Journal of Marketing*, (July 1963) pp 30–35.
6. Wind, Yoram J., *Product Policy: Concept, Methods and Strategy* (Addison-Wesley Publishing Co., 1982) pp 79–80.
7. Rediffusion Advertising Ltd., 1985.
8. "Cleaning Up the Cleaner Market" *India Today*, (October 31, 1987) p. 79.
9. Sengupta, Subroto, *The Elite Barrier to Consumer Goods Marketing in India* (Advertising Club, Calcutta, 1975).
10. Urban Housewife Study (Clarion Advertising, 1987).
11. "The Fitness Fever" *India Today*, (February 15, 1988) Cover story.
12. Rothschild, Michael L., Marketing Communications: *From Fundamentals to Strategies* (Heath, 1987) p. 167.

13. Crawford, Merle C., *op. cit.*, p. 395.
14. Ries, Al and Jack Trout, *Positioning: The Battle for Your Mind* (Warner Books by arrangement with McGraw-Hill Book Company, 1986) p. 33.
15. Aaker, David A. and Gary J Shansby, "Positioning Your Product" *Business Horizons*, (May–June 1982) pp. 65–62.

Chapter 5

Symbols by which We Live and Buy

POSITIONING WITH NON-FUNCTIONAL VALUES

We buy products to satisfy some physical and material needs. But once the most basic and primitive needs are met—hunger, thirst, shelter, safety—we look to products for some other rewards as well.

The average middle-class family in urban India probably manages with rice bought from the ration shop for most of the family meals, or at best, unbranded rice from the market chosen principally on the basis of price. But when guests are invited, the hostess would stretch her budget to buy the far more expensive basmati rice. Not only does basmati rice make a better dish in terms of flavour, looks and taste but it also earns for the hostess a reward that she particularly values: the esteem of her guests.

As if made to illustrate this point, an ad for Sohna Golden Basmati Rice portrays a wedding situation with friends dressing up a bride-to-be. The headline says:

Great Occasions Demand It

and the copy reads in part:

Some moments are just so rare. So special. Everything's got to be just right. Even the rice you use must be the best...Sohna rice...No lesser grain dare share your most precious moments.

As a sizable section of our society graduates from the ration shop or basic needs level to a somewhat higher standard, more and more products must offer not only physical or functional satisfaction but psychological or non-functional rewards as well. The concept of Maslow's hierarchy of needs is relevant to us in this context. These needs, in order of urgency or importance, are: physiological needs, safety needs, social needs (belonging and love), esteem and status needs, and finally, the highest order of needs—those for self-actualization. The non-functional values of brands must satisfy our social and esteem needs.[1]

Brands are Symbols

Products take on symbolic meaning and we buy them as much for their physical benefits as their symbolic or non-functional ones. This is self-evident when we look at 'badge' products, that is, products which we use in public and whose symbolic meaning rubs off on ourselves in the eyes of the beholder.

When a teenager buys a pair of jeans he is not only buying denim slacks but a label which he will display to the world on his derriere. That label—call it Levi's, if you will—carries a symbolic meaning for himself, his friends and peers. He is quite ready to pay, and does pay, thrice as much for that symbolic meaning than for an identical pair of jeans which has an obscure label or none at all.

It would be incomplete to think that such symbolic meaning attaches only to products of conspicuous consumption. They apply to 'closet' products as well, products whose identity is known only to the user. Others will see the result from the use of that product but will not know—unless they ask—what its name is.

That attractive male in the commercial 'smelt terrific', as a lady admirer says, but she does not know the secret. The commercial takes us into confidence and tells us it was due to Aramusk toilet soap. Over and above the physical qualities of that brand, it is being purposefully endowed with symbolic meanings: Maleness, Success, Self-indulgence (see Chapter 7).

The housewife, hitherto satisfied with washing her children's school uniforms in Surf, takes on the additional chore of giving them that last dip in Robin Liquid or Ujala not only because she thinks it would add extra whiteness but also because it makes her feel like an extra-conscientious mother who spares no effort for the good grooming of her family.

That brands have symbolic meanings was known to academics and practitioners over 50 years ago. Quite often, this symbolic meaning was referred to as the brand image.

In 1949, James S. Duesenberry, discussing the theory of consumer behaviour, put forward the concept that consumption as 'symbolic behaviour' may be more important to the individual than the functional benefits provided by the brand, a remarkably astute and perceptive view from an economist.[2]

Gardner and Levy, writing in the *Harvard Business Review* in 1955, clearly brought out the "social and psychological nature of products" and said that advertising for a brand should be considered in terms of its "symbolic and indirect meanings" as well as its literal communication. The brand name is a "complex symbol that represents a variety of ideas and attributes".[3]

Addressing a conference of the American Marketing Association in 1959, Sidney Levy said something quite remarkable. "The pleasure from buying things", he said, is "*ever more playful*" (emphasis ours). Modern goods are psychological things. The products people buy are "symbolic of personal attributes and goals." They have personal and social meanings in addition to their functions...a purchase involves an assessment to decide whether the symbolism fits or not.[4]

David Ogilvy, in his *Confessions of an Advertising Man* (1963) said:

> *Every advertisement should be thought of as a contribution to the complex symbol which is the brand image.*[5]

Stronger Bonding with Emotions

When the consumer looks around at packaged goods today, she finds quite a few that are 'good enough'. It is this which leads to her 'short-list' or 'evoked set' of brands—those which she considers more or less equal in performance and functional benefits. She will make her brand choice from this short-list. With undifferentiated functional benefits to draw upon, she may even vary her purchases among this short-list; functional benefits alone may not forge a strong enough bond between a parity brand and the consumer. The USP is an elusive pimpernel.

Advertising strategists or planners, but even more so the creative people in an advertising agency, are looking for unique emotional values to add to the brand. They are looking for ways to create emotional involvement because this represents *the stronger bonding area between brand and target consumer.*

Moreover, when differentiated positioning based on physical features and functional benefits becomes less feasible and less persuasive, we have to look for differential advantage on the basis of non-functional or emotional and psychological values of the brand. Symbolisms and symbolic meaning become the instruments for differentiation and for forging this emotional bond with the brand.

> *"A brand that captures your mind gains behaviour"*
> *"A brand that captures your heart gains commitment"*
>
> — *Scott Talgo, Brand Strategist*

BRAND LOYALTY PYRAMID

Also look at the following Brand Loyalty Pyramid. The higher and deeper levels of loyalty are linked to the feelings of liking and commitment for the brand.

The importance of such symbolism and emotional values in brand choice goes up as the 'rationality' of the buying decision goes down. There is comparatively more 'rationality' (or *Samajhdari* as Lalitaji calls it in the Surf commercial) in purchasing laundry detergent powder for instance, and, much less in buying cigarettes, cosmetics, beer, soft drinks, fashion apparel, and the like.

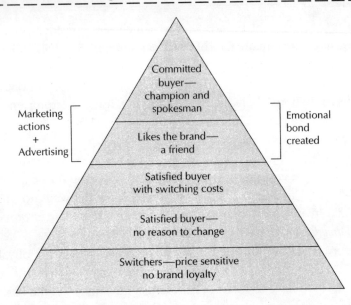

An Australian study in 2001, assessed the extent to which symbolic values become strong differentiators in different FMCG categories (Table 5.1). Understandably, perfumes head the list while potato chips are least likely to benefit from such values.

One may add, however, that there is at least one outstanding example of the mundane and unexciting toilet tissue becoming memorable, entertaining and competitive. The example is Andrex toilet tissue in the U.K. One can also think of P&G's Charmin.

Table 5.1 *Categories where Symbolic Values are Strong Differentiators*

Categories	Agreeing (%)
Perfume	78
Department store	69
Wine	68
Aftershave	62
Instant coffee	47
Beer	46
Cigarettes	40
Toilet paper	30
Toothpaste	27
Potato chips	20

Of the many theories and ideas surrounding brand symbolism there are two, we believe, which have conceptual strength and operational utility. These are the concepts of 'brand personality' and of the 'congruence' or match between 'self-concept' and most preferred brand. We will discuss the latter first.

SELF-CONCEPT AND PREFERRED BRAND

We know intuitively, for example, that in markets offering a wide range of automobiles (such as ours) a car owner sees his automobile as an extension of himself. Research has supported this intuitive judgement. Reporting on a study of choice of automobile models in the USA, Al E. Birdwell concludes that there is a high degree of congruency between the owner's perception of himself and the car he buys: "Automobiles are often extensions of the owner's image of self".[6]

This self-concept or self-image, we should note, is a blend made up of the person's basic physical and emotional characteristics; of the image of his 'real' self; and of his 'ideal' self—the self he would like to be—which includes his aspirations. From this theory the following patterns of buying behaviour may be predicted. Thus, a consumer would:

   1. Buy products consistent with self-image

   2. Avoid products inconsistent with self-image

   3. Trade up to products that enhance self-image

Most branded products, as we have seen, have a physical as well as a symbolic character. Driving much of the consumer's purchasing behaviour is the judgement as to whether a given brand, both as a physical product and a symbol, is congruent with his or her self-image. In short, at the heart of our buying activity is the urge to match our self-image with the image of our most preferred or favoured brand.

In everyday advertising practice we use another term. When an ad has been developed, we ask ourselves: "Will our target consumer identify with this ad?", "Will it urge him to identify with the brand?" At the root of this question is the theory of congruence with self-concept.

Therefore, in positioning a brand with its non-functional values, that is, positioning it with its symbolic meaning, we must ensure that such symbolism helps to support the self-concept of the target consumer. All the elements of the marketing mix must communicate to the target prospect the desired clues for consumer perception and thus create the desired symbolic meaning for the brand.

Brand images are frequently studied in our market. We would expect that where ego-involvement is high in a purchasing action, marketers would also try to get a fix on the target prospect's self-concept.

Departing from packaged goods and looking at the 100 cc motor-cycle market in India, we see a remarkable opportunity for creating brand symbolisms that would reflect the differing self-concepts of their target segments. Indeed, one may hypothesize that market segmentation itself should be done on the basis of differing self-concepts of motorcycle riders.

The major brands are all made with Japanese collaboration: TVS-Suzuki; Hero-Honda; Bajaj-Kawasaki; and Escorts-Yamaha. There are some functional or feature differences among these brands but they may not appear considerable.

One can put forward the hypothesis that the motorcycle rider sees his mobike as "an extension of himself" and that the symbolism which he perceives in these brands, more than minor functional differences, would influence his choice.

Thus, the very arithmetical TVS-Suzuki ad (Exhibit 5.1) comparing its features with those of Hero Honda would stop those motorcyclists who see themselves as very rational and dispassionate, who have confidence in their mechanical know-how and who pride themselves on being cost-conscious. It may leave cold the young man to whom his mobike means the exhilaration of speed, a dash of adventure and the occasional spice of danger.

What clues for consumer interpretation and symbolic meaning are being given by these mobikes in their respective ads? Look at them in magazines and TV and try to differentiate them in terms of a match between brand symbolism and image, and the target consumer's self-image.

Later in this chapter, we will look at a study of 100 cc motorcycles and their owners which probes this question.

The conscious effort to match the brand symbolism being created and the self-concept of the target consumer is more apparent when we look at ads for two new racing bicycles.

The ad for BSA Mach 10 (Exhibit 5.2) shows the sleek, gleaming machine against a black background and the headline proclaims it as 'Elegant by Sight, Electric in Flight'. It seems to be flagging the flamboyant teenager who sees himself as dashing and macho, who has an electric vision of himself flashing past at a speed which draws *ooh's* and *ah's* from his admirers. As the ad says, it's the "Macho Mach... waiting for a bit of muscle".

Exhibit 5.1 *This ad treats TVS-Suzuki as an efficient and economical engineering product (the only symbolic meaning it conveys). It will appeal to those who think of their motorcycle in such rational terms. (Agency: R K Swamy Associates)*

The Hero Hawk is for youngsters—and others slightly older—for whom cycling is a passion. They are concerned keenly about the technical features of their bike. They like to pit themselves against a superb machine and test their own limits. They can't wait for the weekend to stuff their backpacks and set off with a buddy to "push the horizon" (Exhibit 5.3).

And if you look at garments for a moment, contrast the self-concept of the consumer who will consider Allen Solly's 'Friday Dressing' as just right for him versus the much more off-beat image of Weekender garments: 'Wear Your Attitude'.

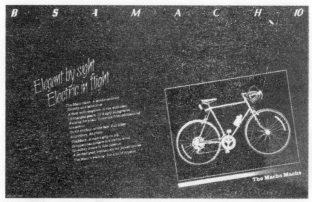

Exhibit 5.2   *Flagging the attention of the flamboyant teenager? The BSA Mach 10 comes across with a clear personality. (Agency: Mudra)* *See p. 135.*

Exhibit 5.3   *This ad reflects the self-concept of the Hero Hawk owner and projects a personality for the bike quite different from BSA Mach 10. (Agency: HTA)*

BRAND PERSONALITY

The second concept that we will take up is that of 'brand personality'. This is a highly promising concept, both in theory and practical relevance, when it comes to positioning brands with non-functional values.

The dividing line between self-concept and Brand Personality is a thin one. What makes good sense is to say that self-concept and the Personality of the brand which the consumer will choose must be closely matched. The really difficult problem is how to create different and distinct Personalities for different brands appealing to the same consumer segment. With colas one might sum up the differences as:

Thums up	:	Tough grown up, Adventurous
Pepsi	:	Young, Irreverent, Fun-loving,
		The Next Generation, (Remember "Nothing Official About It"?)
Coca Cola	:	Perhaps becoming defined with
		"*Thanda Matlab Coca Cola*"

Many brand strategy statements nowadays refer to the 'character' or 'personality' of the brand under discussion. However, brand managers writing these statements often tend to define 'character' for several brands in the Company's line in more or less identical terms. For example, for many OTC remedies, the brand character is monotonously described as 'caring' and 'efficient'. From me-too product features we may end up with me-too brand personalities. For nutritional products aimed at children, and even for laundry detergents, we encounter again and again the character/personality of the 'caring mother' and 'conscientious housewife'. So, how will the consumer make a choice?

The purpose of positioning by brand personality is lost if we are unable to define a desired 'personality' for our brand which is clear and distinct from the personalities of competing brands and sister brands in our own product line.

Problems of Definition

Let us first deal with the problem of definition. What is Brand Image?
Brand Character? Brand Personality?

We earlier quoted Gardner and Levy, in the *Harvard Business Review*
article, as saying that the "brand name is a complex symbol that
represents a variety of ideas and attributes". They then refer to the
brand's *public image, character,* or *personality* and seemingly give
these three terms the same meaning.

David Ogilvy, writing on the Image and the Brand, regards 'image'
and 'personality' as synonymous.

> *The manufacturer who dedicates his advertising to building
> the most favourable image, the most sharply defined
> personality, is the one who will get the largest share of the
> market at the highest profit—in the long run.*[7]

In an earlier book, he wrote:

> *You now have to decide what image you want for your
> brand. Image means personality...the personality of a
> product is an amalgam of many things—its name, its
> packaging, its price, the style of its advertising and above
> all, the nature of the product itself.*[8]

Christine Restall, of McCann-Erickson says:

> *In many markets there are no real differences among the
> competitors. So you begin to explore a more emotional level
> and this is where the brand personality comes in.*

She then draws a distinction:

> *Brand image refers to rational measurements like quality,
> strength, flavour. Brand personality explains why people like
> some brands more than others even when there is no physical
> difference between them.*[9]

It would seem that Restall considers brand personality as being made
up of the emotional associations of the brand, and brand image, of its
physical features and benefits.

Stephen King, formerly of J. Walter Thompson, writes about what
will make a brand successful, says, *inter alia*:

First, it has to be a coherent totality, not a lot of bits. The physical product, the pack and all the elements of communication—name, style, advertising, pricing, promotions and so on—must be blended into a single brand personality.

Thus, King views the 'totality of the brand' as the 'brand personality'. He explains this further:

The added values (of a brand) will tend increasingly to be non-functional values. But they will only work if they are blended with the physical and functional values to form an integrated brand personality.[10]

We believe that the so-called 'character' of brand and its 'personality' hold the same meaning. But the image of the brand, in our view, has a different connotation from its personality.

The brand image represents the essence of all the impressions or imprints about the brands that have been made on the consumer's mind. It includes impressions about its physical features and performance; impressions about the functional benefits from using it; impressions about the kind of people who use it; the emotions and associations aroused by it; the imagery and symbolic meanings it evokes in the consumer's mind—and this includes imagery of the brand in human terms, as if it were a person.

The brand image is indeed the 'totality' of the brand in the perception of the consumer. It is truly a 'complex symbol' and defies over-simplifications that equate it to one of its 'bits'—like its physical features, for example, or its emotional associations alone.

Personality, we think, is that aspect of the brand's totality which brings up in the consumer's mind its emotional overtones and its symbolisms—its characterization, if you will. The great operational utility of the brand personality concept is that when the consumer cannot distinguish brands by their physical features or functional benefits, he is invited to look at their so-called human characteristics. It makes his task simpler in judging whether it's his kind of product; it makes it easier for the consumer to deal with the question, as Plummer of Young & Rubicam puts it: "Do I see myself in the brand?"[11]

To sum up, our view is that the brand image represents the totality of impressions about the brand as selected and adapted by the consumer's perception. It embraces the brand's physical and functional aspects and also its symbolic meanings. The brand personality, on the other hand, dwells mainly in these symbolic aspects.

With differentiated products, the functional benefits of the brand plus its imagery or symbolism help the consumer to make the all-important judgement: "This is my kind of product."

With undifferentiated or functionally equal products, the symbolic aspects of the brand—the brand personality—must bear the brunt of consumer persuasion. It must match the target prospect's self-concept—"I see the brand in myself"—rather better than competing brands.

At the same time, we must respect and acknowledge the fact that seasoned practitioners continue to use the two terms interchangeably. But whichever term they favour, they include in it the *totality* of the brand as seen by the consumer.

Do Consumers Respond?

When you have a good, clear idea of your target consumer, of his or her self-concept, it is possible to think of a personality for your brand which will have congruence with that consumer's self-image.

We saw how advertising planners and creative people breathe life into a brand, give it a human face, as it were, in the example of *Sananda* magazine in Chapter 3. But is this a fantasy that exists only in the advertising person's head? Can it really turn on a consumer or will he simply ignore it?

Stephen King, whom we heard earlier, firmly believes that consumers value brands for *who they are* as much as for *who they do*. They can and do see brands as personalities. He then quotes comments from housewives in the UK who were simply asked to imagine certain brands as people.[12] We quote here only the example of Lifebuoy soap.

Toilet Soaps—Lifebuoy (in the UK)

Interviewer	:	"What about Lifebuoy, if that became a person?"
Housewife D	:	"That's an older man, about fiftyish, somebody whose children are growing up—a very steady job and looking forward to retirement."

Housewife A	:	"I think the sporty type of man, who is always on the tennis courts."
Housewife E	:	"A male worker in his twenties—a dirty job, mining or something."
Interviewer	:	"What would he be like as a neighbour?"
Housewife E	:	"Oh, I should think he would be very good, but people may take him wrongly because he is so abrupt. But underneath it all he is kind-hearted."

In interviews with the consumers in India, we find that they can quite naturally and readily ascribe human descriptors to brands they are familiar with. Some field work in the late 90s, yields the following verbatim comments from consumers. They are the consumer's shorthand impressions about the brand:

Brand		*Some Consumer Verbatims*
Dettol	:	"Guard at the gate protecting my family".
Hindustan Amby	:	'Tough old SOB'. Loyal. Faithful.
BPL 3-door fridge (when launched)	:	"A beautiful woman whom I could hug".
Yamaha 100 cc	:	"Flamboyant. A show-off".
And, of course, Raymond	:	"The Complete Man".

Who Creates Brand Personalities?

Before we look at some detailed Indian examples of brand personification, let us ask: Who creates brand personalities? Where do they spring from? Is there a 'process'?

Perhaps the most famous brand personality of all time is that of Marlboro. We saw briefly how Leo Burnett brought him into being (Chapter 3).

Let us turn now to David Ogilvy who has created more successful and widely recognized brand personalities than any other creative person. Here is an account of one such famous personality: *the Hathaway man.*

Hathaway, the manufacturer of this brand of shirts, hired Ogilvy's agency in 1951. These shirts were sold at a few of the highest-priced men's stores and ads were usually released in the Trade Press to impress salesmen and buyers. Ellerton Jeffe, then President of the Hathaway Company, told Ogilvy: "We cannot spend much money. Our account will be less than $ 30,000 a year. If you will take it on, I will make you a promise: I will never change a word of your copy."[13]

Recalling the incident, Ogilvy says that he 'blanched' at the amount, "but how can you say no to an offer like that? You can bloody well believe I worked hard on that account."[14]

Ogilvy says that when he got the Hathaway advertising business, he was determined to give them "a campaign that would be better than Young & Rubicam's historic campaign for Arrow shirts." And he had to do this on a budget of $ 30,000 against Arrow's $ 2,000,000. As he writes, "a miracle was required".[15]

You have read the story in Ogilvy's book, *Confessions of an Advertising Man* and you have seen that famous ad, *The Man in the Hathaway Shirt*.

How does one develop a campaign after one ad? Ogilvy says in his book:

> *I showed the model in a series of situations in which I would have liked to find myself: Conducting the New York Philharmonic at Carnegie Hall, playing the Oboe, copying a Goya at the Metropolitan Museum, driving a tractor, fencing, sailing...and so forth.*[16]

Thus is a brand personality born and shaped. As you can see, Ogilvy was able to put himself creatively in the target consumer's skin; he was able to dream up a 'personality' that would match the self-concept of those consumers.

Sales went up from below $ 2 million in 1950 to $ 30 million after 10 years of the campaign. Ogilvy writes in the 1987 Preface to his book, "My eye patch campaign for Hathaway shirts ran for twenty-nine years".[17]

The strategist lays down the marketing parameters; for example: a very expensive man's shirt; excellent quality of fabric, stitching and style; a variety of patterns and colours; available at selected stores; and then briefly defines the target consumer and his self-concept. Hathaway was positioned chiefly against Arrow shirts.

The 'design centre' which then turns out the brand personality is the creative individual's imagination. In exceptional cases, apart from the strategy, the brand personality, too, may be created by a marketing man or even a company president who has the rare gift of intuition. That is how the personality of another famous brand, Charlie perfume, was created. Below are highlighted several of the key positioning and creative decisions taken by Charles Revson, President of the Revlon Company in the USA, which launched Charlie in 1973.

- Revson was quite certain that women wanted a 'life style' product built around a 'liberated' image.
- He felt that women would be attracted by a perfume with a man's name; so he called it 'Charlie'—his own name.
- He had the perfume formulated again and again before he was satisfied.

The brand was launched in 1973, built around the Charlie image which Revson had sketched. Almost overnight, Charlie became the best selling American fragrance.[18]

'Input' and 'Take-away'

Advertisers and advertising agencies in India are well aware of the concept of brand personality, but with some exceptions, less so, perhaps, of the need to track the difference or the 'fit' between the advertiser's 'input' and the target consumer's 'take-away'.

The 'input', as the phrase suggests, is the 'personality' that the marketer wishes to attach to his brand. The 'take-away' is the impression of that personality which actually enters the target consumer's head and how close it is to his self-concept.

In March 1989, several students at the Indian Institute of Management, Calcutta (IIMC), conducted small-scale surveys on the personalities of various brands, as part of their course on Advertising Management. Without laying claims to statistical validity, these pilot studies did bring up some interesting observations and insights on what consumers are actually 'taking away'.

Instant Coffee

In one such study,[19] Nescafe was compared to Gold Cafe—both 100% pure instant coffees, both heavily advertised and both premium-priced.

Thirteen female and eight male respondents on campus were interviewed, using a 'loosely structured' format with open-ended questions. The respondents were asked to describe the personality of the brands in terms of 'Mr Nescafe' and 'Mr Gold Cafe'. This group of respondents (Group A) based their observations mainly on the advertising of the two brands to which they had been exposed. Another group of respondents, eleven in all (Group B) made observations based also on other factors such as 'history of the company', 'marketing strategy', etc., one might describe them as an 'MBA Group'. We report below extracts of the findings from the first group (Group A) because these reflect the consumer's point of view better.

Mr Nescafe

He is visualised as a young man belonging to the upper middle class. He is well educated and professionally qualified. He is ambitious and 'wants to go places'. His ambition is backed by competence; he is of high calibre and full of self-confidence. He is an outgoing character and the milieu in which he lives calls for a life style of doing the 'in-things', buying designer garments, etc. He is more likely to read Robert Ludlum and Arthur Hailey and has no serious inclination towards art and culture.

As a young man on the move, he takes more than a passing interest in his health and plays games like squash, tennis, etc. On the whole he emerges as a fun-loving, westernized, upwardly-mobile person, keeping up with the times.

Mr Gold Cafe

"Our respondents", says the study report, "more often than not preferred to refer to Mr Gold Cafe as a 'gentleman', rather than a 'guy'. There seemed to be a subdued sense of awe while describing this person." Mr Gold Cafe was pictured as an older person, possibly greying at the temples and exuding sophistication (In fact, the model was the Nawab of Pataudi).

Professionally, he has achieved much in terms of prestige within his organisation as also financial standing. He continues to nurse higher ambitions. He is a man of experience who has learnt to control his emotions. His sophistication is expressed in his finer tastes, appreciation of art and classical music. Being a person of middle age, he does not indulge in rigorous physical work-outs but prefers games like golf to keep in shape. The overall picture that emerges is one of a sophisticated, rich and middle-aged professional with refined taste and impeccable social grace. He is restrained in the expression of emotions in social settings but shows a liberal amount of affection for his wife and children (Exhibit 5.4 shows a Gold Cafe ad). This brand is not active any longer.

Exhibit 5.4 *The ad which launched the only successful competitor to Nescafe. It gave the brand a personality of sophistication, taste and impeccable social grace, according to one study. (Agency: Clarion) It is not known why the owners allowed the brand to languish.*

Motorcycles

Another group of students set out to assess the fit between the images of motorcycles and the self-concepts of their owners.[20]

First, the student researchers made a fairly extensive study of the literature. They decided to replicate (on a modest scale) the methodology developed by Naresh Malhotra to measure self-concepts, product-concepts and person-concepts.[21] Since Malhotra's study (in the USA) involved automobiles, his scaling method seemed to them to be appropriate.

Using, with minor modifications, the 15 scale items developed by Malhotra, the IIMC students administered a questionnaire to 40 owners of 100 cc motorcycles: 15 were owners of Hero-Honda; 15 of Escorts-Yamaha; and the remaining 10 of TVS-Suzuki. All the respondents were within 18–40 years of age, well-educated, urban and middle class males.

There were questions also on the perceived physical attributes and functional benefits of the three machines.

When the findings were put on graphs, it appeared that Escorts-Yamaha showed the closest fit between brand image and self-concept of the owners. The students were conscious of the limitations of their survey, including the small sample size and other problems of methodology. But even if their findings are regarded as a pilot study and merely indicative, they may provoke the search for more data. We have reported here in summary, this is what they found regarding the brands, the brand personalities and self-concepts of the owners.

We saw an ad for TVS-Suzuki earlier in this chapter. In that ad the brand has positioned itself by attributes which are similar to those claimed by Hero-Honda and it has positioned itself directly against the latter. Thus, TVS-Suzuki is apparently talking to a segment whose self-concept has moved it towards Hero-Honda. The battle is one of degree—'more' economical, 'greater' cost-saving.

Would it be better for TVS-Suzuki to position itself on the strength of a unique personality—one that is distinct from the somewhat flamboyant, vain personality of Escorts-Yamaha and also distinct from the thrifty, almost parsimonious character of Hero-Honda?

We had a brief glimpse of such a personality when the brand was launched in 1983 with the theme of 'the spirit of Suzuki' taking over the Indian roads.

Escorts-Yamaha

The bike was rated as powerful, stylish and speedy; low on mileage and economy, but high on durability and reliability.

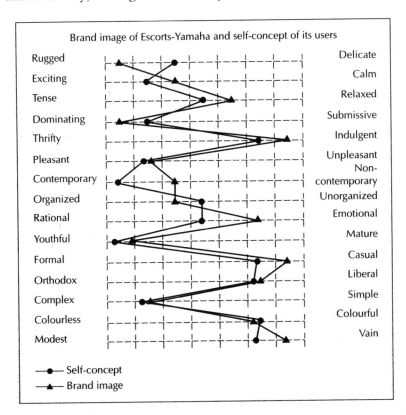

Figure 5.1 *There seems to be a close fit between the self-concept of Escorts-Yamaha owners and the image they have of their motorcycle. If anything, the machine could be made to appear more 'contemporary'.*

Brand personality: It was described as rugged, dominating, youthful, indulgent and vain. Also, but to a lesser extent, it was complex, colourful and exciting. It has (says the report) a very clear-cut and well-defined personality.

Self-concept of owners: They view themselves in terms of concepts very similar to what they used to describe the personality of their machine, but to a lesser degree. They are dominating, tough, youthful, highly indulgent and also sociable.

In a social setting they are very visible and they see themselves as opinion leaders. They are also flashy, vain and given to showing off (Figure 5.1).

TVS-Suzuki

It is stylish but less sturdy and less fast than the other two. It is also reliable, durable and easy to ride.

Brand personality: Rational, colourful, youthful and also rugged. Unlike Escorts-Yamaha, the TVS-Suzuki is quite 'relaxed'.

Self-concept of owners: He comes through as a somewhat laid back individual, one who 'takes it easy'; he is colourful but that has not made him flashy or vain. He perceives himself as mature while his mobike appears to be more youthful. He sees himself as a complex character while his mobike is more simple and uncomplicated.

Hero-Honda

(Exhibit 5.5, Plates 9–10)

It is seen, in terms of product attributes, as a 'balanced' motorcycle, lying in between Escorts-Yamaha and TVS-Suzuki. For example, it is stylish but not as much as Escorts-Yamaha. It gives the most mileage and is highly economical. Readers will recall that memorable line: "Fill It. Shut It. Forget It".

Brand personality: It is thrifty, dominating, contemporary. It is urged but not as much as the other two. On other characteristics (such as 'exciting', 'tense' 'youthful', 'emotional') it gets a rating which is midway between the bi-polar scales.

Self concept of owners: They see themselves as rational, complex and liberal. They usually take a balanced view and are neither too colourful nor too vain. However, they see themselves as somewhat indulgent while their mobike is seen as parsimonious or thrifty. They see themselves as prone to excitement but they describe their mobike as placid (Figure 5.2).

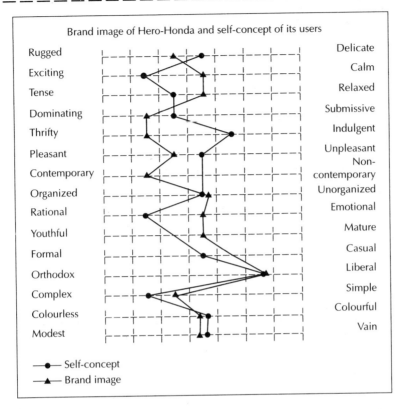

Brand image of Hero-Honda and self-concept of its users

Rugged	Delicate
Exciting	Calm
Tense	Relaxed
Dominating	Submissive
Thrifty	Indulgent
Pleasant	Unpleasant
Contemporary	Non-contemporary
Organized	Unorganized
Rational	Emotional
Youthful	Mature
Formal	Casual
Orthodox	Liberal
Complex	Simple
Colourless	Colourful
Modest	Vain

— ● — Self-concept
— ▲ — Brand image

Figure 5.2 *By contrast with Escorts-Yamaha, there seems to be a gap between the self-concept of Hero-Honda owners and the image they have of their mobike. What they seem to be saying is that thrift can be carried too far!*

The author gratefully acknowledges the enthusiasm with which the IIMC students plunged into these studies. It is our hope that by drawing attention to the potentially valuable findings that can emerge, more such studies will be undertaken—with larger samples and greater rigour—and published for the benefit of the academic world as well as practitioners.

If we look at bicycle ads today, we see that bicycle advertising is usually all about personality. Here is a small sample of bicycle ads.

Write Your Own Story

Of Guts & Glory

And the World Will Say

'Bravo'

"Got adventure in your blood?

Got a dream to chase?

Get on the new Hercules Bravo and challenge the limit.

Test ride it today!"

(The model featured is Akshay Kumar)

And Another:

"Your first pimples have shown up. You have asked for a pocket money bike. You feel like staying out more. Your time is arriving, race towards it and give it a hug, man.

Hero Siren

Overtake Childhood."

Motorcycle ads, understandably, present specific functional features which are in line with the personality being presented. Take two recent examples.

Karizma

Ready for take off

Jet Set Go

And features which support this imagery.

(Exhibit 5.6, Plate 11)

Likewise, a recent ad, for the Bajaj Eliminator:

"Goosebumps ahead!

"Come January 2001, the formidable cruiser-styled Kawasaki Bajaj 'Eliminator' will be hitting Indian roads. And when it does, every strand of hair on your body will welcome it with a standing ovation."

The uncharitable critic may say that both machines appear to be talking to motorcycle buffs with the same self-concept but will they find in the two ads two sharply defined personalities? It all seems to be coming down to a war of words, rather than the creation of sharply defined personalities. You should debate this.

Let us close this chapter with another study by IIMC students in 1995 in which they used two simple methods for exploring Brand Personality, viz. asking respondents to write a 'Brand Personification' (that is, if this brand were a person, what kind of person would he be?) and 'Brand Obituary' (i.e. write an obituary for this brand as if it were a person).

They did this for two brands of cigarettes: 'Classic', one of the most successful ITC brands; and 'Jaisalmer', a Godfrey Philips brand which had a similar quality of tobacco and similar smoking characteristics. This brand is no longer active. The findings are highly entertaining and in this author's view, brought out some valuable insights despite the small sample size.

Jaisalmer vs. Classic

- *Qualitative Study*
- *15 respondents*
- *Brand Personification + Brand Obituary*

Jaisalmer

- *Around 35 years of age*
- *Regal bearing*
- *Proud*
- *A man of passion/appealing to women*
- *Takes part in adventure sports*
- *Doesn't read; listens to Indian music*

Classic

- *Older—40–45 years*
- *Sober, conventional*
- *Snobbish, cultivates aristocracy*
- *Goes to clubs; plays golf*
- *A high level executive*
- *Married with 2 kids*
- *Listens to western classic music*
- *Reads what is considered intellectual*

Brand obituary...

Jaisalmer

- *Died fighting for his pride/trying to protect a lady*
- *Buried in the deserts of Rajputana*
- *He left behind no (legal) family of children, but a large number of moist eyes and heavy hearts*
- *He died as he had lived—alone and proud*

Classic

- *Died in a nursing home*
- *Survived by wife; 2 children and a pet dog*
- *His ex-colleagues sent a floral wreath and a condolence message*
- *There will be a memorial service on...*
- *He died as he had lived—quietly*

Isn't it a remarkable coincidence that shortly afterwards, ITC brought about a dramatic change of the Classic Brand Personality? One assumes that much larger and more scientific research led ITC to the conclusion that the then personality of Classic was out of synch with the temperament of its actual smokers who would respond to a more lively and more contemporary personification of the brand. An important signal of the 'Classic' metaphor remained, Polo, indeed a 'Classic' sport, and introduced by the Raj.

We conclude this chapter with the thought that for long-term success in competitive markets.

Brand Personality is the Stronger Bond

The strategic purpose in creating a brand personality is to evoke from the target consumer the response:

"I see myself in the brand"

"I see the brand in myself"

"This brand is for me"

And this becomes the basis for a bond or a relationship between consumer and brand which is stronger than if it were founded on cold functionality alone.

SUMMING UP

Except for the most basic necessities, consumers buy products both for their functional benefits and their symbolic meanings. That brands are symbols has been known for a long time. Research has proved that consumers do attach symbolic associations to brands. This is most commonly seen with products whose consumption takes place in view of others, e.g. clothing, cigarettes, soft drinks, etc. Consumers choose those brands, the symbolic meanings of which make them feel "this product is for me".

Among the theories about such symbolic meanings, one of the most practical and relevant appears to be the theory of congruence between the symbolic associations of a brand and the consumer's self-concept. That is, consumers prefer to buy those products and brands that match best with their image of themselves.

Another theory which is also very relevant is the concept that brands can be, and are, likened to people; they acquire human characteristics, as it were. This is known as 'brand personality'. Consumer research does tend to show that consumers buy products for *what they do* and also for *who they are.*

Thus, the marketer attempts to endow his brand with a 'personality' that matches the self-concept of the target consumer.

Seasoned practitioners believe that brand personality and brand image signify the same thing—the totality of the brand, including its physical and non-functional values.

This writer believes that *brand image* is the term that signifies the totality of 'the complex symbol' which is a brand, including its physical and emotional associations. But *brand personality* refers more to the symbolic and emotional characteristics of a brand.

In the context of a high degree of physical similarity between brands of packaged goods—and even many durables—differentiation and differentiated positioning can be achieved mainly through distinguishing brands by their personality.

Some examples are given of how consumers personify brands and the process of creating a brand personality is discussed with reference to David Ogilvy's Hathaway shirt campaign.

The need to study the 'fit' between the personality which a marketer intends to add to his brand and how his consumers actually perceive it is emphasized. Some small-scale studies from the Indian scene are reported.

REFERENCES

1. Maslow, Abraham H., *Motivation and Personality* (New York: Harper & Row, 1954).
2. Duesenberry, James S., *Income, Savings and the Theory of Consumer Behaviour* (Harvard University Press, 1949).
3. Gardner, Burleigh B. and Sidney J. Levy, "The Product and the Brand" *Harvard Business Review*, (March–April 1955).
4. Levy, Sidney J., "Symbols by Which We Buy" *Advancing Marketing Efficiency*, (American Marketing Association, 1959).
5. Ogilvy, David, *Confessions of an Advertising Man* (Atheneum, 1963).
6. Birdwell, Al E., "A Study of the Influence of Image Congruence on Consumer Choice" *Journal of Business*, (January 1968).
7. *The Unpublished David Ogilvy* (Sidgwick & Jackson, London, 1988).
8. Ogilvy, David, *Ogilvy on Advertising* (Orbis Publishing, London, 1983).
9. McCann-Erickson's 'MBA' Training Programme on 'Strategic Planning and Research'.
10. King, Stephen, Director in Charge of Account Planning and Research, J. Walter Thompson, UK, when delivering a speech on "What Is a Brand?" at the 1970 Advertising Association Conference.
11. Plummer, Joseph T., Young & Rubicam, USA, "How Personality Makes a Difference" *Journal of Advertising Research*, (December 1984–January 1985).
12. King, Stephen, op. cit.
13. Glatzer, Robert, *The New Advertising* (The Citadel Press, New York, 1970).
14. *Ibid.*
15. Ogilvy, David, *Confessions of an Advertising Man*, op. cit.
16. *Ibid.*
17. Ogilvy, David, *Confessions of an Advertising Man* (Pan Books, 1987).
18. Cravens, David W., Strategic Marketing (Richard D. Irwin, Illinois, 1982). This account is taken from Chapter 7, 'Marketing Program Positioning Strategy'.

19. IIMC students who worked on the coffee project are: Atul Bhatnagar, Bhaskar Basu, Alka Dayal, Harish Agarwal, Padma Subramanium, Prabha Sadanivasan, Shilpa Shirgaokar, T. Bose, Anindya Mukherji, Chevula Nageshwari, Naval Bir Kumar, Rajan Khanna.

20. IIMC students who worked on the motorcycle project are: L.N. Naik, M.P. Tangirala, T.V. Rao, U. Wailong, Babu Shankar, P.A. Ananth, R.J. Kini, Vinay Sambare.

21. Malhotra, Naresh K., "A Scale to Measure Self-Concepts, Person-Concepts and Product-Concepts" *Journal of Marketing Research*, (November, 1981).

22. IIMC students who worked on the jeans project are: Sidhesh Kaul, Deepak S. Rao, R.M. Unni, Sanjay Sachdeva, Santosh Pandit, Hari Bhaskaran, Vikrant Gadgil, Sughosh Moharikar.

Positioning Successes – Case Studies

VICKS VAPORUB

The Rewards of Single-mindedness

"If there is one factor that is responsible, more than any other, for the success of Vicks VapoRub in the market place, it is proper positioning of the product".

Gurcharan Das, Marketing Controller,
Richardson Hindustan Ltd.

History and Origin[1]

In mid-1973, while reviewing the phenomenal progress of Vicks VapoRub, Mr. Das pointed out that the positioning decision did not come spontaneously. Much debate and deliberation had preceded it.

Richardson Merrell, USA, came into being in 1905 when a small-town chemist of North Carolina started marketing a product called

---

* This case was originally published in 1976. The Company has since become Procter & Gamble India Ltd., and Mr Gurcharan Das is its President.

Vicks VapoRub. From this small-town operation, Richardson Merrell grew into a multi-national, $500-million enterprise.

In 1951, Richardson Merrell opened a branch office in India called Vicks Products Inc. which was later converted into Richardson Hindustan, an Indian Public Limited Company with 45 per cent shares held by 10,000 Indian shareholders. Richardson Merrell retained 55 per cent of the equity.

Like its parent company, Richardson Hindustan Ltd. (RHL) was a heavily marketing-oriented pharmaceutical and consumer product company.

The Vicks VapoRub Position

In the early 1950s when Richardson Merrell first looked at it, the market in India seemed promising for Vicks VapoRub. Since the "balm market" was fairly extensive in India, specially in south India, the company expected little resistance to the introduction of the product. All that was needed was to sell Vicks VapoRub as a balm.

The company then took a longer, harder look at the situation. The balm market at that time consisted mainly of four to five brands with Amrutanjan as the accepted leader. Should Vicks take a plunge against the leader and the other well-entrenched brands? Or, should it carve out for itself a distinct niche? Vicks VapoRub had a distinct position in other markets all over the world, i.e. *a rub for colds.* But here was an admirable opportunity to cash in on a countrywide acceptance of balms, rather than fight for acceptance of a new concept in the consumers' mind. Technically or therapeutically the formula of Vicks VapoRub did not prevent its use as a multi-purpose ointment.

The final decision, however, was not to position the product as a multi-purpose balm but to stick to its worldwide position as a rub for colds. Once this was done, the position was brought into sharper focus. Whereas balms were multi-purpose ointments used for colds, aches, pains, sprains, insect bites, etc., Vicks VapoRub was positioned specially as a rub for colds. The company realized that this definition would limit its use; nevertheless, it decided to go ahead as it would bring the product into sharper focus.

Further, knowing that the typical Indian family centred round the child and also realizing that the health of the child was the prime concern of the parent, Vicks VapoRub was positioned as a rub for the child's cold. This was felt to be the best way of getting it into the homes. Besides, this meant further distinguishing it from a balm, because a balm was much stronger and therefore preferred for adults. Vicks VapoRub's milder formulation was more suited for children.

The company also knew that the most frustrating thing to parents was to have a child suffering from cold and not being able to do anything about it. The situation was all the more harrowing when the child could not sleep and lay awake throughout the night in great discomfort. Therefore, while balms were used at all times of the day, Vicks VapoRub was specifically positioned as a rub for a child's cold to be used at night.

Finally, whereas balms were mainly used on the forehead for colds, or on the specific area of pain, Vicks VapoRub was positioned for use on the "nose, throat, chest, all over the back" and this became an integral part of the VapoRub message. The scientific rationale behind this was demonstrated in advertising as the famous two-way action: (1) *The inside action*: As the rub was applied to the skin, the heat of the body and the rubbing action made it release vapours which, when inhaled, opened clogged passages. In fact, it was this phenomenon that gave Vicks VapoRub its distinctive name. (2) *The outside action*: On being rubbed on the skin, it acted as a counter-irritant. The heat and the rubbing broke down congestion just below the rubbed area.

So, RHL ignored the temptation to position Vicks as a balm. In fact, while balms were multi-purpose ointments, preferably for adults, used at all times, on all parts of the body, or on the forehead for colds, Vicks was launched in the Indian market as a Rub for a Child's Cold to be used at Night on the Nose, Throat, Chest and Back.

Balms	*Vicks VapoRub*
Multi-purpose	Colds
Adult	Child
Day-time	Night
Forehead (colds)	Nose, throat,
Specific area of pain	Chest and back

This positioning was maintained and reinforced in every communication to the consumer, to the trade and within the Company (Exhibit 6.1).

Exhibit 6.1
Richardson Merrell (as the Company was then called) positioned Vicks VapoRub as a rub for a child's cold to be used at night.

Thus, Vicks VapoRub was not competing against balms but against all other cold remedies. A consumer research study revealed that consumers could be classified according to different types of cold remedies they used. This classification was found to be correlated to some extent with their 'worldview'; for instance, it was found that the more modern consumers preferred tablets and the more traditional consumers opted for home remedies. In fact, on this basis, the company created a 'modernity index'—a hypothetical ladder—on which they found a distinct rung for Vicks VapoRub. Its place was in the middle of the modernity ladder, but somewhat more on the modern side as shown below:

Ladder of Remedies for Colds

		Examples
↑	Antibiotics	Terramycin
Modernity Index	Cold tablets	Coldarin, Cosavil, Dristan
	Analgesics	Anacin, Aspro, Saridon
	Balms	Amrutanjan
	Home remedies	Masala Tea, Kadha, Rasam

This ladder, of course, varied in different parts of the country; for instance, in certain parts, Vicks VapoRub was thought to be the most modern form of medicine; and in other parts, it was considered old-fashioned and traditional. Recognition of this modernity index and the resulting segmentation was of considerable use to the company in formulating the advertising and marketing strategy.

Later Progress

In a short span of time, Vicks VapoRub had not only overtaken all the balm brands, but had shot up to become the largest selling medicine for colds. From being the largest selling cold medicine in the sixties, it became the single largest advertised medicine. As a single brand in a particular form, it became the largest selling medicine in India.

In fact, with the success of Vicks VapoRub, Richardson Merrell quickly converted their American branch in India into an Indian Public limited company—Richardson Hindustan—which diversified its product line considerably, dealing with not only Vicks Products, but also other consumer and pharmaceutical products. It also made a commitment to the Indian economy by going into the manufacture of menthol from a medicinal herb, called *Mentha-Arvensis* (a variety of mint). This became a highly successful operation involving over 20,000 farmers and made the country self-sufficient in menthol, which had previously been imported. This was really an instance of vertical integration, because menthol was a major raw material for Vicks VapoRub and Richardson Merrell is the world's single largest consumer of menthol.

Understanding the Indian Environment

Though the positioning of Vicks VapoRub in India was very similar to what was being done in other countries, a proper understanding of the Indian environment contributed substantially to the success of Vicks VapoRub. All over the world Vicks VapoRub had been promoted mainly as a winter remedy and had been pushed mostly in winter, simply because the incidence of cold was greatest in that season. This pattern was followed in India in the early stages. Later, research showed

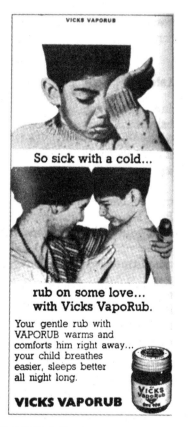

Exhibit 6.2 *Research showed that incidence of colds was very high during the monsoons. Hence this type of ad.*

Exhibit 6.3 *The emotional link— the power of touch—was introduced through this ad. This emotional bond is found in all subsequent VapoRub advertising.*

that people were equally susceptible to colds in the monsoon. Therefore, to tap this opportunity, Vicks VapoRub was recommended as a remedy for "monsoon cold". A special set of advertisements was built around this "monsoon story" (getting wet in the rain, sneezing, colds, etc.)—(Exhibit 6.2).

Another major marketing success for Vicks VapoRub came when the company realized that the Indian market needed, besides the 19 g bottle, a smaller, economy pack. The 19 g bottle, which was sold at Rs 2, was expensive for the poorer and small-town consumers. They were aware of Vicks VapoRub. They were favourably disposed to the idea of using it. However, they could not afford to spend as much as Rs 2 at a time for such a product. Therefore, RHL came out with a 5 g tin which, after initial resistance, was a total success. Sales have spiralled considerably after this move. Another outcome of RHL's comprehension of the Indian environment was a set of advertisements in which they showed a series of typically Indian actions which demonstrated warmth and affection through the sense of touch. They related this to the Vicks VapoRub story by stressing the fact that by virtue of its rubbing action, it made use of the "Power of Touch" (Exhibit 6.3).

Success of Positioning Strategy

RHL attributed the success of Vicks VapoRub in India to proper initial positioning. In addition, there were other correlated factors that also contributed to its wide consumer appeal.

Over the years, the top management resisted the attempts of various brand managers who wanted to redefine the position of Vicks VapoRub as a multi-purpose ointment, because they felt that this would weaken the main strength of Vicks VapoRub. However, some modifications were made in the original definition of the Vicks VapoRub positioning. Having once introduced Vicks VapoRub into homes by appealing to the parents' concern for the health of their child, it was later recommended for use by adults too. This was done for the obvious reason of broadening the target group because the product had already been established in the Indian household. Besides, research showed

Plate 9

HERO HONDA *CD-Dawn*
Public Ka Naya Transport

1

The film starts with a bus pausing at a stop to pick up passengers.

2

The conductor is left aghast when he does not spot even a single soul.

3

Cut to the shot of a train where the same scene is repeated—no life.

4

Autorickshaw drivers suffer the same plight as they have nothing better to do than doze.

5

Just than a bike vrooms in wiping the silence away from the scene...

Exhibit 5.5
(See p. 148)

(Contd)

Plate 10

6

... and pushes straight
into the bus depot.

7

As he collects the parking slip
from the attendant it becomes
clear that the idle bus conductor
has changed jobs to become...

8

...a parking attendant.
He announces proudly
pointing to the bike
"public ka naya transport".

9

A 'parking full' signboard is installed
in the parking space as the MVO adds...

10

*...Naya Hero Honda CD-Dawn, keemat
siraf Rs 31,899/-, Public ka naya transport.*

Exhibit 5.5

(Courtesy: JWT) (See p. 148)

Plate 11

Exhibit 5.6 *Motocycles are purchased for their functional and non-functional values. But this 'Karizma' ad surely appeals to the deeper psychological urges of the motorcycle buff rather than his functional needs.* (Courtesy: JWT) (see p. 150,)

Plate 12

FRANKLIN TEMPLETON
INVESTMENTS

Copy common
for all ads

Cautions about investing in equity funds in today's environment, yet want the long-term growth they offer? The Franklin India Bluechip Equity Fund (FIBCF) is just for you.

Consider this Rs 1 lakh invested in this fund in 1993 would be worth over Rs. 4.05 lakhs today. The same amount in a bank deposit would be worth Rs. 2.43 lakhs. Also, the Bluechip fund has delivered a strong 19.37% p.o. return since inception and 17.08% return last year, a year the equity market was down * (Past performance may or may not be sustained in future.)

The fund carefully chooses those companies with consistent track record and attractive growth potential investing across multiple sectors to reduce risk. And with the BSE Sensex currently at a low of about 3000, this could be a good time to invest in equity funds for the long-term.

FRANKLIN INDIA BLUECHIP FUND
Performing consistently for you

Exhibit 6.12
(Courtesy: Contract Advertising)
(See p. 181)

that adults were, in fact, using Vicks VapoRub. Further, day-time use was also recommended.

Figure 6.1 shows the sales growth of the company from 1966–67 to 1973–74.

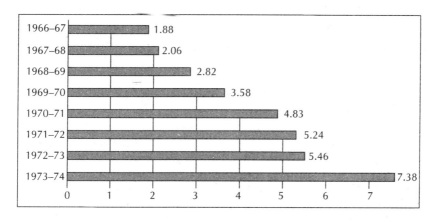

Figure 6.1 *Eight-year sales record of Richardson Hindustan Ltd., in Rupees crores.*

Update: 1989

The above case study was first published in 1976 as an example of competitive brand positioning. More than a decade later, it still stands out as a model of how to use positioning concepts to gain competitive advantage.

Even though the ingredients and attributes of Vicks VapoRub were similar to those of multipurpose balms which dominated the market, differential advantage was secured through positioning strategy. It was differentiated by (a) *target user*: child, (b) *usage occasion*: colds, and (c) *manner and time of application*: at night, on the nose, throat, chest, and back.

Much has changed in the meantime. The company itself has become part of P&G worldwide and is now called Procter & Gamble India Ltd. But one thing has remained unchanged. The single-minded positioning of Vicks VapoRub has continued to this day. See, for example, the script of a current TV commercial (Exhibit 6.4).

TV Script

Product	:	Vicks VapoRub
Execution	:	Birthday
Length	:	30 seconds

Visual	Audio
1. Opens on a wet boy coming home with a bouquet of flowers. He sneezes as his mother opens the door.	Mother : Your cold has got worse, why did you go out? Son: Happy Birthday, Mummy.
2. Application of VapoRub on the boy's chest, neck and nose by the mother.	FVO*: Vicks VapoRub works two ways.
3. Animation of vapours rising from chest to nose.	One— It opens a blocked nose to give breathing relief and eases cough due to colds.
4. Animation of internal action on the back.	Two— It relieves body aches and pains.
5. Mother comes to the boy who has just woken up. Relief on the boy's face as he takes a deep breath.	Mother: Now, how is your cold?
6. Pack shot; window showing relief on boy's face.	MVO*: Breathe in relief. Feel the relief with Vicks VapoRub.

* FVO : Female Voice Over
* MVO : Male Voice Over

Exhibit 6.4 *TV commercial for Vicks VapoRub.*

The rewards for such consistent and competitive positioning have been many. Mr. S. Khosla of P&G India Ltd. has provided updated information based on a major Usage and Attitude (U & A) study in 1983–84.

- Unaided awareness of Vicks VapoRub is very high; both in urban and rural India it is nearly 80%.
- In urban markets, the 'ever-used' figure is 85%, and 'used for the last cold', 57%.
- Even in rural markets, usage ranges from about 50 to 75%.
- 90% of urban dealers stock Vicks VapoRub.
- Vicks VapoRub is the premier cold remedy in the country. It has the highest usership level for 'the last cold' among sufferers.

The sales of Vicks VapoRub have doubled from Rs 8 crore (Net of Excise) in 1980–81 to over Rs 16 crore in 1987–88.

Competitors have tried to assail this position; for example, Rubex and Anoleum, promoted as 'the gentle cold rub' from Amrutanjan Ltd , 'makers of trusted household remedies for 80 years'. The ad for Anoleum showed a mother and infant —a clear echo of VapoRub's position. None of them have posed any real challenge.

Expanding Volume

The original case study, when it was published in 1976, ended with questions like the following in the context of expanding the market.

- Would the communication of Vicks VapoRub as a cold remedy for adults weaken its perception as a rub for colds for children?
- Should the company promote a brand extension for adults or should it use the present product for the adult market as well?

The updated information suggested that the market for the usage position of a cold rub for children might be reaching near saturation, at least in the towns. Further volume growth with this position might be no greater than the population growth of children. Therefore, extending Vicks VapoRub's usage to adults is a tempting solution.

Even earlier, the Company had occasionally used ads addressed to adults but had not emphasized such usage. Recent research showed that in households purchasing Vicks VapoRub, application of the product for adult colds was quite frequent, although much less than for children. In the Company's view, consumer behaviour suggested that in the urban markets, at any rate, there was no perceived inconsistency between usage of Vicks VapoRub for children's and for adults' colds.

Soon after the U&A study of 1983–84 brought up these findings, it was decided by the company, said Mr Khosla, to continue the momentum of volume growth by identifying two key areas.

The first decision was to expand usership among adults. New advertising was developed and aimed over TV in tandem with the existing child-oriented commercials, one of which we saw in Exhibit 6.4.

विक्स वेपोरब प्लस

जब जुकाम के कारण सर दुखने लगे तो सिर्फ़ सरदर्द के बाम से काम नहीं चलेगा!

सर्दी-जुकाम में आपके विश्वस्नोय विक्स जानते हैं कि आपके जुकाम के साथ-साथ सरदर्द की तकलीफ़ भी आती है.

तभी तो विक्स ने खास आपके लिए बनाया एक ज्यादा शक्तिशाली फ़ॉर्मूला: नया विक्स वेपोरब प्लस.

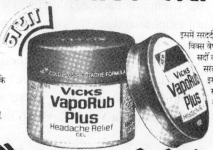

इसमें सरदर्द की दवाई के साथ-साथ विक्स वेपोरब की आज़माई हुई सर्दी की औषधि भी है - जो सरदर्द के बामों में नहीं! इसलिए यह जुकामवाले सरदर्द की जड़ यानी जुकाम तक असर करता है. सरदर्द और जुकाम दोनों से तुरंत आराम दिलाता है.

सरदर्द और ज़ुकाम-दोनों से आराम

Exhibit 6.5 *An ad in Hindi for Vicks VapoRub Plus positioning the brand as giving relief for headaches due to colds. The copy distances the brand from straight-forward headache balms. The base line says: Gives relief from both colds and headaches. (Courtesy: Procter & Gamble)*

The second was a line extension decision: launching a new product branded as Vicks VapoRub Plus. The opportunity was that balms are used for aches including headaches. Colds are often accompanied by headaches. Thus, there seemed to be a vacant position which the new brand could fill better than its competitors—"a rub for aches, specifically headaches due to colds".

To match this position, a significant product change was needed. "In order to ensure that no negative impact was made on VapoRub's existing strength of congestion relief," said Mr Khosla, "a new product was developed and introduced as a line extension—Vicks VapoRub Plus" (see Exhibit 6.5).

In Chapter 10, we shall examine in some detail the dangers and benefits of brand extensions. You can begin by asking yourself whether the new product should have been launched as an extension of the existing brand and using the same brand name with a 'Plus' added, or should it be given a new identity altogether?

COMPLAN

Too Much of a Good Thing?

The problem of marketing Complan is somewhat unusual. It is, and it is perceived as, 'far superior' to competing products. And that is precisely the problem. As one housewife remarked, "It's too much of a good thing. Do I really need all that?"

The origin of Complan explains its vastly superior formulation. It was developed by Glaxo Laboratories as a complete and balanced nourishment for serious medical and surgical patients unable to take normal food. Introduced into the Indian market in the early sixties, Complan was first promoted 'ethically', that is, to doctors who then prescribed it for their patients. This ethical positioning as complete and balanced nourishment obtained very good support from doctors and a growing, if modest, tonnage of sales was achieved. However, after some time growth levelled off.

In 1970, Glaxo set up a Family Products group in the Company with the object of promoting some of its ethical brands over-the-counter, that is, promoting them directly to consumers with mass media advertising. It was judged that this would greatly increase their sales volume. Complan was one such product and it more than justified those expectations—for a while.

Positioning by Competitor

In its very first public appearance, Complan adopted the strategy of 'Positioning by Competitor'. It positioned itself directly against milk.

> *'Your body needs 23 vital foods', said the first ad. 'Milk gives 9. Complan gives all 23' (Exhibit 6.6).*

Notice the semi-clinical look of the advertising which reflects the transition from ethical to consumer promotion.

The copy gives considerable factual information about these 23 nutrients and how they affect bodily functions; e.g. protein to build up and repair tissues and cells; calcium for healthy teeth and bones; folic acid to form new blood cells; vitamin A for the eyes, etc.

This advertising and the position assumed by the brand created a high degree of awareness and trials. The consumer offtake of the brand rose from a volume index of 100 in 1969–70 to 298 in 1973–74. The steady growth also reflected that a considerable number who tried the brand stuck to it and repeatedly purchased it (Figure 6.2).

Despite the success of this strategy, there was cause for rethinking. What really did this positioning imply? Taken to its logical extreme, it meant that Complan should displace milk from the dining table. In India, particularly, milk has a unique position in the consumer's psyche. It is regarded as the source of life, growth and health; it is almost an object of reverence as a necessary ingredient in many religious rituals.

Moreover, with Operation Flood well under way, milk, in the form of powder and also as fresh milk from the Mother Dairies, was being given a great deal of marketing and advertising support. Fighting milk would not be a cakewalk. And, as a socially aware corporate citizen, Glaxo wondered whether it should be in the business of 'knocking' milk which formed such a vital part of the nation's health and nourishment plans. Very wisely, this positioning strategy for Complan was abandoned.

In fact, here was a classic instance of looking afresh at a key positioning decision: Which product class are we competing in? If not milk, then the logical product class definition had to be other malted milk-foods like Horlicks, Viva, Bournvita. This can also be described as the health beverage product class.

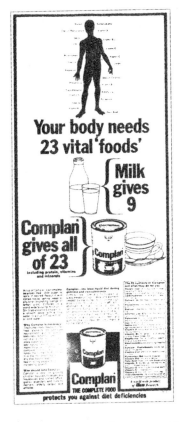

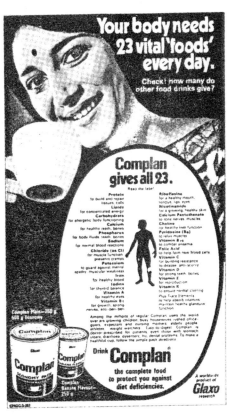

Exhibit 6.6 *Complan 'went public' with this ad—a strategy of positioning by competitor, comparing its nutritional contents with that of milk.*

Exhibit 6.7 *Later, Complan positioned itself against Horlicks, 'the great nourisher'. The ad invited the reader to compare the labels of both products and judge which gave more nutrition.*

Positioning vs. Horlicks

The strategy seemed to be readymade! How should we reposition Complan? Why, against Horlicks, of course, the leader in the health beverage category? Just ask the consumer to compare the label of Complan, so packed with all good nourishing things, with the label of Horlicks whose list of ingredients runs out after naming a few.

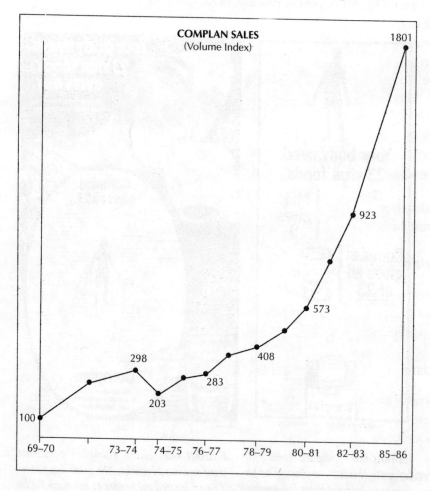

Figure 6.2   *But for a dip in 1974–75, Complan sales by volume have showed uninterrupted and, at times, spectacular growth. Much of this growth has been attributed to its positioning strategy and advertising which steadfastly reinforced this strategy.*

The positioning strategy was similar to what had proved to successful earlier—positioning by attributes and by the main competitor. Research data also showed that many Complan users were earlier users of Horlicks. 'The great nourisher'—Horlicks—was to be treated as the reservoir from which would flow a steady stream of consumers to Complan.

The new headline in the Press ads (1973–74) said: 'Your body needs 23 vital foods every day. Check: how many do other food drinks give?' The consumer was urged to read the label on the Complan tin and to compare it with the label of his present brand, assumed to be Horlicks (Exhibit 6.7).

This strategy bombed. The year 1974–75 was the first time when sales of Complan declined (Figure 6.2). A thorough review seemed called for.

Review of Strategy

Sales data as well as consumer research, including group discussions, brought some key problems to the surface.

Price

Complan's price was almost twice that of Horlicks. Consumers agreed that Complan was a superior source of nourishment but they also felt it was 'too much of a good thing' for them. Did they really need it?

Taste

Its taste was almost universally disliked, violently so by children, who were often forced to drink it by health-conscious mothers. Even a spoonful of sugar couldn't make it go down!

Strategy

Was Complan on the right track in its preoccupation with fighting the competitor, Horlicks, head-on? Would it be better for Complan to achieve a perception in its own right? Instead of making Horlicks the standard of comparison, should one try to create a unique position for Complan and then ask consumers to judge if Horlicks or any other competitor could be substituted in that position?

Dialogue with the Consumer

Complan's dialogue with the consumer had evidently broken down. Several interviews had the following pattern.

Mother : 'I know Complan is good for him (my son), but he can't stand the taste.'

Elderly person : 'My doctor asked me to take Complan after my illness; now that I am all right, enough is enough.'

Housewife : 'Complan is good but we can't afford it. I think we'll switch over to Horlicks. It costs only half as much.'

Interviewer : 'Madam, why do you use Horlicks?'

Housewife : 'Well, all of us work hard and I feel a bit more reassured if we take something extra, besides normal food. And it's such a well-known product and a sort of family tradition, you see.'

Interviewer : 'But Madam, Complan gives you so much more nourishment than Horlicks.'

Housewife : Well, we're not a sick family, you know. What we need is a bit of extra nourishment, not a daily dose of medicine'.

A large mass of research data brought out one priceless nugget: In the Horlicks household there were more than two users of the product on the average. In the Complan household, the average number of product users was far less. This seemed significant—that Complan was perceived as something more special than Horlicks and was therefore more selectively used.

While other brands like Bournvita and the industry were growing, Complan was not. But the more significant data was that even if there were few additional converts, there was steady re-purchase of Complan by many households indicating that it had a core of loyal users despite its seeming handicaps.

Why did they stick with Complan? Research plus judgement provided the answer. There were many households with children who were fussy eaters and mothers constantly worried about their lack of nourishment. There were workaholic husbands who skipped breakfast or lunch. There were elders and convalescents for whom the housewife felt responsible when they went off their food. And there was this marvellous woman herself, busy taking care of others and thoroughly exhausted at the end of her daily chores.

The New Look of Complan

Complan strategy went through a radical change. It was now decided to position it—not by competitor—but by target user and usage occasion.

Complan's position could now be stated as follows:

> *Complan is ideal for totally fulfilling the nourishment needs*
> *of people who cannot or do not eat enough, because only*
> *Complan is complete with 23 vital foods for the body.*

Exhibit 6.8 (1975–76) is an unambiguous example of advertising designed to serve a clear-cut positioning strategy. The cinema commercial (TV became available at a later date) dramatized these usage occasions more vividly: the problem eater child tossing his food aside; the husband rushing off with his uneaten breakfast on the table; the convalescing elder who has no appetite for food; the harassed housewife herself.

In such situations, to what could the worried mother and housewife turn? What health drink would assure her of all the nourishment that was needed in these special, but everyday situations? The ads clearly presented Complan as a product which was unique and complete in its nourishment value. It was no longer 'too much of a good thing' but the only brand with enough good things to give her the reassurance she needed. Could this position be adequately substituted by any other brand? No way.

Not only Complan advertising, but the product itself wore a new and more attractive look. The package design was cleaned up and modernized. The product's taste was improved through a change in the manufacturing process.

New flavours were introduced: Chocolate, because of its universal popularity, especially with the young; Cardamom Saffron, a typically Indian flavour with images of health and goodness; the Strawberry flavour was reserved for later introduction—as a delicious, iced drink. And the price was increased!

Exhibit 6.8

With this ad, Complan broke away from comparison with Horlicks to carve out its own distinct niche as the only complete health beverage to suit specific occasions and users.

The Take-Off

In a very real sense, this repositioning strategy, together with product improvements, provided the thrust for a take-off in sales. From an index number of 203 of sales volume in 1974–75 (1969–70 = 100), sales shot up to an index of 408 by 1978–79—a doubling of volume in four years. The availability of full-fledged commercial TV in 1978 and the heavy use of this medium by Complan gave the brand further thrust.

It became clear that price was not the barrier to growth. By positioning Complan in a unique slot, consumers were persuaded to see that it had no real substitute and a new price–value perception was created for the brand.

A Sharper, Narrower Positioning

We had mentioned in Chapter 4, when discussing Positioning by User, that good brands are invariably versatile in terms of usage and benefit segments. If you read the fine print in the earlier ads for Complan this versatility would become apparent. Take the very first ad with which Complan went 'public' (Exhibit 6.6). The copy reads:

Who Should Take Complan

> *Complan is ideal for growing children, busy adults (especially housewives and rushed office-goers), expectant and nursing mothers, elderly people and athletes.*

It had long been surmised that the actual users of Complan were predominantly children of school-going age. Later research corroborated this belief. It was found that close to half of the actual users of Complan were of school-going age. This was a far younger age profile than for other malted milk beverages.

It is noteworthy that with sales rapidly increasing, the next repositioning exercise brought about a much more focussed and narrower positioning by target user, instead of broadening its user positioning. This calls for a great degree of strategic clarity and courage.

The next ads positioned Complan single-mindedly for 'growing children' and were created and released by Lintas in 1981 (Exhibit 6.9).

Sales data (Figure 6.2) show that Complan's growth was accelerated following this most recent re-positioning. But, with hindsight, you may wish to go more deeply into the reasons for this sharply focussed positioning for growing children and apparent indifference to other users, such as the elderly and the busy, active adult.

Exhibit 6.9 *A sharper, narrower positioning strategy is reflected in this ad — Complan for growing children. (Agency: Lintas)*

You should note, however, that Complan was consistently advertised to the medical profession through ads such as in Exhibit 6.10. Also note that a much higher percentage of Complan sales came from chemists as compared to other malted milk drinks.

New Questions

You may now wish to debate the following issues.

- Complan is the only beverage positioned for children which does not have a chocolate base (It has a variety, the most popular one, in chocolate flavour). An analysis of competitive advertising shows that all the 'brown' beverages which have a chocolate base—Bournvita, Maltova, Boost, and Nutramul—are also positioned for children.

- Moreover, a new product, Sapan's Active 25 has been introduced recently and positioned directly against Complan (Exhibit 6.11). The ad claims that it has 'real chocolate' and 'it's got the one thing your kids will love. Taste.'

- In early 1989, Cadbury's launched Enriche for children between 2 and 10 years of age, with the claim of having 26 vital ingredients and as a 'Total Nutrition Food'.

- How should Complan reinforce its position against such competitors? Complan, as we have seen, is versatile in its positioning opportunities. Should its positioning for other target users—expectant mothers, convalescents, the elderly and even weight-watchers (as an earlier ad suggested)—be confined to

Exhibit 6.10 *Despite going over-the-counter, Complan has consistently addressed the medical profession through ads like this in medical journals.*

Exhibit 6.11 *A new product, Active 25, has positioned itself directly against claiming to give 25 essential vitamins and nutrients—Complan (Agency: Rediffusion)*

the medical press only? Or could one expect even faster growth if the brand were positioned for all these target segments through consumer advertising? Can positioning theory help us to find an answer?

- Special analysis (1988) based on independent household panel data has shown something very significant. Households which have received a much higher exposure of Complan's TV advertising (as recorded in the housewife's diary) compared to Horlicks, invariably purchased more Complan than Horlicks.
- Does this seem to call for experimentation with heavyweight TV advertising to medium and light Complan users to judge if the extra expenditure pays off in higher market shares and profits?
- Does it also suggest that the Media Planner for Complan should look for segments where it can command higher TV exposure than Horlicks within the available budget?

FRANKLIN INDIA BLUECHIP FUND*

Background

In September 2002, the market sentiment towards equities as an asset class was extremely poor and investor confidence was at an all time low. In the case of equities; since stock markets had been down the last couple of months people were reluctant to invest, not seeing any signs of recovery and for the reason that they had burnt their fingers in the past.

News of corporate governance issues in the US, border tensions in India coupled with limited demand for large-cap stocks in the light of continuous selling pressure from bodies like UTI to meet redemption pressures as also FIIs who had reduced their India exposure, simply meant that demand was less than supply.

While all research pointed to the fact that equity markets were poised to take off, stock market valuations looked attractive and fundamentals of the economy were looking strong, it did not help investor sentiment in any way, even though equities made ample sense.

---

* Based on the entry for the Effie Awards 2003. *Courtesy:* Mr. Rohit Srivastava, Contract Advertising.

The opportunity/challenge for us was really to reinstate belief in the equity market and demonstrate that it was the right time to get back into equities with an investment option like the Franklin India Bluechip Fund, given the following support:

- It had consistent performance: The oldest private sector equity mutual fund which has a nine year track record and despite market volatility had time and again consistently generated a good return and outperformed its benchmark, the BSE Sensex.
- Equities have the potential to give the highest return the long-term, one of the most important aspects when investing to meet financial goals. The Franklin India Bluechip Fund has an unparalleled track record having given 21% p.a. return over a 9 year period.
- FIBCF's investment universe comprised equality large cap bluechip stocks that have strong financials, good fundamentals and strong management focus as investors seek safety in stocks of proven companies. These by their steady nature were usually the first to rise up when markets look up, while preserving value in falling markets.

Marketing Challenge

The Worst Time for Equities:

- The much hyped IT bubble had burst and the UTI fiasco added fuel to fire.
- Consequently the stock market crashed and was in as bad a shape as after the "Harshad Mehta Scam".

Some Statements from Financial Newspapers:

- Sensex is currently at the same levels as it was 10 years ago (*Financial Express*, 15.11.02)
- 41 UTI schemes have Rs. 11,655 cr. negative reserves (*Business Standard* 1.02.02)

Equity Mutual Funds: A category that no one wanted to buy:

- Investors had completely lost faith in—Equity Mutual Funds (MFs), Direct Equities and any new age instrument which promised higher returns at some risk.

Some Statements from Financial Newspapers:

- 'MF for sale' or should that read 'dreams turned ashes'? (*Economic Times*, 28.01.02)
- MF's Equity Investments Held Up as Inflows Drop (*Financial Express*, 15.11.02)

- As a result an MF, which invested in equities, would be the worst possible combination.

An Overcrowded Market:

- There were over 100 equity funds in the country vying for the same consumer.
- These included funds from some of the most well established and trusted institutions.

Add to this the foreign status of FT.

Campaign Objects

The objective was to become the preferred equity fund by driving investments into Bluechip in terms of—

- Sales
- New Accounts

Target audience

- 30–60 yr. old, male, SEC A & B
- All the investors who had exited MFs/Shares post the fiasco and had thus grown skeptical of Equity MFs and Direct Equity Markets. They had declared them 'Unsafe'.
- Potential investors, who influenced by the market sentiment, were only looking at FD and other conservative (safe) investment options.

Creative Strategy

A skeptical investor:

- The investor was evaluating everything with extreme skepticism.
- He was stricter than ever in his evaluation criteria. Even a rock solid track record might not have been enough.
- He refused to look at an instrument if it so much as mentioned the word "RISK" or "HIGH RETURNS". Thus he was returning to Fixed Income instruments like Fixed Deposits, and was foregoing returns for higher safety.

Bluechip—A radical choice:

- At a time like this, the conventional wisdom suggested a choice of Fixed Income or Debt Instruments—avenues, which would ensure capital preservation. Because these would address the consumer need immediately. But this would at best be a short-term measure.

- The consumer had lost faith in the market. Thus the only real solution was to reinstate his belief in the market, rather than in a particular fund(s).
- Bluechip could do the above but was a radical choice, since the fund itself was part of the much-maligned equity market. But being among the most consistent funds even through the turmoil, it was the only hope to pull back the consumer.

Bluechip—The Two Options:

- Talk about the "Consistent High Returns" of Bluechip—a benefit, which directly addressed the consumer need. But will the consumer empathise with this? Will they take it on face value and trust us (an MF)?
- Second, confront the consumer's current mindset of "overcaution" and use consistency as a support.

Since the real problem was the consumer mindset, it was required that we address it instead of promoting the product promise. *Therefore the creative strategy was to position Bluechip as* **"The fund for the Overcautious Consumer"** (Exhibit 6.12, Plate 12–13). Consistent returns would act as a support.

Other Communication Programs

No other communication programs were used in conjunction with this Advertising Campaign.

Starting January 2003, we started the 'Equity Incentive Program' for the distributors. Other communication programs included PR, Web advertising and POPs.

Media Strategy

Small media budgets:

- Bluechip had a very limited budget of Rs. 2 crore.

Dominate or spread thin:

- With this kind of a budget we consciously decided to stay out of TV and dominate the press and outdoor for reach.
- Also we decided to focus only on eight markets where the FT presence was strong. The sales force would then close the loop.

Media selection and role:

- Press and Outdoor built reach. We chose a mix of national and vernacular newspapers to reach both metro and semi metro investors.
- Prime time radio was used for frequency.
- Good POPs support was also provided at the retail end.

The media strategy was sales focussed. The message had to reach the audience the right number of times, so as to generate enquiries, which the FT team would convert to sales.

Media Used

- Trade/Professional Magazine
- Point-of-Purchase
- Sales Promotion
- Radio
- Consumer magazine
- Out-of-Home
- Interactive/On-Line
- Newspaper
- Public Relations

Evidence of Results

This evidence must relate directly to campaign objectives. If the objective was to increase sales, indicate sales response to the campaign. If the campaign attempted to bolster corporate image, how did your measures show this? You need not disclose confidential information. Proof of performance may be indexed if desired. Please be as specific as possible in documenting all evidence. Provide sources of data, research involved and the time period covered for the results provided so that it can be verified by the EFFIE Committee.

ABN AMRO FREEDOM CREDIT CARD*

Marketing Challenge

Crowded Market
- Current base of over 5 million cards in circulation. With a card per cardholder ratio of 1.35.
- 13 issuing banks already. The big 4 (Citibank, Stanchart Grindlays, SBI and HSBC) controlling 75% of the market.
- Average per card spend still at a low of Rs 1,400 per month.
- All types of cards, i.e. classic, gold, platinum, co-branded, affinity, with all features already present in the market.

ABN AMRO Bank—A late entrant
- *No company brand image:* ABN AMRO Bank had no historical retail equity in India that is so critical for consumers to buy into any financial product.
- *No retail presence:* Very low base of 200,000 customers being serviced out of just 10 branches.
- *The Bank's first mass retail product in a crowded market:* The Freedom card would be the flagship for ABN AMRO's entry into mass retail financial services.

The Opportunity
- Low penetration levels. Restricted to SEC A and partly B.
- One of the fastest growing card markets in the world with a c.a.g.r ranging between 25 and 30%.
- But this rate of growth had begun to plateau over the last 3–4 years. Prospects either wary of getting credit cards or not feeling eligible enough to get one.
- Very little product differentiation and innovation.
  The marketing challenge was, despite being the 14th player, to stage an entry into this category that would be noticeable, impactful and credible.

---

* Based on the entry for the Effie Awards, 2003. *Courtesy:* Mr Rohit Srivastava, Contract Advertising.

Campaign Objectives

To sell 35,000 ABN AMRO Freedom Credit Cards in the first year of launch.

Target Audience

The ABN AMRO Freedom Credit Card was targeted at young men, 20–34 years, living in a metro or a mini metro belonging to SEC A and B. While being eligible, they had chosen to stay 'uncarded'.

Creative Strategy

Research proved that while a credit card was attractive to the eligible yet uncarded people, *they regarded it as the temptress that would make them lose control over their purse strings.* It was this specific insight that the product was developed to deliver on. With features such as *flexi-limit* and *Active alerts*, the ABN AMRO Freedom Credit Card promised "Control over your money".

The creative idea was "Live without Fear" and this is what the advertising communicated right from the card design to the TV commercial, press ads, outdoor and PoS.

Other Communication Programs

The advertising campaign was accompanied with some prelaunch public relations program, direct mailers to the bank customers and PoS at the 11 ABN AMRO Bank branches in India.

Media Strategy

Media selection was pivoted around the creative route besides the regular media parameters of reach, involvement, response requirements (key for Credit Card advertising) and the inherent medium strengths/weaknesses.

Since the creative approach was to dramatise the fear of overspending, Television was chosen as the lead medium since its ability to evoke the emotion of "Fear" was far superior to that of Print.

Print was used to achieve launch impact. It also served as a reminder medium and helped drive responses/card enquiries.

The launch campaign ran from July 11, 2002 to August 31, 2002.

Evidence of Results

- By December 31, 2002, ABN AMRO Bank had achieved its entire first year's sales target of 35,000 Freedom cards (within 5 months of launch).
- By the end of the first year, i.e. July 2003, ABN AMRO Bank had sold over 85,000 Freedom Credit Cards.
- There was an overwhelming response at the call centre number flashed in advertising. Total calls—53,000 in 75 days after launch.

Enquiries

Period	No. of calls at call centre
July 13 – July 30	36302
August 1 – August 31	111815
September 1 – September 30	1

Card enquiries crossed 20,000 in the first 8 days itself.

Sales/Card issuals (there is a time lag of 4–6 weeks between enquiry and card issual)

Sales Target: 35,000 Freedom cards to be issued by March 31, 2003.

Freedom cards issued by December 31, 2002: 35,031

Freedom cards issued by July 31, 2003: 85,000

ITC HOTEL SONAR BANGLA SHERATON AND TOWERS

Set amidst wide open spaces and yet a bare 15 minute drive from the centre of bustling business Kolkata, ITC's Sonar Bangla Hotel has positioned itself clearly at the very top of the ladder. It is a "Luxury and Quality" hotel.

In line with this positioning strategy, the hotel does not accept airline crew, for instance. Its average room rate is said to be about Rs. 1500 more than the Taj or Oberoi.

Mr. Ranvir Bhandari, General Manager of the hotel, stated: "We have positioned ourselves as a destination, and not just an hotel."

This is an unusual concept of positioning for an hotel. It lifts the hotel from the status of a place where you eat, sleep and talk business to a place which you enjoy and take pleasure in for its own sake. Perhaps this is the ultimate positioning for an hotel.

To support this position, the Hotel has created a spa which is rated "as one of the best in the world", and the reputation of this spa spreads by word-of-mouth.

The unusual feature of clear sparkling pools of water visible from the public areas as well as the private rooms adds to the special touch of coolness and serenity.

With an average room rate of Rs. 4,500 (in 2003) you might expect occupancy to be somewhat low. But evidently many of its patrons also look upon this hotel as a 'destination' which is why the Hotel achieved 50% occupancy rate in the first year itself, meeting its target.

The Hotel provides unmatched conference facilities. It offers, for instance, a staggering 22,000 sq feet of space for conferences and has created, as Mr Bhandari said, "a seamless co-existence of work and stay." Interestingly, the conference facilities are physically at a distance from the residential rooms so that they do not impinge on the latter in any way.

The hotel has seven (7) restaurants, including the world famous 'Bukhara' named here as the 'Peshawri', and also the well known 'Dum Pukht' and 'West View'.

The hotel attracts guests through word-of-mouth and this is where the staff plays such a critical role, making the excellence of its service a source of attraction for new guests.

In addition, as an ITC Hotel, it draws upon the resources of Sheraton worldwide, its contact with travel agents and also the Internet.

The Hotel has a formal feedback system from guests. During the first half of 2003, for instance it collected 4,655 feedback forms filled in by guests. Some specimen guest comments are quoted on the next page.

A question that some might ask is, despite this positive feedback about the Hotel, does Kolkata have the potential to justify such a large investment in such a 'Luxury' hotel? The occupancy figure that has been quoted seems to say 'Yes'. Moreover, Mr Y.C. Deveshwar, Chairman, ITC, explained the expectations of the Company as follows:

It was only because of the State's latent potential that ITC invested nearly Rs. 250 crores on setting up this hotel. The opening up of the Nathula Pass and the recent protocol signed between India and Thailand would strengthen West Bengal's cause of emerging as a Gateway to the East. "Those who would come here now with the capital would be just in time. The early bird will be the one who will catch the worm."

(*The Times of India,* October 18, 2003)

Some guest comments on ITC's Sonar Bangla Sheraton Hotel:

Richard Saldanha
Executive Director
Bennett, Coleman & Co. Ltd.

> *"My stay here has exceeded expectation. You have set new standards in India and the East."*

Anindita Sengupta
Lawyer

> *"Service is exceptional & the decor is great. Keep up the good work."*

Shekhar Sen
Mumbai
"Keep it as beautiful as it is"
Kesyan Mohan
New Delhi

> *"The over stay has been very rewarding, the staff have been trained very well to be courteous and polite."*

Atul Chand
ITC Ltd.

> *"Sonar Bangla is definitely going to be the crowning glory of Kolkata; just keep up the good food and service."*

Sanjay Bhutani
Schlumberger Measurement & Systems
New Delhi

"Excellent facility, and makes the guest feel a privileged one."

His Divine Grace, BS Tirtha Goswamy Maharaj
Sri Gouranga Ashram

"A wonderful and unique experience."

HP GAS

1. Brand name   :   HP GAS
2. Product Type   :   LPG (Domestic Cooking Gas)
3. Category   :   Service
4. Campaign Title   :   Ji Haan Services
5. Campaign   :   National Campaign

Marketing Challenge*

After many years of an oligopolistic marketplace, the domestic LPG segment was finally opened to private players. However it was still not a level playing field. That's because the government LPG players like HP Gas, Bharatgas and Indane still had the advantage of government subsidies in terms of pricing. This coupled with their advantage of reach made the government LPG manufacturers the preferred choice.

In the category, the dealer was the front for the consumer—the decision maker as to when he got the connection and then when he got the gas refill.

However, things are soon to change. With government subsidies being withdrawn, it is expected that service delivery and brand image would be the key drivers for brand consideration in the coming years when the private players made an entry.

In this scenario, HP Gas had no clear personification. It was seen as just another Public Sector company supplying LPG. There was no clear brand differentiation amongst the PSU players too.

The challenge for HP Gas was to change the "LPG category" negative perceptions and create a brand identity.

---

* Entry for Effie 2003. *Courtesy:* J. Walter Thompson.

Campaign Objectives

Hence the need for HP Gas was:

- to take the lead in building a distinctive brand
- creating a unique identity for the product in a market where it is treated like a commodity
- thereby modifying the negative image perceptions linked to the category.

To enable the above to happen, the company had to undertake the task of influencing both the internal and external audience—dealers and consumers.

The task was further compounded by the sheer volume—over 17 million consumers and over 1800 dealers spread across the length and breadth of the country.

Target Audience

Core Target Audience

The communication target audience straddled different segments:

1. *Current HP Gas users:* prevent switching and use more LPG in lieu of kerosene
2. *Non-LPG users:* make them positively pre-disposed towards LPG and bring HP Gas into their consideration set.

Profile

Research[1] among housewives threw up an interesting insight.

- The household manager performs many tasks. She receives help from other family members/hired help for most of these tasks.
- However the cooking task is something that she handles on her own.
  - 72% are responsible for cooking and cook themselves.
  - And 54% don't receive any help in cooking.

Creative Strategy

Brand Position: *Given the fact that the housewife has no help in the kitchen the aim of the brand was to position itself as her "expert helper" in the kitchen. This was supported by the brand service delivery of*

---

1. Millennium Woman Study 2001.

immediate new gas connection, refills in 24 hours and 8 am to 8 pm booking and delivery service.

Desired Response: *A helper who provides efficient service and is accessible and reliable* (Exhibits 6.13, 6.14, 6.15, Plates 13–14).

Solution: The position of the "expert helper" was brought alive in the brand mnemonic and the brand statement: "*Ji Haan*". Each creative execution made a specific service come alive and linked it back to the brand position.

Sadhu	— Immediate new connections
Maid	— 8 am to 8 pm gas delivery
Bhai	— Cylinder refill delivery within 24 hours

Other Communication Programs

Due to the scale of the operations, it involved perception change at two levels: internal and external. The internal audience involved the employees and the dealers, while the external audience involved the consumer.

For the employees and the dealers, an extensive range of interactive sessions were held before the consumer launch. Secondly, since it was the first time the service was being branded, it was critical that the HP Gas have one identity—from the boy doing home deliveries, to the dealer signages, the delivery trucks, cash memos, uniforms, bulk tankers, and so on. Top help do the same, a comprehensive brand identity manual was developed and implemented across the country.

In stage two, the consumer launch was done across 55 cities with an extensive PR exercise followed by an aggressive multi-media launch—press, outdoor and TV.

Media Strategy

Due to the phased manner of the launch, it was decided to selectively use media.

At the launch in each centre, it was the strategic use of multiple media, i.e. PR, outdoor and daily print. When the rollout reached a critical mass, TV was used for efficiencies in getting reach. The total media spend for the same was approx. Rs 3.18 crores.

Media used

Television, Newspapers, Point-of-purchase, Out-of-home, Public Relations

Total media expenditure: (Rs 3.18 crores approx)

Rs 2.5 crores to Rs 5 crores

Evidence of Results[2]

- Unaided brand recall: 86% (16% pre campaign)
- 8% top of mind ad recall (any ad)—the 4th highest among all categories. Competitive brands like Bharatgas and Indane at 0.1% and 0.2% respectively
- Category aided (LPG) recall at 35%—4 times higher than closest competitor
- Correct message takeout: 77%
- HP Gas as a brand is seen as a "well behaved, responsible, high profile, kind at heart person"
- "*Ji Haan*" mascot: seen as desirable and positive. A customer-friendly brand
- Market share movements[3]
- New connection acquisition rate: 27% (up from 23% prior to campaign)
- Market share: 24.8%

TEEN HASEEN*

Marketing Challenge

The soap category has seen a degrowth in the last two years. Consumers in this category typically flirt between brands frequently and also downgrade to lower priced soaps. In such a scenario Lux faced severe competition.

---

2. HP Gas Brand Track 2003 and AC Nielsen Study 2001.
3. Industry records.
*. Entry for Effie 2003. *Courtesy:* J. Walter Thompson.

The challenge was to offer the consumer a choice of three distinct variants, so that if the consumer was looking for a change, she did not have to look outside the Lux portfolio.

In 2001, Lux was a 70,000 tonnes brand (around 14% of the total soap market of 4,88,457 tonnes) of which the three—Lux variants: Lux Pink almond, Lux Black honey, Lux White milk cream were in the ratio 78 : 12 : 10.

Lux Pink was the favourite among consumers and most of them were not aware of the existence of the other variants. Therefore, in order to drive awareness of variants and retain consumers within the Lux portfolio it was critical to incentivise and induce her through a special initiative.

Campaign Objectives

The objective was to increase awareness and induce trials of the other two variants—Lux Black with honey and Lux White with milk cream.

Target Audience

18–35-year-old women, who are Lux Pink users, and are always on the look out for alternatives either in terms of variety or values.

Creative Strategy

Consumer understanding indicates that to a consumer a bath is as monotonous as a routine can get. However, if the bathing experience is made to look different and exciting, it would overcome the boredom that this routine induces. In order to seduce the consumer to adopt the different variants on Lux, all the three Lux variants were banded together in a special pack of three and sold it at a discount of Rs 3/-. This special pack was called '*Teen Haseen*' Lux to offer three distinct bathing experiences from Lux.

- **Lux Pink with almonds**, cued energy and youthfulness

- **Lux White with milk cream**, cued luxurious indulgence
- **Lux Black with honey**, cued sensuality

Other Communication Programs

Trade Incentivisation:
- **'Tak Dhina Teen':** A special event around movie stars was organized for trade where three famous film stars present as Lux brand ambassadors, performed live. This was done in seven cities across the country. In order to hype up the event, Lux tied up with B4U—a leading TV channel to promote and telecast the event. There were PR write-ups on the same as well.
- **Point of sale material:** Product displays, innovative posters, shelf cards, shelf strips, streamers was used to create high visibility.
- **Packaging:** For the first time the back-of-pack on the soaps carried each of the three variants to build awareness of the three variants.
- **Lux White milk cream and Lux Black honey communication:** Edits of this successful campaign were run for rest of the year focussing on the Lux White milk cream and Lux Black honey variants in select geographies.

Media Strategy

TV, press, and in-shop activity was used to ensure high salience, visibility and excitement generation.

The **television** campaign was not just to generate excitement around the three variants, but also to communicate the thematic values of the brand, viz. the goodness of nourishing ingredients that enhances beauty. Lux also sponsored movies featuring Lux film stars as brand ambassadors.

A **Press** campaign was run in Maharashtra, Karnataka, Punjab, Rajasthan, Delhi, Bangalore, and Tamil Nadu to ensure high salience.

Evidence of Results

The 'Teen Haseen Lux' campaign was run between April and June 2002.

'Teen Haseen Lux', contributed to Rs. 6,817 lakhs in value terms and 8,386 tonnes in volume terms, and lead to an increase in the sales of the other two variants of Lux:

- The volume sales of the **Lux Black honey** variant grew by 40% between 2001 and 2002.
- The volume sales of the **Lux White milk cream** variant grew by 24% between 2001 and 2002.

Taking the communication on Teen Haseen Lux forward, edits of this campaign were run for rest of the year focussing on the Lux White milk cream and Lux Black honey variants in select geographies.

MINI LUX

Marketing Challenge

The soap market had shown de-growth in the last two years. A key factor was downgradation to heaper soaps across markets. Lux had to face severe competition due to this in the rural market and among the low-income group in the urban market.

The reason Lux was getting out of reach for this consumer was the Lux price point at Rs 11/- for 100 gm, whereas the lower priced soaps like Nima rose/Breeze were available for Rs 7/- for 100 g.

Given the scenario that the entire spend or more than 40% of the rural consumers on soap per purchase visit was Rs. 11/- and that more than 70% of the rural consumers used less than 50 g of Lux, the challenge for Lux was to be accessible to the consumer through a smaller pack size at an affordable price.

Campaign Objectives

The objective was to grow the rural market and the low-income urban market aggressively by building awareness and inducing trials through

Plate 13

Exhibit 6.13 *(See p. 190)*

Exhibit 6.14 *(Courtesy: JWT) (See p. 190)*

Plate 14

~~Com~~promise

Refills within 24 hours.

~~Non~~ co-operation

8 am to 8 pm refill delivery.
All seven days of the week.

~~Im~~possible

Immediate new connections.

Now, 'No' is not an option
At HP Gas we are sensitive to all your needs.

For more information contact our Customer Service Cell at 3321285.

For new connections the refundable deposit for a cylinder is Rs 700/-
and for a regulator is Rs 100/-. Other charges as applicable.

your friendly gas

In case of a gas leak :
• Switch off the regulator • Do not switch on or off any electrical switches • Never light a matchstick • Open all the windows

*Services available in Delhi city

Visit us at www.hindpetro.com

Exhibit 6.15   *(Courtesy: JWT) (See p. 190)*

Plate 15

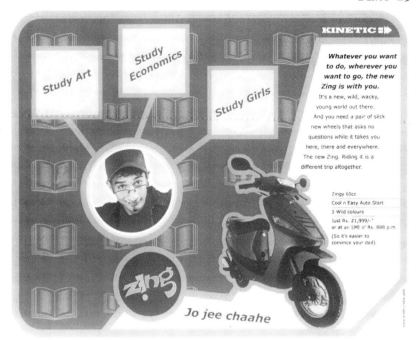

Exhibit 6.16 *(See p. 204)*

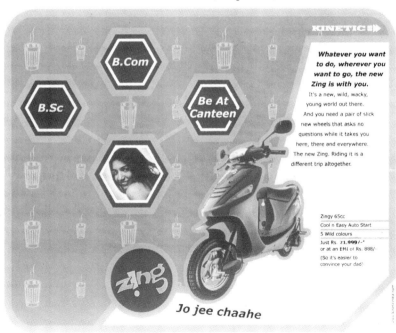

Exhibit 6.17 *(See p. 204)*

Plate 16

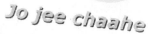

Exhibit 6.18 *(See p. 204)*

the introduction of a smaller pack (50 g) of the pink Lux variant at Rs. 5/-. The 50 g Mini Lux sales target was set at 4,000 tonnes.

Target Audience

A woman in the age bracket of 25–35 years, who lives in rural India, wants to look beautiful. The family soap that she uses is her only cosmetic as she has a very limited budget for household purchases.

Creative Strategy

Lux, with its heritage of film stars—who epitomise beauty in India, is a highly aspirational brand to the rural consumer.

Stemming from the target audience insight—'*Beauty out of my reach*' the communication in this campaign was aimed at focussing on how this beauty was now made accessible through Mini Lux at Rs 5/-.

This proposition was brought to life for the rural consumer through an evocative and memorable jingle. The Mini Lux film cast the Lux Film star—Raveena Tandon along with a little girl version of the film star, who was also introduced to personify Mini Lux.

Other Communication Programs

Rural touch points
- To make the Mini Lux jingle a household tune, it was aired in rural markets in local transportation.
- Innovative and durable in-shop merchandising—tin plates with mirrors and calendars for utility value were created, to ensure their high visibility and presence in a rural shop for many months.

Rural Distribution Programs were specially designed to achieve optimal depth and width of reach in rural areas:
- To drive the sales of Mini Lux through the distribution channel and not just at the consumer level, key rural wholesalers and retailers who were part of the HLL rural incentive schemes were further incentivised.

- An economic barrier existed for the rural retailer to purchase in bulk (the normal Lux carton). To make Mini Lux accessible even to the smallest retailer, smaller cartons were specially designed for Mini Lux.

Media Strategy

Mass media vehicles relevant to the rural and the low-income urban consumers were used in a phased manner to ensure an effective and continuous presence.

Phase one of the communication strategy involved maximum weights to television and in **phase two** maximal weights were given to the radio jingle of Mini Lux to reinforce the communication.

National Terrestrial TV was the lead medium. Special entitlements such as sponsorship of the Friday Super-hit movies through the year were taken.

In addition, **Radio** was used across seven states to increase the reach of the communication at times during the day when the consumer would be most receptive to the message.

Evidence of Results

In a scenario, where the soap market had witnessed a degrowth of 12% in volume terms and 6.47% in value terms over 2001 and 2002, Lux witnessed a 17.4% increase in volume terms in 2002 over 2001.

Against the target of 4,000 tonnes that was set for this initiative, Mini Lux went beyond and actually garnered volumes of 4856 tonnes in 2002. This contributed to 40% of the incremental volumes of 11,896.43 tonnes for Lux in 2002 over 2001.

DAIKIN AIRCONDITIONER

Circa 2001: A flashback to the US$ 4 million air-conditioner industry in India

The new leaders in the Indian cooling market were the charismatic and international LG, Samsung and the all-American Carrier. The

Courtesy: Mr. Ram Sehgal and Mr. K. Subramanian, Rediffusion—DY&R.

homegrown warriors (Voltas and Blue Star), with more than thirty years of local expertise, were attempting a spirited comeback. Not to forget the villains of the drama were the unorganized and unbranded sector with nearly 25% of the market.

The Government of India, with its adverse taxation policies (an excise duty of 32% and an import duty of 35%) nearly doubled the cost of any branded air-conditioner. And the ubiquitous Rain Gods that lashed the country, naturally mitigating the summer heat, ate away the potential sales.

In this action packed drama entered the Japanese novice, Daikin a premium split airconditioner. It was internationally known as a flawless, well-engineered product but it was unheard of, unproved and untried in India.

An additional factor that had to be kept in mind was the considerable price premium at which Daikin was pegged (more than 25%); this too in a market traditionally known for its frugality, and where for the most part, an air-conditioner itself was a luxury. And here was a brand, which was not only marketing a 'luxury' product but had the temerity to price it even higher than other brands, making the task of rationalizing the purchase so much more difficult for the consumer.

The challenge, therefore, was not only to create the consumer's preference for this 12th brand of air-conditioner in the country, but also to actually cajole as much as 25% price premium (over the rest of the category) out of him.

To address this challenge, should it flash the "I am International" tag and hope that this had enough appeal to lure him? A number of big global brands like Ray-Ban, Kellogg's and KFC had tried this route without much success! Or, should it follow the international Daikin doctrine of endorsement and say, "Daikin cools the Sony Headquarters" or "Daikin cools the G8 Summit"—a proposition that cued in the superiority of the product drawback in both the routes was that the Indian consumer might just turn around and say—"So what's in it for me?"

So what should this first time campaign for a new product launch do?

Planning the Campaign

A four-pronged sequential campaign was felt to be critical to best address the marketing challenge.

The first thing Daikin needed to do was to create a context and position for itself in the minds of its prospective customers. This required the campaign to start with mass media in order to generate awareness that this is not 'just another air-conditioner'.

The next step was to generate interest among the specific target audience that the brand had to attract, the high net worth individuals and the specialist influences like architects, interior designers and air-conditioning consultants. This was done through specific specialist magazines and premium publications.

Phase III was to zero-in on "hot" targets. They were targeted through direct mailers to reiterate the product superiority and make them an offer they could not refuse!

Finally, to give the product touch and feel experience among its core audience, the brand participated in expositions and exhibitions.

Campaign Objectives

The campaign was formulated with a few key objectives.

The discerning Indian consumer would need a very strong hook to buy this untested brand and NOT buy the other more familiar, trusted brands that he was comfortable with. Hence, it needed to establish a compelling, persuasive, relevant yet differentiated reason for the consumer to choose the brand.

It needed to create an aura of an extraordinary, technologically-flawless product and hence rationalize the extra premium for the brand.

And while doing this, the campaign had to be impactful enough to help the brand garner a 15% share of the premium split air-conditioners segment in the very first complete year in market. This share was critical for the brand to continually invest and grow in India. More so, when the air-conditioner was the only product selling under this brand name, unlike other consumer durable brands that had entire portfolios from microwaves to televisions.

Marketing Communication Strategy

There were three key pillars to the communication strategy.
The first key pillar was an important insight that had been obtained from consumers. Consumers desired a more mythical overall 'sense' of technology instead of being overawed by the actual technology and the various scientific specifications that go into making the product. Hence, the flawless engineering of Daikin, while being the product characteristic, had to translate into a consumer sensible tangible manifestation of technology.

A look at the competition indicated that most of the communication clearly fell into two distinct clusters.

At one end, there were those that talked about the generic benefit of cooling and comfort, which were implicit in any premium brand. However, Daikin was only talking to those who had well internalized the generic benefits of an air-conditioner.

At the other end of the spectrum were those that extolled some very exaggerated and unreal virtues such as 'Healthy Air' (LG) and 'Perfection' (Hitachi). However, conceptually, our audience had a mindset of a 'Bullshit Detester'—someone who had a mind of his own and would not be taken in by glib tall non-sensical claims of mass-market durables. Hence, the brand needed to give the consumer a distinctive 'tangible' reason to choose it.

Societal trends over the last few years had meant that the category of airconditioners was moving from being a luxury product to being an essential aid to comfortable living. In a world of urban stressful living, all that one yearns for is some cool comfort, but more importantly peace and quiet; this provided the way in which one could get both without compromising on either.

Tie all this with the subconscious observation of the irritating constant hum of the air-conditioner and we arrived at the platform of 'Complete Silence'. And perceptually, Daikin was able to deliver this proposition because it was at the forefront of cutting-edge technology.

Media Strategy

Since this was the first year in the market, the brand had a very sparse media investment plan of INR 35 million (US$ 0.7 million) as opposed to the category's INR 720 million (US$ 14.4 million). In comparison, LG (the leader in the category) spend upwards of INR 120 million (US$ 2.4 million) on air-conditioners alone. This also does not account for the monies that they invested in advertising several other categories that had a natural rub-off on air-conditioners too.

This challenging media investment meant that one had to be more focussed, smart and creative while formulating the media strategy.

The media selection was very sharply focussed on the business executive given that he was psychographically most likely to be the conceptual target audience we had defined. Only night slots were taken on television. Weekends were avoided. Business and specialist publications were chosen for the correct audience profile. Strategically chosen outdoor locations in arterial business districts were added. Sponsoring programs such as the Union Budget and the Oscars on television added to the impact.

Finally, the convention of advertising for air-conditioners only in summer months was avoided. Consciously and intentionally there was disproportionate focus on the rest of the year. This decision was taken to avoid category clutter that would have happened if only the summer months were chosen, specially given the fact that Daikin was a new brand competing against big established players.

This selective strategy gave the brand maximum reach within the defined audience, minimal spill over, high impact visibility and premium imagery.

Creative Strategy

How does one demonstrate 'Complete Silence'—an abstract and intangible phenomenon?

Should one merely state the fact that this product did not make any noise, supported with various facts and figures? This might have conveyed the product's promise, but would it have broken through the media noise?

The communication targeted an evolved and discerning consumer. It was critical that the campaign had to be thought-provoking and clever enough to catch his attention while communicating the benefit of "Complete Silence" in a way that was relevant to him.

The humour needed to be subtle keeping in-line with our entire postioning. To further cue in the exclusivity of the product, we needed to use premium imagery in the campaign, which would appeal to only the specific intended audience.

A whole array of characters that typified noise were chosen and an unexpected twist was added in order to emphasize the lack of sound in the product. Examples of these were well-known signifiers like the Gandhian monkeys (speak no evil, see no evil, hear no evil), Van Gogh's cut ear and the Munch's 'Scream'.

It was decided to take the platform of "Complete Silence" beyond the positioning, right up to the execution.

The entire thematic appeal of the communication was deliberately elegant and understated in a media situation where the consumer was constantly bombarded with exaggerated competitive claims. Hence the use of muted colours, antiques in the visuals, highly evolved paintings, and subdued font.

Silence was also emphasized in the layout with very little copy, clean visuals, and minimalistic headlines. The product visual itself was depicted in a very subtle, un-instrusive manner.

Evidence of Results

The results were there for all to see!

As opposed to a target of 15% share of the premium split air-conditioners segment in 2002, the brand achieved a market share of 22%.

In the complete splits market of nearly 20 players (with Indian stalwarts like Voltas and Blue Star and international giants like Samsung and Carrier), Daikin is now only second to LG in the first complete year of presence in the market.

In an industry that measures its achievements in total tonnage of airconditioning sold, Daikin achieved a tonnage of 35,000 tonnes in 2002 as opposed to the leader LG achieving 40,000 tonnes.

However, the market realization per ton was much higher for Daikin as compared to LG, a reaffirmation of the fact that the consumer was willing to pay a premium for the brand Daikin.

In-house qualitative research has proven that the key influencer segment considers Daikin as an industry 'benchmark'. The trade has significantly more confidence in the brand, a fact decoded from the observation that at least four significantly large distributors have shifted to Daikin from competition.

Daikin International awards one of the countries they are present in as the 'Daikin Country of the Year' on the basis of four key indices: brand development, sales achievement, customer satisfaction and dealer satisfaction. Daikin India received this award in 2002 in its very first complete year of operation.

Additionally, the client has adopted the concept of 'Complete Silence' across their internal systems, their dealer meets and press conferences' have adopted the mantra of 'Complete Silence' while meritorious dealers are given certificates carrying the tag 'The Silent Achiever'.

And lastly, when the national sporting icon 'Sachin Tendulkar'—who is revered and adored as much as a Michael Jordon in this cricket crazy country—decides to depend on Daikin for his theme restaurant, we know that we have been successful in what we set out to accomplish.

BRAND: KINETIC ZING

Marketing Challenge

1. Facing a 10-yr-old entrenched market leader:
   (a) TVS Scooty had been the undisputed market leader for the past 10 years.
   (b) It had almost become generic to the category.
2. An extremely volatile category:
   (a) Several extremely well-established two-wheeler players had tried and failed to make an impact. They got exited after

Courtsey: Contract Advertising.

promising starts. Hero Winner, LML Trendy, Bajaj Sunny, Bajaj Spirit and Bajaj Saffire—to name a few.
3. A consumer who preferred the tried and tested:
   (a) The market for this category is semi metros and small towns, which is quite conservative and doesn't like too many risks.
   (b) Brand history and reputation are important factors in decision making.
   (c) Thus, most consumers ended up buying Scooty, which among other things enjoyed excellent owner feedback.
4. No product USP:
   (a) On a feature-to-feature comparison—Zing was a parity product. Anyway, with established competition, a performance claim would have been just that—a claim.
   (b) Kinetic could no longer leverage Honda's equity, since their association had just ended.

Perhaps the market did not want any new products. Yet, Kinetic wanted an assured presence in this segment.

Communication Objective

To permanently enter the consideration set of consumers and become the most preferred brand by:
(a) Winning 20% of the market share in the first year of launch.
(b) To be a strong no. 2 brand in the category within the first year of launch.

Target Audience

The youth, who was the user and the joint decision maker in the purchase.
(a) 18-yr-old school/college goers, SEC A and B
(b) Living in semi-metros and small towns, e.g. Ahmedabad, Jaipur, Nasik, etc.

Creative Strategy (Exhibits 6.16, 6.17 and 6.18, Plates 15–16)

An apologetic category:

- In the two-wheeler category, scooterette was the bottom of the rung—in terms of power, overall appeal, speed, price, etc.
- Attitudinally, a scooterette was associated with girls rather than boys, the sweet and boring rather than smart and sharp types, weak rather than strong, losers rather than winners. It was a 'Compromise'.

The market leader was adding to the problem:

- Scooty's advertising (the largest player—70%) attempted to make 'scooterette even more sweet'.
- Dearth of fresh communication attempts to lend any sort of attitude to the category.

The consumer actually wanted an attitude:

- As a category, the two-wheeler promised a 'World of Freedom' to the 18-year-old, who was till recently dependent on cycle, bus, train, his friends or parents. It made his mobile and independent.
- This 'Freedom' gave him serious 'Attitude' versus those who still depended on cycle, parents, bus, etc.

But the consumer had almost written off the scooterette as far as fulfilling his need for 'An attitude' was concerned. Rather, he was buying it from jeans, college campus, MTV, cafe joints, etc. The scooterette purchase was as compromise, an apologetic purchase.

Taking the compromise out of scooterette:

- Only 'an attitude' could convert a compromise to pride of ownership.
- And 'Freedom'—the category attitude—was still unappropriated.

  In terms of the product proposition also, 'Freedom' would starkly differentiate Zing from Scooty.

  Freedom was defined as—an opportunity to do whatever you want to do, no rules, no formats, no gyan...*Jo Jee Chahe*. The creative strategy was to associate **Freedom as an attitude with Kinetic Zing**. This would also take Zing beyond the rational feature comparison.

Media Strategy

A typical scooterette media strategy would be to reach both the decision makers—youth (user) and father (buyer). We consciously stayed away from this and focussed only on media vehicles which enjoyed higher involvement of youth.

A limited budget:
- Given the size of the task, the budget of Rs 2 cr. was really small.

Innovations:
- Teaser ads in press were designed to generate buzz and excitement in the market.
- Contests carried across TV, Internet (C2W) and Radio further added to the buzz.

Dominate the youth media vehicles:
- A mix of music channels like B4U, MTV, and VTV, and outdoor sites near colleges were chosen for reach. Radio and ads in youth magazines (e.g. JAM) were used for frequency.
- We advertised in vernacular newspapers to reach the small town audience.

Evidence of Results

Pre Campaign: Scooty had 70% of the market while Saffire and Spirit together had 30%.

Post Campaign

Zing won 27% of the market share within 9 months of its launch thus achieving 135% of its target, 3 months before the estimated time period. Zing not only achieved both its objectives, it overachieved them, as shown below:

- Zing became a strong No. 2 in 9 months of its launch, thus displacing Spirit and Saffire from this slot. Scooty, Spirit and Saffire all three lost significant market shares to Zing.
- Scooty's market share was down to 57% while that of Saffire and Spirit was down to 16%. Zing had won 27% of the market.

Chapter 7

A Fresh Look at Advertising Objectives

ADVERTISING MUST POSITION THE BRAND

What is the role of advertising in the context of positioning? A landmark definition of advertising was developed for the Association of National Advertisers of the USA by Russel H. Colley. It brought a greater degree of clarity to management thinking on advertising decisions. It emphasized that advertising pulls a consumer towards purchasing action through changes in his or her knowledge and attitude responses. It laid the foundation for a practical and widely used model: DAGMAR or 'Defining Advertising Goals for Measured Advertising Results'.[1]

Colley's definition is:

> *Advertising is mass, paid communication, the ultimate purpose of which is to impart information, develop attitude and induce action beneficial to the advertiser—generally the sale of a product or service.*

This is a comprehensive definition. You cannot fault it.

But we could attempt another definition that is more operational that specifically takes into account a competitive marketplace, and that recognizes the increasing difficulty of creating distinct brand identities. We could say, for example:

Advertising is the discovery
And communication
Of a Persuasive Difference
For a brand to the target prospect.

There are three critical elements here. Advertising must communicate a *difference* for the brand. It must be a *competitive* and persuasive difference. Such a difference may not fall into the communicator's lap in the form of a readymade USP. In the absence of strong functional superiority or distinction, he must search and *discover* where such persuasive differentiation lies.

The possible routes were examined in Chapters 4 and 5. We discussed there that the essence of positioning strategy is to create differential advantage for the brand. We might, therefore, crystallize our thinking by saying that the central task of advertising is to place the brand in the desired position in the prospect's mind.

That is, advertising has one overriding task: to position our brand in the prospect's perception or perceptual space, in relation to competitors, so as to create distinctness and preference.

We could rightly say that the entire marketing mix should be geared up to serve our brand's positioning objective. Advertising, however, has to carry the major burden in packaged-goods marketing with decreasing product differences.

Recent articles in the *Journal of Advertising Research* note this new orientation to the objectives of an ad campaign. This new approach acknowledges that the principal role of advertising is to influence positioning.

A truly successful advertisement has to be strongly associated with its brand, be memorable, and be influential enough to affect the final position of its brand (Keon).[3]

Ogilvy is quoted over again in a thought-provoking new volume entitled, *The Unpublished David Ogilvy.*[4]

Ogilvy recalls:

My original Magic Lantern started with the assertion that Positioning and Promise were more than half the battle.

Reiterating his views on what makes great campaigns, Ogilvy voices his two most important concerns.

Do all your campaigns execute an agreed positioning?

Do they promise a benefit which has been tested?

Setting Objectives, Measuring Results

Advertising objectives are usually set, at present in terms of awareness, knowledge or comprehension of benefit and the degree of conviction or buying intention for the brand. This is basically the DAGMAR model. Colley gives several hypothetical examples. To take one.[5]

One of the smaller overseas airlines, based in the USA, set itself the target of increasing passenger loadings by 10%. To this end, the advertising goal was defined as communicating the image of a luxury airline to an additional 20% of target prospects in one year. Benchmark and post-campaign surveys revealed the following:

	Before ad campaign(%)	After 6 months(%)	After 12 months(%)
Awareness (Have heard of Co.)	38	46	52
Image (Luxury, all-jet overseas service)	9	17	24
Preference (Would seriously consider for next trip)	13	15	21

Brand images before and after a campaign are often studied in India and expressed in profile charts (see Chapter 11). However, such measurements of an old campaign do not capture, in a manner usable by the manager, the relative positions of our brand versus major competitors on the critical dimensions; neither do they give us a practical fix on how close our brand has moved to its desired spot in the consumer's perception, following the campaign.

The DAGMAR model for testing pre- and post-exposure comprehension of the brand benefit and the ad campaign's ability to persuade—as in the example given by Colley—has on its side, simplicity and ease of application. But it also fails to track our brand's movement in the consumer's perception in relation to competing brands and in relation to the *ideal* which our target segment is seeking.

We have noted in Chapter 2 how perceptual mapping gives a reliable picture of the relative positions of competing brands in the target consumer's perceptual space. We have also seen that in the same 'joint space configuration' or map we can plot positions of brands as perceived at present and the preferred position or ideal point of our target segment. If in a perceptual map of a category, we find that point A (present perception of our brand) is at a distance from A^- which is the ideal point of consumers who matter to us, advertising's task is to move our brand from A to A^+ in that segment's perceptual space (Figure 7.1).

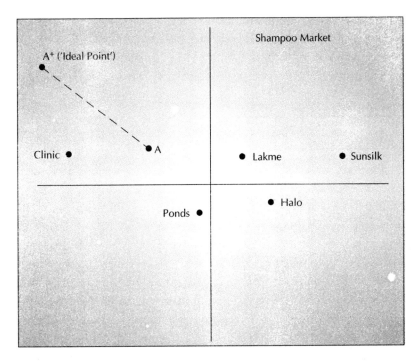

Figure 7.1   *Perceptual mapping such as this depiction of the shampoo market helps to define the advertising task in clear terms. It also helps to measure the effectiveness of the campaign with reference to this task. This is an illustrative example. It is rare for advertising objectives to be spelt out in this fashion.*

How is this theoretical concept translated into practice? As we said in Chapter 2, there is apparently no published literature on perceptual mapping based on Indian marketing and advertising cases. Nor is it clear if marketing companies and ad agencies in India generally set advertising objectives in terms of positions to be occupied in the target segment's perceptual space so that pre- and post-campaign measurements can be made through such perceptual mapping. We must fall back on some highly instructive case studies from overseas.

From Theory to Practice

The reader is referred to as an excellent example discussed in an article captioned, "How Advertising can Position a Brand" by Smith and Lusch.[6] The case relates to the L&M cigarette brand marketed by the Liggett & Myer's Company in the USA.

In early 1974, the company judged that its L&M brand was "not properly positioned" and that it had to be "repositioned in the full-flavour category". The company began with product-feature changes to match the desired position: a new blend of tobacco and a new cork filter. The pack design was also changed.

The mainstay of the repositioning effort was "a massive advertising campaign" in selected test markets. As *Advertising Age* described it, the new campaign comprised a series of ads in which "a rugged, powerfully built shirtless man (was) seen clearing an area and building a cabin in the wilderness". Persumably, it was thought that a 'Marlboro type' campaign would propel the L&M brand into the full-flavour category where Winston and Marlboro were firmly positioned.

Thus, a desired position for the L&M brand relative to competition was set by the company. The objective of the new ad campaign was also set in terms of that repositioning task, viz. to change the L&M brand's present position in target smokers' minds to the new one—"a full-flavoured cigarette".

So, what happened?

Measuring Position Change

Using MDS (Multidimensional Scaling) techniques, Smith and Lusch tracked the positions of various brands before and after the new campaign. Here we shall summarize what they found among two samples of smokers: One was the control sample in a region where the new campaign was not released, and the other was an experimental sample where the repositioning exercise was on and respondents were exposed to the new campaign.

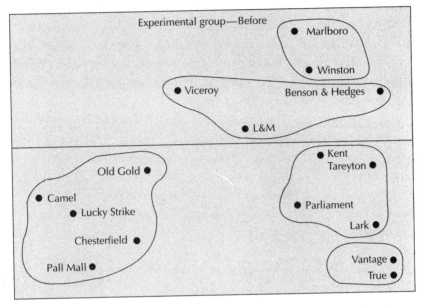

Figure 7.2   *The cigarette brands under study were found to be in five clusters, before the new campaign for L & M cigarettes.*

Figure 7.2 shows the perceptual map of brands among the experimental group before the campaign. Here we find five clusters, each including brands that were perceived to be somewhat similar. L&M was clustered with Viceroy and Benson & Hedges and not with the acknowledged full-flavour brands, Marlboro and Winston. The control group's perceptions were found to be quite similar. These findings matched the company's assessment.

The same questionnaire was administered to the same respondents in the experimental group after that group had been exposed to the new L&M ad campaign for six weeks, and to the control group which had not been so exposed.

In the second round of the survey, the control group yielded the same five clusters that had been observed at the benchmark stage. This was expected.

For the experimental group, the post-campaign perceptual map is seen in Figure 7.3. The clusters are visually the same as in the pre-campaign stage with the exception of Kent. The brand of interest, L&M, had not moved noticeably closer to the Marlboro-Winston cluster as was intended. The researchers concluded that "L & M did not move significantly in relation to Marlboro during the six-week period of the ad campaign for the smokers in their sample". This is a new way of judging advertising effectiveness.

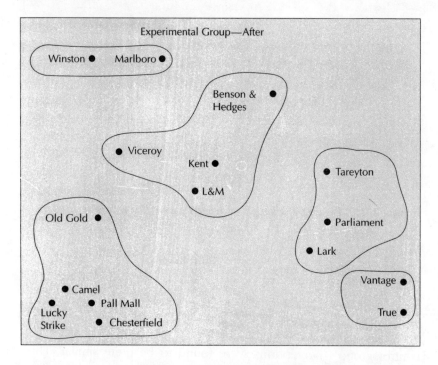

Figure 7.3 *Post-campaign mapping, as in this figure, shows that the L & M brand had not moved significantly closer to Marlboro, as was intended. This was the authors' conclusion based on a statistical analysis. (Figures 7.2 and 7.3 have been reproduced with permission from an article entitled "How Advertising Can Position a Brand" by Robert E Smith and Robert F Lusch in the Journal of Advertising Research, February 1976).*

Repositioning an Indian Cigarette

A somewhat similar exercise has been undertaken by a company in India to move an old-established, once-prestigious brand from a state of relative decline and a diffused, indeterminate position to a new one, which in the company's view would rejuvenate the brand.

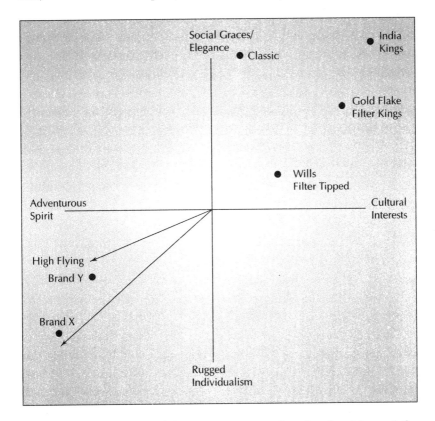

Figure 7.4 *This is one of those rare instances when the advertising task for a brand (Brand X) was set in terms of the position it should occupy in the target consumer's perceptual space. The two vectors displayed on this hypothetical map are 'High-flying Life Style' and the vector along which Brand X has to be positioned.*

The company spelt out the advertising goal for the brand—which we will call Brand X—with the help of a hypothetical positioning map seen in Figure 7.4. The map was drawn using research data and a good dose of managerial judgement. It was believed that the vertical axis could be interpreted as 'social graces/elegance' at one end and 'rugged individualism' at the other.

The horizontal axis reflected 'culture' and 'adventure' activities and interests at either end. This axis could also be interpreted as 'indoor-outdoor'. The brands being observed for this exercise are seen positioned on the map. The company was clear that Brand X should compete primarily with Brand Y and must be positioned in the same quadrant bounded by the dimensions of 'outdoor' or 'adventure' and 'rugged individualism'.

However, Brand X needed to be given a distinct identity. This could be done through a distinctive pack, a more aromatic blend and by attaching to it an attribute (shown as a vector on the map) which was quite different from the attribute of 'high flying' life style associated with Brand Y.

What could this vector be? To describe it, said the company, the technique of 'lateral association' could be used. Thus, "If Brand Y were to become a magazine what would it be"? Clearly, it would be *Penthouse, Debonair* or something similar.

On the other hand, if Brand X were to become a magazine what would it be? The answer: *National Geographic.*

Thus, the task of advertising was to create for Brand X a personality that would position it along this new vector (new, because no other brand was plotted there). The effectiveness of advertising that was created would be measured against this desired position.

We believe that positioning theory offers us a new approach to the determination of advertising objectives and for pre- and post-exposure measurements of an ad campaign. The further we move from the USP as a reality in advertising, the greater must be our reliance on positioning strategies to differentiate our brand, and on perceptual mapping to evaluate the worth of an ad campaign.

We will now examine a case in which a premium toilet soap brand in India was conceived to fill a vacant position in the market. All the elements of the marketing mix were designed with the single-minded objective of occupying that position—the brand name, perfume, shape, colour, price, size, pack and choice of outlets. Advertising was given the specific task of situating the brand indelibly in the desired position in the target consumer's mind. Mr. Ram Ray, Chairman and Managing Director of Response ad agency, describes the exercise.

ARAMUSK

A Relevant New Proposition for an Untapped Audience

The Shaw Wallace Group entered the consumer market with a Consumer Products Division to make and sell detergents, soaps and cosmetics.

In this context Shaw Wallace in late 1984, wanted to be reckoned as a major toilet soap company with more than one national brand of premium toilet soaps.

Enter Response

The agency, Response, worked on a Soap-Scan to identify new segments and opportunities which had not been previously exploited.

The Soap-Scan showed, on the whole, that toilet soaps were positioned on the dimensions of 'Feels Good' and 'Does Good'.

Feels Good			Does Good	
Just feels good	Feels good and also does good	Does good and feels good	Does good, may feel good	Does good
Lavender	Supreme	Pears (glycerine)	Neem (antiseptic)	Neko (medicated)
Dew			Cinthol	
Moti	Pond's Cold Cream		(deodorant)	
Gold Mist	Raindrop			
Mysore Jasmine	Green of Apple			
	Liril			
	Mysore Sandal			

Detailed study of these brands under Soap-Scan led to the following conclusions:

- Pure fragrance appeals do not fetch high volume.

- The ingredient hook is weak or strong depending on consumer perception of specific *do-good* properties of the ingredient claimed.
- Medicated soaps have restricted appeal.
- The dramatic success of Liril suggests the scope for adding a psychological dimension to the *feel-good* appeal.
- The point of difference is made by the imaginative appeal within the *feel-good* area.
- Such new positions are likely to cut across demographic groupings and break the artificial price barrier suggested by 'Popular' and 'Premium'.

Creating such a new position was determined to be the master key to success.

A Soap Exclusively for Men—An Untapped Market

Scanning the entire spectrum of brands, the agency found that there appeared to be nothing that was exclusively or even predominantly MALE, with the single exception of Lifebuoy, which again had little upward mobility from blue-collar *Janata* usage.

Why this gap? It could be that the industry leader, Hindustan Lever Ltd., was not interested in the tonnages possible. And everyone else played safe behind them.

By and large, most brands are pitched at females and, so the agency believed, taken on sufferance by males. Since the era of male-adornment products had come to stay, there had to be latent dissatisfaction on this count.

The Product

To break into the difficult premium soap market in India, one needs a product with features that are highly distinctive both conceptually and physically. There appeared to be room for a soap with a superior finish, select appeal and deluxe price. The agency came up with a concept to fill this vacant position.

A deluxe male soap
With a musk perfume
Abundant creamy lather
Beige colour
Cushion shaped cake
Man-size grip
Priced at around Rs 7.50 for 100 g
With an exclusive golden seal that also keeps the soap dry.

The Target Group

Affluent, well-travelled, suave men of the world and those who aspire to be like them.

Communication Task

Develop a mix of benefits in which advertising creates the right personality and design packaging for the soap that matches the profile. An invitation to an exclusive man's preserve.

Agency Response

1. Generate a name that would telegraph (a) class and (b) the most distinctive feature of the soap, its perfume—*Aramusk*.
2. Design packaging that fully exploits the exclusive nature of the product.
3. Design advertising that would communicate the offering of a premium toilet soap experience, but that would go beyond just soap—to keep open the possibility of a new world of expensive and exclusive men's personal products.

Note how the product features, the price, the packaging and the brand name were all designed to reinforce the desired position. It was then the task of advertising to *situate* the brand as intended.

Another certain something that's extravagantly male.

Introducing Aramusk. Bath Soap For Men.

Exhibit 7.1 *Aramusk was test-launched in Delhi with this ad. The soap and the pack appeared in colour. A strong association was created as an exclusive men's product. (Agency: Response)*

Creative Execution

Instant noticeability and immediate association with an exclusive men's product through use of illustrations of antique artifacts and the brand payoff, 'Extravagantly male'.

The Launch

The product was test-launched in Delhi in December 1985 supported by press advertising (Exhibit 7.1), hoardings and point-of-sale material including dispensers and show-window kits. A direct mail operation introducing the product to members of top Delhi clubs was also carried out.

In May 1986, a dipstick survey in Delhi showed:

1. Awareness was very high.
2. The main source of awareness was advertising.

Plate 17

Exhibit 7.4 *Gold Flake Filter will reflect "a more individualistic personality (compared to Wills Filter)...Someone more culturally "inclined"* (Agency: Clarion)

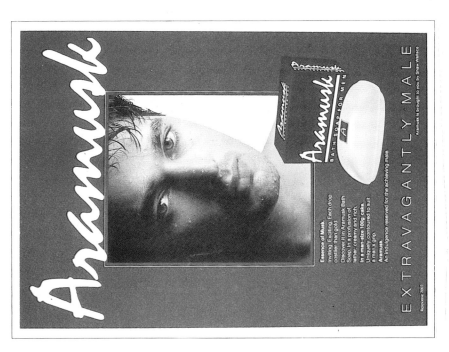

Exhibit 7.3 *The new campaign—a younger, sporty, sophisticated and more sensuous image for the brand.* (Agency: Response)

Plate 18

Exhibit 7.6 *Positioning Gold Flake Filter Kings for 'the gracious people'.* (Agency): *Clarion*)

Exhibit 7.5 *This new ad for Gold Flake Kings was pre-tested and scored well all round. (Agency: Clarion)*

3. The usership was greater amongst younger men.

4. The main message recall was 'For men only', placing it firmly in our target position.

5. More than two-thirds of the audience found the ad impressive, interesting, stylish, and different.

6. The product was identified as being exclusive, expensive.

7. The advertising was difficult to identify with. A number of people did not feel the product was meant for them. Possibly it was a little cold and somewhat abstract.

8. It did not appeal so much to men in the 20–30 age group (who, paradoxically, were the largest group of triers).

The agency worked on a revised campaign which projected a younger, active, sporty, sophisticated, more sensuous male image while the brand payoff steadfastly remained 'Extravagantly male'.

The new Press ad is seen in Exhibit 7.3 (Plate 17), and a detailed treatment of the TV commercial is given in Exhibit 7.2.

This campaign, launched in September 1986, was instantly successful in achieving widespread awareness among the target audience with minimum exposure. Marketing efforts—particularly, sales promotion—perhaps need to be undertaken to address the brand's current priority—greater trial.

Client	:	Shaw Wallace, Calcutta
Product	:	Aramusk Bath Soap and Talc for Men
Purpose	:	30-second TV Commercial for National Network
The Treatment	:	This film, using tight shots, intimate angles, slight

slow motion and a roving camera, follows and exposes an active, selective, refined, affluent, 30-year-old man, from the moment he returns home and enters his room to the moment he actually has a bath with Aramusk.

Atmosphere as well as suspense are critical. These are created through dramatic lighting and low-angle tasteful shots that give the viewer an insight into the kind of person they are watching (but not what he is planning to do).

The music for this film is tailor-made, Modern Jazz rather than Pop.

In this man's room, the floors are polished wood, the bathroom floor and walls have beige (Aramusk soap colour) tiling on them; this highlights the differences between two rooms. Dark brown (Aramusk pack colour), towels on towel rack.

The Idea: Film opens with powerful, big, black Doberman. Dog is sitting on the floor facing heavy wooden door which can also be seen in the shot. Low light comes from a corner table lamp. Car headlight beam coming from outside a large French window sweeps across the room. Dog looks up.

Key is heard turning in lock. Door opens and dog gets up slowly and pads to door. Camera follows.

Entering through the doorway, a pair of expensive but well-used tennis shoes. They pause mid-stride as man pats the dog. Legs in shoes belong to man who is definitely fit. Man's hand turns on stereo. Music starts. Suddenly we notice a small piece of pink paper on the floor. Hand enters frame from top and in one swift and easy movement, lifts one out of frame. Legs begin to walk. Camera follows from side. Walk is springy—full of life.

Man's hand places pink note under the table clock. Note in a feminine scribble reads, 'What were you wearing last night? It smelled terrific. Coming by tonight at 8.00 to find out! Signed simply *Me*. Clock shows 7.55.

Back to man's feet. He removes shoes without using hands. T-shirt flies into frame and settles on rocking chair. Low bathroom light comes on. Bare feet pad onto new surface: beige colour tiles.

Hand closes shower curtain. Camera follows. Shower is heard. A man, revelling in his bath, is seen in vague silhouette. Hand comes out of shower, we follow it to the bathroom sink. Hold. Hand goes out of frame. We see a bar of Aramusk, well-lathered, big.

Clock strikes 8. Man ties bathrobe belt. Camera freezes on his face. Doorbell rings.

Camera pulls back to reveal steamed bathroom mirror, superimposed by *Extravagantly Male, Aramusk*. Camera lowers slightly to reveal a pack of Aramusk soap on the mirror-shelf.

Exhibit 7.2   *TV film advertising Aramusk. (Agency: Response, Calcutta)*

The Aramusk brand now belongs to the Henkel Company in Chennai. In the period since the case was written we have not seen much advertising support for the brand although it still lingers on the shelves.

We will conclude this chapter with a note on O&M's approach to Positioning and Brand building written by Mr. S.R. Iyer, former Managing Director of O&M in India, which appeared originally in the first edition of this book.

SUMMING UP

Advertising's task has hitherto been defined in terms of creating awareness, comprehension and conviction—the DAGMAR model.

The author suggests a modified definition which is more operational and more attuned to creating distinctness and persuasiveness for the brand in relation to competitors in the consumer's *perception*.

A cigarette example from the USA is quoted to illustrate the value of such an approach. The objectives for the brand's advertising were mentioned in terms of its desired position in relation to competitors and effectiveness was measured by the same yardstick.

A cigarette example from India is also mentioned, but it is believed that such an approach is not yet common in India.

The launch of a premium toilet soap brand in India is discussed in some detail. Here, the starting point was the search for a vacant position in the market followed by a product concept that could fill that position.

Then came a detailed product design in which the product features, brand name and packaging were all fashioned to serve this single-minded positioning objective.

Advertising's task was identified as lodging the brand in the desired position. The first approach was found through research to be ineffective. Thereafter, the new campaign focussed more clearly and more imaginatively on creating the perception of a luxury soap which was *extravagantly male*.

In the author's view, positioning theory and perceptual mapping offer a more relevant basis for setting advertising objectives and for measuring advertising effectiveness in today's competitive markets with decreasing product differences.

Academics have talked about positioning since 1966. But what made practitioners sit up and take notice was a full page ad released by Ogilvy & Mather, with the signature of David Ogilvy, in the *New York Times* on April 7, 1971. Trout and Ries hailed this ad as heralding the era of positioning (see Exhibit 7.7).

Take a closer look at Ogilvy's ad. This is how the ad opens:

The most important decision. We have learned that the effect of your advertising on your sales depends more on this decision than on any other: *How should you position your product?*

Should you position Schweppes as a soft drink—or as a mixer?

Should you position Dove as a product for dry skin or as a product which gets hands really clean?

How to create advertising that sells

by David Ogilvy

Ogilvy & Mather has created over $1,480,000,000 worth of advertising, and spent $4,900,000 tracking the results.

Here, with all the dogmatism of brevity, are 38 of the things we have learned.

1. The most important decision. We have learned that the effect of your advertising on your sales depends more on this decision than on any other: *How should you position your product?*

Should you position SCHWEPPES as a soft drink — or as a mixer?

Should you position DOVE as a product for dry skin or as a product which gets hands really clean?

The results of your campaign depend less on how we write your advertising than on how your product is positioned. It follows that positioning should be decided before the advertising is created. Research can help. Look before you leap.

2. Large promise. The second most important decision is this: what should you promise the customer? A promise is not a claim, or a theme, or a slogan. It is a *benefit for the consumer.*

It pays to promise a benefit which is unique and competitive. And the product must *deliver* the benefit you promise.

Most advertising promises *nothing.* It is doomed to fail in the marketplace.

"Promise, large promise, is the soul of an advertisement" — said Samuel Johnson.

3. Brand image. Every advertisement should contribute to the complex symbol which is the brand image. Ninety-five percent of all advertising is created *ad hoc.* Most products lack any consistent image from one year to another.

The manufacturer who dedicates his advertising to building the most sharply defined personality for his brand gets the largest share of the market.

4. Big ideas. Unless your advertising is built on a BIG IDEA it will pass like a ship in the night.

It takes a BIG IDEA to jolt the consumer out of his indifference — to make him *notice* your advertising, *remember* it and *take action.*

Big ideas are usually *simple* ideas. Said Charles Kettering, the great General Motors inventor: "This problem, when solved, will be simple."

BIG SIMPLE IDEAS are not easy to come by. They require genius — and midnight oil. A truly big one can be continued for twenty years — like our Eyepatch for Hathaway shirts.

5. A first-class ticket. It pays to give most products an image of quality — a first-class ticket.

Ogilvy & Mather has been conspicuously successful in doing this — for Pepperidge, Hathaway, Mercedes-Benz, Schweppes, Dove and others.

If your advertising looks ugly, consumers will conclude that your product is shoddy, and they will be less likely to buy it.

6. Don't be a bore. Nobody was ever *bored* into buying a product. Yet most advertising is impersonal, detached, cold — and dull.

It pays to *involve* the customer.

Talk to her like a human being. Charm her. Make her hungry. Get her to participate.

7. Innovate. Start trends — instead of following them. Advertising which follows a fashionable fad, or is imitative, is seldom successful.

It pays to *innovate,* to blaze new trails.

But innovation is risky unless you pretest your innovation with consumers. Look before you leap.

8. Be suspicious of awards. The pursuit of creative awards seduces creative people from the pursuit of sales.

We have been unable to establish any correlation whatever between awards and sales.

At Ogilvy & Mather we now give an annual award for the campaign which contributes the most to *sales.*

Successful advertising sells the product without drawing attention to itself. It rivets the consumer's attention on the *product.*

Make the product the hero of your advertising.

9. Psychological segmentation. Any good agency knows how to position products for *demographic* segments of the market — for men, for young children, for farmers in the South, etc.

But Ogilvy & Mather has learned that *psychological* segmentation of the market.

Our Mercedes-Benz advertising to fit nonconformists who scoff at reject flimflam appeals to snob

10. Don't bury news. It is easy consumer in a product when it is other point in its life. Many copy instinct for burying news. This is tising for new products fails to tunity that genuine news permit

It pays to launch your n BOOM-BOOM.

11. Go the whole hog. paigns are too complicated of marketing objectives. To get views of too many men or too many things, they achi

It pays to boil down promise — and go the whole promise.

What works

12. Testimonials Testimonial commercials if done cessful — if you are ... tive. But avoid ... no natural consumer testimonials. It is from your presentation.

13. Problem solution. Then that prob ... in sales ... you can ... moron.

14. ... visual demonstrations in the marketplace.

It pays to ... It drives the promise home.

15. Slice of life. These playlets are ... most copywriters detest them. But they have sold a lot of merchandise, and are still selling.

16. Avoid logorrhea. Make *your picture* tell the story. What you show is more important than what you say.

Our Mercedes-Benz commercials drown the viewer in a torrent of words. We call this logorrhea (rhymes with diarrhea).

We have created some great commercials *without* words.

17. On-camera voice. Commercials using on-camera voice do significantly better than commercials using voice-over.

18. Musical backgrounds. Most commercials use musical backgrounds. However, on the average, musical backgrounds reduce recall of your commercial. Very few creative people accept this.

But we never heard of an agency using musical background under a new business presentation.

19. Stand-ups. The stand-up pitch can be effective, if it is delivered with straightforward honesty.

20. Burr of singularity. The average consumer now sees 20,000 commercials a year; poor dear. Most of them slide off her memory like water off a duck's back.

Give your commercials a flourish of singularity, a burr that will stick in the consumer's mind. One such burr is the MNEMONIC DEVICE, or relevision symbol — like the crowns in our commercials for Margarine.

... cartoons. Less than five percent ... als use cartoons or ... ban live com-

28. Simple ... Your headline should *telegraph* what you want to say — in simple language. Readers do not stop to decipher the meaning of obscure headlines.

29. How many words in a headline? In headline tests conducted with the cooperation of a big department store, it was found that headlines of ten words or longer sold more goods than short headlines.

In terms of *recall,* headlines between eight and ten words are most effective.

In *mail-order* advertising, headlines between six and twelve words get the most coupon returns.

On the average, long headlines sell more merchandise than short ones — headlines like our

"At 60 miles an hour, the loudest noise in this new Rolls-Royce comes from the electric clock."

30. Localize headlines. In local advertising it pays to include the name of the city in your headline.

31. Select your prospects. When you advertise a product which is consumed only by a special group, it pays to "flag" that group in your headline — MOTHERS, BED-WETTERS, GOING TO EUROPE?

32. Yes, people read long copy. Readership falls off rapidly up to fifty words, but drops very little between fifty and five hundred words. (This page contains 1909 words, and you are reading it.)

Ogilvy & Mather has used long copy — with notable success — for Mercedes-Benz, Cessna Citation, Merrill Lynch and Shell gasoline.

"The more you tell, the more you sell."

33. Story appeal in picture. Ogilvy & Mather has gotten notable results with photographs which ... tell a story. The reader glances at the photo, asks himself, "What goes on here?" Then ... copy to find out.

... Rudolph called this *magic element* ... al." The more of it you inject into your ... ch, the more people look at your adver-

... easier said than done.

Before & after. Before and After advertisements are somewhat above average in attention ... ell.

... form of "visualized contrast" seems to ...

5. Photographs vs. artwork. Ogilvy & Mather ... nd that photographs work better than draw- ... almost invariably.

They attract more readers, generate more appetite appeal, are more believable, are better remembered, pull more coupons, and sell more merchandise.

56. Use captions to sell. On the average, twice as many people read the captions under photographs as read the body copy.

It follows that you should never use a photograph without putting a caption under it, and each caption should be a miniature advertisement for the product — complete with brand name and promise.

57. Editorial layouts. Ogilvy & Mather has had more success with editorial layouts than with "ad" layouts.

Editorial layouts get higher readership than conventional advertisements.

58. Repeat your winners. Scores of great advertisements have been discarded before they have begun to pay off.

Readership can actually *increase* with repetition — up to five repetitions.

Is this **all** we know?

These findings apply to most categories of products. But not to all.

Ogilvy & Mather has developed a separate and specialized body of knowledge on what makes for success in advertising *food products, tourist destinations, proprietary medicines, children's products* — and other classifications.

But this special information is revealed only to the clients of Ogilvy & Mather.

Ogilvy & Mather

2 East 48th Street, New York, N.Y. 10017

Exhibit 7.7   *Released by Ogilvy & Mather in the New York Times on April 7, 1971, this ad was hailed by Trout and Ries as heralding the era of positioning.*

The results of your campaign depend less on how we write your advertising than on how your product is positioned. It follows that positioning should be decided before the advertising is created. Research can help. Look before you leap.

Would it surprise you that Ogilvy's first commandment on "How to Build Great Campaigns" in his *Confessions* (published in 1963) was:

What you say is more important than how you say it...your most important job is to decide...what benefit you are going to promise.

In his 1971 ad, "Large promise" has become the 'second most important decision' after "positioning"—the result, says Ogilvy, of the constant tracking of the effects of O&M campaigns.

How do marketing companies in India view positioning? We have seen some important examples in other chapters.

For ITC, positioning is a critical decision because of their many brands and the danger of cannibalization.

For Richardson Hindustan, now Procter & Gamble, positioning has been the key to the marketing success of Vicks VapoRub (Chapter 6). A highly successful packaged goods company in India says:

For an existing product, think positioning before making any important changes in marketing mix elements (advertising, package, promotional programme, etc.)

For a new product, decide on one or more positioning ideas as a starting point for concept development and testing.

Positioning can never be a substituted for creativity or sound marketing judgement but it should be the vital starting point for both.

Another equally successful company writes in its manual:

Brand positioning is a series of decisions which in total cause consumers to recognize that the brand is designed to meet a very clear, specific purpose.

One of the key criteria of good positioning is that the decisions are wholly consistent with each other.

Another is that the decisions are limiting: not only do they define what the brand consists of, they also deny managers the freedom to move from those decisions. In short, they lock a company into a strategy of marketing behaviour that will, over time, develop a brand's personality (Emphasis ours).

A strong brand franchise is a priceless asset. We tend to take it for granted. Virtually all companies have the ability to build a strong brand franchise regardless of the business they're in.

The foundation for building a brand is a sound competitive advertising strategy—a major component in the effort to gain the cutting edge through advertising.

Brands fail for many reasons—bad products, bad research, bad pricing, bad distribution, bad advertising and bad luck.

But I submit the reason why most brands fail is bad thinking, which really means bad strategies. If your strategy—if what you are saying and where you are saying it—is correct, you'll be successful sooner or later. Even if the advertising is pedestrian, if it communicates a good strategy, you will have a winner. But if your advertising is brilliantly saying the wrong thing, you will fail.

So, what is the role of advertising in relation to the building of brands?

It is to build and maintain strong brand franchises.

A strong brand franchise, as I mentioned earlier, is one of the most priceless assets in a company's balance sheet. It is priceless in the literal sense—you won't see the value of that franchise listed by an accountant. Yet it has the ability to generate revenue year after year; it has the ability to command a higher price; it could provide a strong platform to launch new products; it gives you leverage with distributors and retailers; it can have line extension possibilities; and so on.

To build successful brands it would seem logical that what is required is sound thinking and strategies calculated not to lose. A good strategy ensures you won't lose. A great strategy makes it easier to hit winners. A great strategy is what gives you the *cutting edge*.

Advertising strategy is what we are talking about. So the first question is: How does it differ from positioning? How does it differ from *brand image*?

The effect of your advertising on your sales depends more on "how you position your product" than on anything else. The dictionary says that position is "the place held by a person or thing". When you position your product, *you place it in a certain way in the consumer's mind.*

This is crucial in today's context. Consumers do not weigh the merits of all the products they see. Life is too short to test-drive every two-wheelers, sample every soft drink, and visit the retail showroom of every textile mill.

The first objective for today's marketer is entry into the target consumer's shortlist of considered brands. Product advantages no longer guarantee your brand will make it.

Once you have that all-important decision, you need a strategy to get you there. Positioning is the result. Strategy is the instrument that gets you there.

For example, Lux is positioned as a beauty soap. The strategy focusses on how Lux cares for your complexion. The use of filmstars is purely an executional element.

A strategy, by the way, must never be limited to, or describe, a single campaign.

David Ogilvy, who invented the concept of positioning, is of the view that whilst positioning is important, there are other elements that are equally important. Like: a great idea, a persuasive promise, credibility, pleasantness and consistency with the brand's desired image.

In 1955, David Ogilvy made a speech to the American Association of Advertising Agencies. Here are some of the things he said:
_Sure, deals will get you display space in the stores. But they can cost too much. And they don't build the kind of indestructible image which is the only thing that can make your brand part of the fabric of life...
Let us remember it is almost always the total personality of a brand rather than any trivial product difference which decides its ultimate position in the market._

Now we have it straight. _Positioning_ is placing your product in a certain distinct and preferably unique way in the consumer's mind. _Strategy_ is how to get to that positioning.

Brand image describes a product's personality, beyond its physical characteristics.

An advertising strategy is a _plan of action_ of make consumers do something. It is like a _route map_ that takes into consideration the _target consumer_, a creative strategy and a _media strategy_.

Let us now look at what goes into a strategy that will lead to outstanding creative work and provide long-term direction for a brand. The following in my view are vital:

1. The objective of the advertising programme.
2. A three-dimensional portrait of the target audience.
3. The benefit of the product to the consumer.
4. Some support for why your product delivers that benefit.
5. A statement of the *tone and manner of the message.*

So, what go into a copy strategy are—audience, benefit, support and brand image. What comes out is a *positioning* for the brand.

The three ads reproduced in Chapter 4—Sunlight powder, Cadbury's chocolates and Titan watches—exemplify, each in its own way, O&M's approach to positioning and advertising strategy (Exhibits 4.31, 4.32, 4.33, Plates 7–8).

REFERENCES

1. Colley, Russel H., *Defining Advertisement Goals for Measured Advertisement Results* (Association of National Advertisers Inc., 1964).
2. Seggev, Eli, 'Testing Persuasion by Strategic Positioning' *Journal of Advertising Research*, February–March 1982).
3. Keon, John W., 'Copy Testing Ads for Imagery Products' *Journal of Advertising Research*, (December 1983–January 1984).
4. *The Unpublished David Ogilvy* (Sidgwick and Jackson, London, 1988).
5. Colley, Russell H., op. cit.
6. Smith, Robert E. and Robert F. Lusch, 'How Advertising can Position a Brand' *Journal of Advertising Research,* (February 1976).

Chapter 8

Positioning through Celebrity Endorsement

In a pioneering study of Celebrity endorsements in India by FCB–Ulka (refer to "Cogito", June 2002), the match between celebrity and brand has been studied by developing a Compatibility Index and a Trait Index. The unaided association between the celebrity and the brand has also been measured.

This quantitative survey was conducted among 200 consumers in Mumbai, Delhi and Bangalore.

A big worry about Celebrity endorsements is that consumers will remember the celebrity but not the brand. However, some of the better known brands have fared positively. One sees from Table 8.1 that consumers, for the most part, correctly associate the celebrity with the brand.

The compatibility index means that consumers see a suitable match between the celebrity and the brand. We see that some brands have a high degree of 'match' with the respective celebrities; others do not. The 'Trait Fit' index is based on the match between the top five brand personality traits and top five traits of the Celebrity's Personality. Preity Zinta's score at 4 is the highest and this has been indexed as 100. Sachin may have a fit with Pepsi on only one trait, viz 'friendly'; so his score is 1. In the table, we see an index of 100 for Preity. Sachin's score will be one/fourth of Preity's—hence 25.

Is this complexity of practical value? As the study says: "... the Compatibility Index seems to be a better indicator of the overall suitability (of a celebrity and a brand) than the Trait Fit Index".

For 'overpowering' celebrities such as Sachin and the Big B, a high compatibility index seems to follow naturally. As the study says:

"It seems powerful celebrities are able to overcome the personality gap with the brand, traits be damned!"

Do Celebrities break through the ad clutter? Of the top six ads recalled—Pepsi, Coke, Thums Up, Home Trade, Cadburys and Tamarind, all have used celebrities except Cadbury's. The study concludes with the dictum that 'youth brands' should use the latest heartthrob. In a serious category "choose someone who radiates maturity and credibility."

A STUDY BY FCB-ULKA

So what do we have to say?

Compatibility Index seems to be more important than Trait Fit Index *(Exhibits 8.1, 8.2 and 8.3. Plates 19 & 20)*

While it is very difficult to concretely say what incremental gain each creative would have delivered, with or without a celebrity, a higher Compatibility Index in some form reflects an existing or potential positive effect of the celebrity. It definitely does help in creating an association with the brand, for one (See Table 8.1).

Table 8.1

Brand	Celebrity	Unaided Association	Compatibility Index	Trait Fit Index
Thums Up	Salman	93	93	100
Coke	Aishwarya	89	98	75
	Hrithik	83	100	50
Tamarind	Hrithik	76	76	75
Pepsi	Sachin	73	95	25
	Preity Zinta	38	68	100
Adidas	Sachin	73	85	25
	Leander	29	41	25
Samsung	Tabu	54	68	25

If a celebrity has a high (more than 70) Compatibility Index, it seems to get reflected in high Unaided Association with the brand (the converse could also be true).

And that's irrespective of the Trait Fit Index. Sachin has a low Trait Fit (25) with Pepsi (See Figure 8.1).

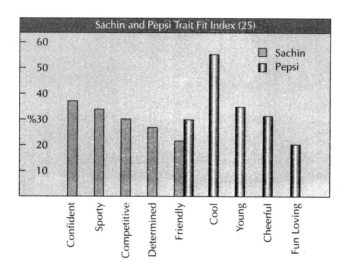

Figure 8.1

But he still enjoys a high Unaided Association (73) with it. Similarly in the case of Hrithik and Coke, there is a low Trait Fit Index (50) yet there is a high Unaided Association (83)! On the other hand, Preity Zinta despite a very high Trait Fit Index (100) with Pepsi has a low Compatibility Index (68) and thereby low Unaided Association with it (Salman Khan is a rare example of a high Trait Fit Index and a high Compatibility Index).

Since the Compatibility Index seems to be a better indicator of the overall suitability (of a celebrity and a brand) than the Trait Fit Index, let's try and understand what makes for a high score on the Compatibility Index.

If you are a 'Desh Ki Dhadkan'... well that is about enough!!

When a celebrity falls in the league of Sachin or Amitabh Bachchan, who are larger than life, then a high Compatibility Index seems to be a natural corollary. To illustrate...

Sachin Tendulkar is seen as a Confident, Sporty and Competitive person. But the brands he endorses have their own personality traits which may be different from Sachin's. Pepsi is about being Cool and Young. On the other hand Visa is 'Family Oriented and a Solution Provider. However, these differences do not seem to impact Sachin's Compatibility Index with either of the brands (See Table 8.2).

Table 8.2

Sachin	Compatibility Index	Trait Fit Index
Pepsi	95	25
Visa	90	0
Adidas	85	25

Similarly with a Trait Fit Index of only 50 with Coke, Hrithik has a high Compatibility Index of 100 (See Figure 8.2).

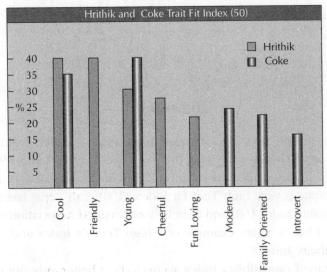

Figure 8.2

In fact, a celebrity's aura can be so overriding that even the negative traits tend to get ignored. For example, there may be some negatives associated with Shah Rukh Khan (e.g. too proud) but his 'aura' ensures that the consumer sees an overall fit for Santro (73) and Clinic (73). This, despite a Trait Fit Index of 50 with Santro and 25 with Clinic.

It seems powerful celebrities are able to overcome the personality gap with the brand, traits be damned!

The above is quoted from "*Cogito*" (June 2002) published by FCB-Ulka.

Chapter 9

Celebrity Endorsement

Beware of 'Pester Power1'!

But Everybody Loves 'Celebs'.

The 'New Generation 2002 India' study carried out by Cartoon Network gives us some surprising facts. It shows that 'Pester Power' (i.e. the power of the Super kids) is considerable for the purchase of:

Chocolates	Chewing gum
Soft drinks	Bicycles
Toothpaste	Hair oil
Shampoo	

And even Refrigerators, Cars, TVs and Computers.

Understandably, the Pesterers love Celebrities. At any cost you have to bring Celebrities into your Ads to position and promote your brands.

But it's not the Super kids alone. From Alcohol and Automobiles to Bank Loans and Polio, at least 14 categories regularly feature Celebrities in their Ads (Study, courtesy MICA).

In this exhaustive study, MICA students detail the brand and endorser, the way the celebrity is being used, how the brand is being positioned and what is being communicated. Readers can obtain the full report from MICA. Some extracts from this excellent report are given in Annexure 1.*

A recent estimate notes that one quarter of all commercials screened in the USA include Celebrity endorsers.

In UK, one in five (20%) marketing communications campaigns feature celebrities (*Journal of Advertising Research*). In India, they not only feature in TV commercials and print ads but also in 'Events' and door-to-door campaigns.

Emami, which launched their "Beauty Secrets by Madhuri" range of toiletries in 2002, have devised a novel sales promotion scheme to back up their media advertising which features commercials with Madhuri explaining the unique features of the toiletries in the range. The scheme was called: "Madhuri On Your Lips".

While many brands in India have joined the Celebrity brand wagon, it is not clear whether they have observed some of the basic criteria on the productive choice of celebrities. What are these criteria?

1. MATCH-UP BETWEEN BRAND IMAGE AND CELEBRITY IMAGE

This is the essential starting point. The best example is that of Kapil Dev and Boost, the match-up is perfect. Don't select a Celeb who does not have this 'fit'.

On a more subtle plane, we have the example of musician and composer A.R. Rehman demonstrating how Airtel mobile phone service gives your crystal clear music even at a distance and with a lot of surrounding noise. He doesn't say a word about Airtel. He doesn't need to. The visuals and sound tell the story.

Madhuri Dixit testifying to the goodness of a shampoo named after her and which gives shiny, clean, bouncy hair is again a natural match-up.

Emami have long used Sourav Ganguly to endorse Sona Chandi Chyavanprash, one of the 'Star' products in their Brand portfolio. The brand has made significant headway (as we note later in this chapter).

---

* The students involved are Paramita Roy Sarkar, Paramita Chaudhuri, Prakriti Kamalakara and Megha Pahwa.

Why then are they changing their 'Celeb' to Sunny Deol? Try to figure that out.

Sachin has endorsed 12 brands in 2002: Pepsi, Boost (both good matches), Visa Cards, Adidas (both good matches); Gillette (Okay); MRF (perhaps, using the analogy of the cricket bat). But what about TVS Victor, Fiat Sienna, Home Trade? Similarly with Shahrukh Khan endorsing of brands from Pepsi (good match) to Home Trade (?)

This match-up is critically important because the process of persuasion is believed to be:

- Transfer of meaning from the celebrity (what the celebrity stands for), to the brands, and from the brand (the image of the brand) to the consumer (how does this meaning match his self-concept?).
- The key to celebrity selection is the identification of meanings that the celebrity may pass on to the product.

An excellent study by Manokamana Chawla of MICA reports that consumers remember Shahrukh as endorsing 3.34 brands, although he has endorsed 15 brands over the years (7 during 2002). Thus the advertisers of the other 11 or 12 brands have apparently lost a lot of money. Can it be that for the many forgotten brands the reason was an inadequate 'match-up'?

Surprisingly, Raveena Tandon's endorsement of the Rotomac ball point pen (where is the match-up?) seems to have benefited the brand. According to Imran Mohammed of EMPI Business School, following Raveena's endorsement, "Rotomac today is a name to reckon with in the writing instruments industry."

At this writing, there could be a rather difficult problem of match-up in respect of their new range of toiletries branded as "Beauty Secrets by Madhuri". Should Madhuri come through as the embodiment of glamour, i.e. physical attractiveness or as a very beautiful woman who is willing to share her secrets with her audience (the 'expertise' criterion which we discuss below)? Both are logically sound but which Madhuri 'position' would carry more credibility?

2. FAME, POPULARITY

Brand Managers seem to believe that famous celebrities can benefit any product that they endorse. Sachin and Shahrukh Khan were both roped in to endorse 'Home Trade,' an electronic shopping site. This enterprise has since gone bust. Simple lesson: the most famous 'celebs' cannot compensate for a brand or enterprise which is fundamentally inferior or unviable.

On the other hand, celebrities who have a special aura can probably carry it off with almost any product which has reasonably good quality. In 2002, Sachin endorsed 12 brands, from tyres to biscuits to motor cars and toothpastes. Shahrukh Khan endorsed seven brands from Pepsi to motor cars and noodles. Amitabh endorsed five from motor cars to fountain pens. It may be argued that they are so popular with consumers and so well liked that no one asks if the celebrity is knowledgeable about the product category, or whether there is a match between the brand and the celebrity.

'Kaun Banega Crorepati' (Do you wish to win Rs 1 crore?) was a hugely popular contest running on Star Plus in 2002. Amitabh Bachchan was the compere, one of the main reasons for attracting a massive number of viewers.

What the 'Celeb' can achieve is to draw attention to your brand, probably induce trial and then it is up to the brand. Nobody on earth can compensate for an inferior brand over a period of time.

A most instructive example is Amitabh Bachchan's endorsement of personal bank loans from ICICI. You might expect that a consumer seeking a bank loan to build a house would seek advice from someone whom he regards as knowledgeable in such matters—a reputed columnist in a trusted business paper, for example. So what benefit has Amitabh Bachchan—by no means a financial 'expert'—brought to ICICI by endorsing their personal loans: "the best deal"?

We can get at least a glimpse of an answer from a pilot study carried out by Direct Marketing Services (DMS), a Kolkata based research agency.

The ICICI Bank Example

A small study with 50 samples (drawn from corporate executives, self-employed professionals and businessmen aged below 40 years) was carried out in Kolkata city between April and June 2003 to test out the effectiveness of the Amitabh Bachchan endorsed ICICI Bank loan advertisement campaign.

Plate 19

Exhibit 8.1 *(Courtesy: JWT) (See p. 228)*

Plate 20

Exhibit 8.2

(Courtesy: JWT) (See p. 228)

Exhibit 8.3

(Courtesy: JWT)
(See p. 228)

It was found out that more than 90% of the respondents could recall having seen the ICICI ad. No other bank ads received a mention over 10%. This was particularly interesting in view of other banks also having continued their ad campaigns during the period.

When it came to the Top of Mind (TOM) Bank, ICICI and SBI were found to be the only two banks receiving close to 30% mentions as against less than 10% mention for any other bank.

More than 85% of those sampled could recall Amitabh Bachchan as the 'brand ambassador' for ICICI. Further, most of the respondents were positively inclined to the use of Mr. Bachchan as they felt his personality and popularity was boon to the image of ICICI. He was perceived to be effective, competent and trustworthy in communicating to the consumers about loan facilities being offered by ICICI Bank.

The success of the celebrity endorsement is further boosted by the claim of more than one-fourth of the respondents that in future they would approach ICICI Bank first for such loan facilities like car loan, house loan or other personal loans.

Note the characteristic of 'Trustworthy' which consumers readily associate with the 'Big B'.

3. TRUSTWORTHINESS

Do you remember a famous spoof ad which featured Richard Nixon, former President of the USA and the author of the infamous Watergate scandal? The ad showed a photo of Nixon and asked:

Would you buy a used car from this man?

A totally opposite example is provided by Amitabh Bachchan. You would have seen the TV spots in which he urges parents to have Polio vaccine given to their children. In a news item in *The Times of India* (29.05.03), titled: "Wanted a hero for polio drive, the paper says that the TV spots with Bachchan "have worked wonders for Uttar Pradesh", and comments that the absence of a super star in the West Bengal campaign has cost the state dear. Apparently, Sourav Ganguly is to be roped in. What more evidence do we need to appreciate the importance of trustworthiness as a criterion for choosing a celebrity when the stakes for the consumer are high?

4. EXPERTISE

Common sense, backed by research, suggests that consumers will heed advice on a technical product or a specialised product like financial instruments, if they regard the Celebrity endorser as highly knowledgeable on the subject. Would they regard Rahul Dravid as an expert on automobile lubricants? He likens the first ten minutes when a batsman is at the crease to the first ten minutes when you start your automobile engine. Good analogy but would that be enough to make one switch from Servo to Castrol?

The all-time classic example of Expert endorsement is provided by Colgate. They have a consistent programme of detailing dentists through their field force. Their packs always carry the logo of the IDA (India Dental Association). Above all, they invariably have a dentist featuring in their commercials.

The late Hafeez Noorani, then Marketing Manager of Geoffrey Manners, and Manohar Benegal, then Advertising Manager, strongly believed that the line: "Forhan's: The toothpaste created by a Dentist", (which always appeared on their packs and in their advertising) played a significant part in making Forhans the No. 2 toothpaste brand in India—although far behind Colgate in market share—in the late 60s.

Why do motor cars and auto accessories quote words of praise which appear in reputed automobile journals? When consumers recognise an expert in a technical or semi-technical category, they are much influenced by expert testimony. This is the reason why infant cereal food brands like Farex and Nestle's Cerelac spend so much effort in detailing paediatricians. A Fiat Palio commercial carries an implicit endorsement from Michael Schumaker, the No. 1 racing driver in Formula I today.

When Sachin Tendulkar takes up a cricket bat and explains what he looks for—like balance and stability—and uses the analogy to promote MRF tyres, this is an example of expert recommendation, although in the form of an analogy.

Roobina Ohanion, writing about her research findings in the *Journal of Advertising Research* (Feb/March 1991), concludes:

"The fact that the perceived expertise of the source was consistently related to respondents' intention to purchase the product emphasizes the importance of using expert celebrity spokespersons in image advertising."

5. PHYSICAL ATTRACTIVENESS

Some would say that this is Criterion No. 1. Whoever endorses your product must be physically attractive. Of course, you would rather not have an ugly, obese, thoroughly unattractive person as an endorser (however much of an expert), but this criterion is absolutely critical when you have a non-technical product, and especially a product that relates to personal appearance and grooming. Everyone intuitively knows this.

In fact, this criterion is an essential element in what is called "source credibility" which is made up of *expertise, trustworthiness,* and *attractiveness*

It would be impossible to find a celebrity endorser of brands in India who is not physically attractive (leaving aside, possibly, some highly technical products like medicines or machinery).

In view of the widespread use of celebrities by advertisers in India, some research firm may well emulate 'Marketing Evaluations', a US company which annually determines a 'familiarity' and 'likeability' rating of top male and female personalities (refer to the dissertation of Imran Mohammed of EMPI Business School).

What Practitioners Look For

In a study conducted among U.K. ad agencies, practitioners rated the following as important criteria for celebrity selection:
- Cost and likelihood of hiring the celebrity
- Celebrity trustworthiness
- Controversy risk
- Prior endorsements
- Celebrity familiarity and likeability

The risk of celebrities overshadowing brands and the stage of celebrity life cycle were only somewhat important (Madhuri advocates, take heart!).

The Bottom Line

At the end of the day, what knowledge do we have of the incremental effect on the brand's strength that celebrities can have? Can they really help to position and promote brands?

Let's start with a legend: Michael Jordan. "His effect has been calculated to have contributed around $ 10 billion to the U.S. economy during the 14 years of his NBA career"! (_Fortune_, 1998)

If we descend from the stratosphere to everyday ground realities, we have already seen the dramatic effects of Amitabh Bachchan's endorsement of ICICI loans and Polio. He really was able to position ICICI loans as a "good deal".

The undisputed benefit is that a celebrity ad breaks through the clutter and draws attention to the ad and the brand. As the "Cogito" study points out, celebrities do not usually overshadow the brands, because respondents were able to make a correct unaided association between brand and celebrity, and they help to bring about a high degree of recall (close to 90% for Pepsi and over 70% for Coke.)

Take a look at a relatively new brands—Emami's Sona Chandi Chyavanprash. In a short period after launch, the use of Sourav Ganguly has brought the awareness level of the brand to a high 79% against such stiff competition as Dabur's brand. There has not yet been a comparable effect on market share.

Chyavanprash Brand	_Awareness (%)_	_Market Share Ratio_
Dabur	90	17
Sona Chandi	79	1

Emami's new range of toiletries—"Beauty Secrets by Madhuri"—has achieved 98% awareness of its ads soon after launch among a pilot sample of target consumers in one important market, Kanpur.

The "Cogito" study shows an over 80% recall of Pepsi ads; over 70% for Coke; 40% for Thums Up.

The "Interest" Curve

Speaking during the launch of the 'E.T. Club' in Kolkata, Mr. Shiloo Chattopadhyay, Managing Director of the well known research company—Taylor Nelson Sofres Mode—has put forward an interesting theory about the value of celebrity advertising during the fairly prolonged period between the intention to purchase a durable (say, a TV set) and actual purchase.

Celebrity advertising draws attention to the brand and helps to keep alive interest when the consumer, let us say, is in a "passive" state. As the time of actual purchase draws near, the 'interest' curve rises reaching a peak at the time of purchase. After purchase, the interest curve declines, but not precipitously. In other words, continued celebrity advertising can keep your durable brand in the consideration set of the buyer at all stages of the purchase decision.

Speaking on the same occasion, Mr Ram Ray, Managing Director of Response Advertising, made a thoughtful observation.

"Product + Celebrity = Brand; Product + Celebrity + Message = Instant Connect."

A celebrity, he said, gives "Instant Personality to a Brand".

Conclusion

Is all this elaborate analysis really necessary? Or shall we simply conclude, as the researcher writing in "Cogito" has done:

"Get a Sachin or a Hrithik or Amitabh Bachchan or Shahrukh Khan to endorse your brand. Voila, you've hit the nail on the head"!

THE TATA INDIGO CASE STUDY

"Every successful brand is a rational grain of information enclosed in an emotional envelope".
— **John Philip Jones**

Background to the Launch

With car penetration in India at a low of 4.2% of all urban households, carmakers in the country have largely concentrated on trying to *build* a market for cars by getting new users into the fold. Thus most of the action has been focussed on the lower priced, entry-level, value

This case has been contributed by Mr M.G. Parameswaran, Executive Director of FCB-Ulka.

hatchback (A and B) segment. The Indian *sedan* market, on the other hand, had seen limited volumes as the choices available in this segment were traditionally higher priced and way beyond the reach of the Indian car buyer.

While the hatchback is a crucial volume generator for a carmaker, the real money is in selling higher priced sedans which helps earn substantial margins. Thus, manufacturers have tried to gradually nudge the consumer into a higher bracket of cars by lowering price points and offering affordable finance, leading to the emergence of the value luxury or the entry level C (Rs 4–7 lakh) segment. While the Maruti Esteem has historically been the unequivocal leader in this segment, new and aggressive launches by global majors such as Ford (Ikon) and Hyundai (Accent) caused the market to explode as the duo fuelled and fed on the Indian consumer's rising aspirations. Making most of their early mover advantage, the two global brands grabbed a stronghold of the market. A subsequent relaunch by Esteem in 2001, by Fiat (Sienna) in 2002 and frequent upgrades by Opel (Corsa) have all failed to challenge the domination of the Ford-Hyundai duo. In 2002, the two accounted for 46% of C segment sales.

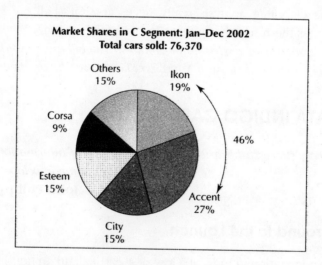

Figure 9.1

By the time Tata Engineering decided to enter the market in December 2002, the C segment was in the firm grip of two international car majors and had become a tough nut to crack.

The Marketing Challenge

Having tasted phenomenal success in the volume driven hatchback market with the Indica V2, Tata Engineering was all set to launch its sedan offering which was seen as a crucial profit generator for the company.

But Tata Engineering's ride into the C segment was not going to be a smooth one. It faced challenges on two fronts.

- Since the Tata sedan was built on the same platform as the Indica, it looked quite similar to the hatchback from the front. Given that the hatchback and the sedan owners differed in their needs and aspirations, it was imperative to distinguish the two cars in the minds of the consumers and create a distinct brand to appeal to the Segment C buyers.
- Secondly, since Tata Engineering's equity as a passenger car-maker was still being built, consumers expected Tata to manufacturer value for money cars and were skeptical about the ability of the carmaker to make luxury cars.

The challenge was to therefore create a brand personality, which would be distinct from the Indica and reflect the needs of the sedan buyer.

The first requirement was a distinct brand name for the new offering. Given that the luxury car reflected the aspirations of a country on the go, the name chosen was the *Indigo-India on the Go*.

Understanding the Consumer

The main target audience for the sedan is the current hatchback owner wishing to upgrade to a bigger car.

Indepth qualitative research amongst current owners and intending buyers of sedan revealed the following key insights about the consumer in the context of car selection and purchase.

- Sedan is a symbol of success
  While small cars (hatchbacks) had utility value, the purchase of a sedan was driven by emotional reasons: the need to gain **peer approval and self-esteem**. *"You can get a car of lesser price with the features of a big car. But you know a guy has arrived when he steps out of a good car"*—Esteem Owner.
- Seeks value but does not want to be seen as compromising
  While the sedan buyer may not want to declare it to the world, he is sensitive to the value he is getting for his money. Sedan buyers are extremely sensitive to features and prices and owners had gone through the rigour of comparing all offerings in the market on a series of parameters before making a final choice.
- A car that pampers him
  While a hatchback owner mainly looks for economy, a sedan buyer is willing to compromise on that for a bit of style. Buyers articulated that looks and comfort (expressed in terms of interior space and smooth drive) were some of the most important parameters of choosing a particular brand of sedan.

In short, the category demanded that the positioning be strongly veered toward the promise to luxury and indulgence backed by a compelling reason why?

Product Insight

The Tata Indigo *(Exhibits 9.1, 9.2 and 9.3, Plate 21–22)* had distinct class leading product advantages—

- The interior space: The legroom and rear seating was the best in the class, perfect for a chauffeur driven drive.
- The only car in its class to have independent 3 link rear suspension ensuring a smooth drive.

These two features ensured that the Indigo would be **extremely comfortable to drive**. Comfort, extremely important to the sedan buyer, was the perfect anchor for the promise of luxury and indulgence.

Positioning Strategy: To connote a feeling of luxury and indulgence based on the pay off of 'comfort'.

Plate 21

Exhibit 9.1

(Courtesy: FCB-Ulka)
(See p. 242)

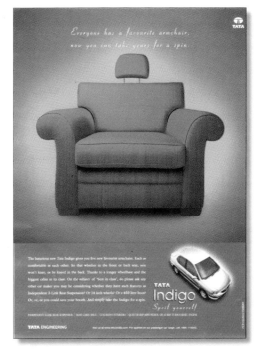

Exhibit 9.2

(Courtesy: FCB-Ulka)
(See p. 242)

Plate 22

Exhibit 9.3 *(Courtesy: FCB-Ulka)* *(See p. 242)*

Creative Strategy

Creative Route chosen: Comfort that indulges you—*Spoil yourself.*

Since the promise of luxury and premiumness was almost a category norm, most sedan advertising was lifestyle-oriented. All sedan ads showed dramatic shots of the car coupled with modern, upmarket user imagery. In a way, sedan advertising was a grey mass—not rooted in any product promise.

While promising luxury and indulgence, it was imperative that Tata Indigo advertising looked and felt different in order to break the clutter and get noticed.

The 'big idea' was to use a metaphor that symbolised comfort in a picture and drive the association of the metaphor with the car. After rigorous research and going through a number of options, a simple, yet effective metaphor was arrived at—a big, luxurious, comfortable sofa that once you look at you want to sink into. The Indigo sofa became the central element of all Indigo communication across press, TV, outdoor, POP, etc. and helped build synergies and enhance impact.

The launch had to be a 'big bang' launch, which would make everyone sit up and notice. Launch advertising was concentrated on the medium that enjoyed high penetration and involvement amongst sedan buyers—the press. For 2 weeks pre and post launch, full page colour ads dominated most popular newspapers in the country. The hype in the weeks before the launch, when Indigo got a lot of press exposure, was compounded by full page teasers featuring the sofa and the headline 'Spoil Yourself' in a bid to drive the sofa-car association. Launch ads backed the sofa-car link with the rational reasons: space, suspension, 14 inch tyres, etc. Different, eye catching and intriguing, research showed that Indigo sofa ads successfully broke the clutter and communicated comfort.

Evidence of Results

1. The Largest Selling Car in its Class

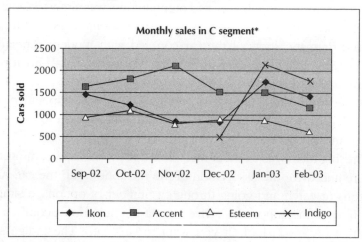

(*Indigo launch on December 19th. Sales recorded in December are only for 12 days.)

Figure 9.2

Within 15 days of its launch, the Indigo has become the largest selling car in the C segment. Having beaten both Ikon and Accent, the Indigo looks well set to achieve its sales target of 20,000 cars by the end of the year.

2. Clutter Breaker

The campaign created strong awareness for the Indigo. Post launch research amongst 191 SEC A male car owners, intending to buy a car in the next one year revealed that Indigo TV advertising scored maximum recall amongst its class of cars.

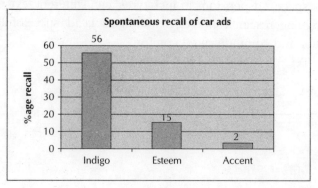

Figure 9.3

3. Message Received

Any issues on whether the ad would be comprehended were laid at rest by these numbers. The Indigo ad clearly communicated that the Indigo was a comfortable and spacious car.

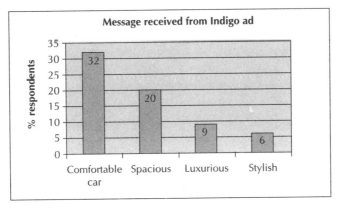

Figure 9.4

LIFEBUOY

Lifebuoy Path to Growth

An Enjoyable and Compelling Experience of Health

Marketing Context

The Indian Personal Wash Market: 2000

Hindustan Lever Limited (HLL) stood as the market leader with a market share of 60% of the total soap market valued at US$ 575 million. This market consisted of four distinct price segments.

Segment	Price Band (US$/kg)	Value % of Mkt.
• Premium	8	21
• Popular	4	43
• Low Price (Discount 22% and Carbolic 14%)	2–3	36

Within the Premium segment, HLL had a share of 41%, with brands such as International Lux, Liril, Dove, Moti and Savlon. Within the popular segment, HLL (70% share) clearly dominated with brands such as Lux Beauty Soap, Rexona and Hamam.

Within the discount segment, HLL's share stood at 49% with brands such as Breeze and Jai. The key competitor here are discount brands from Nirma Company (Nirma Beauty and Nima Rose) with a combined share of 41%.

HLL's Lifebuoy with a 92% market share dominated the Carbolic segment. Lifebuoy has also been one of HLL's most profitable brands. The only other competitor in this segment was Nirma Bath (6%) with a product that was very similar to Lifebuoy and positioned on the health platform.

Over the five years (1996–2000) the discount segment had grown dramatically from a little under US$ 55 million to well over US$ 120 million by 2000. A bulk of this growth had come between 1998–2000. This growth was coming from two sources:

- Share gain from Lifebuoy (driven by better sensorials and price) and the popular segment (driven by price).
- Market growth appropriation from consumers who bathe less than two times a week. (historically a Lifebuoy domain).

As a result of this Lifebuoy, HLL's profit generating star for decades, kept losing consumers and sales dramatically, declining by over US$ 15 million in just one year—2000. The one point agenda for the soap business was "To stop the hemorrhage of Lifebuoy", and restore it on the growth path.

Consumer Trends 2000

1. Increasingly, women were beginning to make the critical purchase decisions even in rural homes. In fact women demanding a more enjoyable choice drove the growth of the discount beauty segment. Even in adjacent categories like shampoos and oral care, the preference for brands like Clinic (Healthy hair), Pepsodent (No germs in the mouth) and Colgate (Strong teeth) have been driven by women who play a key role as the home maker in the family.
2. Disposable incomes were increasing significantly. Given this trend, there was a clear trend of people moving up the benefit chain seeking higher order benefits that went beyond basic cleaning.

Courtesy: Hindustan Lever Ltd.

Lifebuoy: The Brand

"Tea, railways, cricket and Lifebuoy.
Presents from the British that are still very dear to Indians"

Lifebuoy first landed on Indian shores in 1895 at Bombay harbour. Over the past century, the basic brand deliverables had not changed. Targeted at hardworking, down to earth, low-income people who managed to fulfil their basic needs in life it was a basic product with no frills. Positioned as a powerful germicidal/disinfectant soap that washes germs in dirt, it was supported by a strong cryslic (phenolic) smell. It stood as a value for money soap: low priced, a chunky bar and thus long lasting. Its red colour symbolized masculinity, health, vigour and valour.

This was orchestrated with one of the most successful and memorable advertising campaign ever run in India. The communication consistently used the sports metaphor, a universal symbol of good health to communicate the brand message. The brand jingle remains etched in the minds of the Indian consumer: *"Tandurusti ki raksha karta hai Lifebuoy, Lifebuoy hai jahan tandurusti hai wahan"*.

In sum, Lifebuoy stood for *"Washing away germs to keep you fit and successful"* thus playing the role of the basic upgrader over the last five decades. It sought to convert consumers using mud, laundry soap and ash into a personal cleansing product. The brick shape, the tough red colour, the price and its advertising image all consistently built the fact that the brand was a good value, tough cleaning product that was a superb upgrader alternative to proxy products.

Analysis of the Decline: A Static Consumer Experience

The Lifebuoy brand that offered an unchanged consumer experience in India over a century was thus facing rapid erosion in its user base of over 600 million consumers in India. This was almost entirely due to beauty discount soaps which delivered a bathing experience that was clearly superior to Lifebuoy at a cost that was 20% lower than Lifebuoy. In the past, Lifebuoy was the basic brand that upgraded mud and laundry soap users by delivering a basic, tough, cleansing experience. The use of the sporting idiom in communication signified a robust cleaning experience for consumers who came in contact with dirt and mud. However "cleansing" sought by consumers is undifferentiated [*Personal Wash habits and Attitudes Study reveals that every soap cleans ("A soap is a soap")*]. Given that poor experience the Lifebuoy delivered beyond basic cleansing, the brand had come under severe threat from enjoyability driven discount segment brands.

Lifebuoy and Discount Soaps: The Dynamics in 2000

1. Discount soaps are all positioned on a beauty benefit. Every one of these brands has a highly seductive imagery and talk about benefits such as making skin soft, smooth and beautiful.

2. Discount soaps offered a trade margin of 25% when compared to Lifebuoy's 8%. In a fragmented trade environment like India, the trade, particularly in small towns tends to play a key role in brand push.

3. The gs/bath for discount soaps is 6.58 when compared to hard soaps at 7.89. Given this backdrop, Lifebuoy was retailed to consumers at a discount on a per gm basis (Rs 8.50 for 150 g when compared to discount soaps (Rs 6 for 100 g). More importantly, a milled soap formulation is clearly seen to be a superior formulation that delivers better lather, carries the perfume longer, offers better cleaning and does not dry the skin. Given the higher levels of moisture in a hard soap formulation, it loses up to 14% moisture by the time the consumer receives the soap in the home while the corresponding loss for a milled soap is 4%.

4. Discount soaps offer very appealing and enjoyable floral fragrances as a part of their experience. For those consumers who were leaving Lifebuoy, the strong phenolic smell was seen as harsh and unpleasant when compared to discount soaps. However, a change from the phenolic Lifebuoy fragrance to a new fragrance involved a large add-on cost.

1 US$ = approx. Rs 45

ORG Retail Value Shares (% Market Share in Value)					
Year >>>	1997	1998	1999	2000	2001
Lifebuoy	15.4	14.1	14.6	12.8	11.9
Discount soaps	15.5	18.3	20.0	21.4	24.9

The Task Ahead: A Writing on the Wall

To comprehensively turn around the brand for growth and recreate a powerful health and hygiene brand for the family.

Step 1: Concretising a Brand Core for Growth
The first step in the process was to define the brand vision. Very extensive work with consumers on health revealed that health to consumers stood for three distinctive aspects. The prevention of ill health (a universal concern), signs of healthiness (smelling clean, smelling fresh, decent, wholesome, etc.) and wellness (strong associations with food and ingestion). The second step was to understand the growth insight behind six leading brands from around the world. Successful brands such as Neutrogena (*Visibly healthier looking skin*), Nivea (*Care*) and Sebamed (*The right solution for your skin pH 5.5*) have understood that brands can sustain growth provided the core of the brand is clearly defined and understood. Based on this work, a compelling and energising vision was developed which gave the entire team a sense of purpose.

The Growth Insight
Germs are the enemy
Lifebuoy Vision
"Make a billion Indians feel safe and secure by meeting their health and hygiene needs"

Step 2: Defining a Growth Strategy
(a) Delivering a bathing experience that is far superior to discount beauty soaps.
 • Key consumer judgement criteria were refreshing, invigorating, prevention of body odour, pleasant perfume and does not dry skin.

(b) Reposition cleaning by building relevance for germ protection.
- Link germs to common health/hygiene concerns.
- Make the brand more inclusive by positioning Lifebuoy as a family soap.

Lifebuoy Repositioning for Growth

Success through health⟶ *Health protection for me and my family*

Execution: Lifebuoy Relaunch MQ 2002

(a) Step-changing the bathing experience

The product moved from being a hard soap to a high TFM milled soap that delivered a significantly superior bathing experience on the key dimension of "Does not dry skin".

The Cresylic fragrance was changed to a warm, refreshing fragrance that was seen to be significantly superior on "Refreshing", "Invigorating", "Prevention of Body odour" and "Pleasant perfume". This was a huge decision to make considering that the perfume had a 107 year history and was tested in the largest ever perfume test in the history of Hindustan Lever (6500 consumers). The entire team spent weeks with consumers to build confidence and conviction behind this fundamental change in the consumer experience. The packaging was comprehensively changed in line with the brand positioning and moved from being a masculine, rugged looking pack to a softer, family pack.

Lifebuoy New Formulation

- The soap was modified from 41% TFM to 74%, a milled soap formulation
- Soap tablet made attractive
- Better skin feel and overall bathing experience
- Faster and better lathering

To test consumer preferences, both the 41 TFM carbolic soap and the 74 TFM milled toilet soap were put into consumer tests. The tests showed a clear and conclusive preference at 99% significance amongst Lifebuoy users for the 74 TFM formulation. These preferences were critical CVM preference areas—economy, VFM, skin sensorials and feels good to use.

Lifebuoy New Perfume

Perfume houses were briefed to develop and submit fragrances that would connote strong health cues on a milled formulation. The options were evaluated against very stringent action standards. The existing fragrance would be replaced only if the winning fragrance beat current Lifebuoy at 95% significance and was at parity with Breeze Rose, one of the key discount segment brands. The results showed that the chosen perfume not only won on all key perfume attributes in all towns vis-à-vis current but also had significantly higher purchase intention scores. It even beat Breeze Rose.

The current hard soap 41 TFM 150 gms SKU at Rs 8.50 was changed to a 74 TFM 125 gms SKU at Rs 9.00. This change could be done because the new high TFM soap, although being smaller, lasted longer as it did not lose moisture. Thus, cost per wash value equation for the consumer did not become unreasonable.

(b) Gaining re-evaluation of the bathing experience

Based on an analysis of past innovations, the team understood that it was critical to get a very quick re-evaluation of the bathing experience if the brand had to get growth within the year. A comprehensive plan was executed.

1. Compelling launch advertising was created which talked single-mindedly about the fact that the Lifebuoy bathing experience had transformed.

2. To build confidence amongst the trade that plays a very significant role in shaping perceptions of consumers on the fence, over 100,000 retailers were sampled with the New Lifebuoy in the first week of the launch.

3. A massive in-store merchandising effort was undertaken.

4. The team set itself the simple goal of getting 300 million consumers to experience the new Lifebuoy. A massive cross sampling act was undertaken in the first two months with this in mind where the Lifebuoy brand was sampled with leading tea, laundry and even other soap brands.

(c) Creating relevance for germ protection for the family

1. A quantitative study of over 12 potential health and hygiene consequences threw up three key consequences of germs that were seen to be most credible and relevant—stomach infections, eye infections and infected cuts and bruises. The use of the doctor as a major source of authority was identified as an integral part of building the credentials of a strong health and hygiene brand.

2. A multi-media campaign was run that sought to bring the message alive in the most innovative and compelling manner.

   (a) Television advertising was created that linked germs to the three consequences mentioned above. This was a very important part of the overall plan.

Preview Scores on Stomach Film (Theme)		
	Total	*Action Standard*
Contains new information	116	100
Makes you think the brand is different from others	122	
What it says is relevant	128	105
It was believable	125	105
It made you think differently about the brand	120	
Immediate persuasion	108	105

Advertising objective
Only Lifebuoy protects you and your family from infection causing germs

Advertising idea
The family that bathes daily with Lifebuoy is protected from germ infections and won't need to see a doctor again

Execution idea
A doctor gives a simple tip to the mother on how to keep her child protected

(b) A large scale in store visibility package was run for a period of 3 months that exploited synergies with the television campaign.

(c) A massive on ground health and hygiene education campaign (*Lifebuoy Swasthya Chetana*) was run in media dark areas. This was a low cost, scaleable and multiple contact based programme that run across 8000 villages covering over 40 million rural population. The programme focussed on school-going kids who were seen as the key influencers of driving good hygiene practices. In addition, specific attention was paid on creating excitement in the village, building community participation in addition to the education package.

(d) Given the consumer belief that "Visibly clean is safe", a vivid demonstration was created which used a simple three-step routine to bring alive the fact that germs could not be removed by water alone. This was communicated to various constituents of the village including village elders and children. In addition, the demonstration was conducted across the country with retailers. Every salesman in the country was provided a trade briefing kit that brought this message home.

(e) A large scale PR campaign was simultaneously run and Lifebuoy received extensive coverage across 164 media vehicles—Regional Press (95), Mainline Press (35), Business Press (23), Lifestyle Press (1), Websites (4), and Electronic Media (6).

(f) Lifebuoy tied up with WHO/ORS on diarrhoea prevention and was able to contact 30,000 doctors across India. This meant that almost 33% of doctors in key target markets were covered.

(g) The World Health Day was leveraged aggressively on Press by bringing the Lifebuoy health message alive to consumers.

(h) Thematic promotions were run that sought to build synergies with the new positioning. A successful first aid kit promotion was run.

Results: The first steps in creating a powerful health and hygiene for the entire family

After five years of stagnation, the Lifebuoy brand has grown by 31.2 per cent in 2002, adding more than US$ 25 million in a single year. Market shares have moved up by 4% to 17%. The key brand measures—Protection from germs, Recommended by health experts has moved up three fold. The brand pyramids have improved dramatically and are at their strongest ever.

Brand Key Measures

Figs (%)	Protection from germs	Recommended by health experts
2000	19	10
2001	20	14
Q1 02	21	15
Q2 02	30	27
Q3 02	34	33
Q4 02	39	39

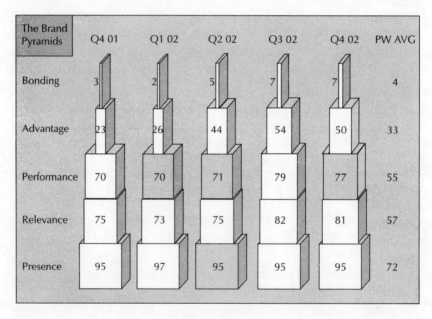

The Brand Pyramids	Q4 01	Q1 02	Q2 02	Q3 02	Q4 02	PW AVG
Bonding	3	2	5	7	7	4
Advantage	23	26	44	54	50	33
Performance	70	70	71	79	77	55
Relevance	75	73	75	82	81	57
Presence	95	97	95	95	95	72

Figure 9.5

MICA BRAND RE-POSITIONING

Background

With liberalization in early nineties, there were changes in the business environment, jump-starting the advertising industry. The industry experienced an overnight transformation of business strategies into being intensely communication driven. In the post-liberalized market place, there was a need for focussed and measurable communication strategies for building brands. Communications strategy became the buzzword. Keeping this in mind, Mudra Communications Limited, the third largest advertising agency in India created the Mudra Foundation for Communications Research and Education in 1991. This foundation set up Mudra Institute of Communications, Ahmedabad (MICA). This institute was the first and the only academic institution in the country, and probably in the Asia-Pacific region, wholly dedicated to the communications industry.

The vision of MICA is "to be the pre-eminent communications management school" and its mission is to "Create through education, training, research, a renewable talent bank of intellectual capital for advertising, marketing, media and all the emerging communication driven businesses".

Hence, in 1991, MICA offered short-term executive development courses in Media Management and Marketing Research. In June 1994, MICA extended to introduce the first two-year Post Graduate Diploma Program in Communications (PGPC). This is the flagship programme of MICA. This programme offers specializations in Marketing Research, Account Planning and Management, Brand Communications and Media Management. One important factor that differentiates the PGPC curriculum from others is its focus on understanding people, cultures of India, economic and political profile of India, language and communications, consumer behaviour and rural communications.

The PGPC students are in demand by the advertising agencies to the extent that MICA became to be known as the 'advertising school', leading to the popular misconception that MICA stands for Mudra Institute of Communications and Advertising. The institute's name also suggests a close association with Mudra Communications Limited,

---

This case has been contributed by Prof. Atul Tandan, Director, MICA.

a reputed advertising agency. Thus being differentiated worked very well for MICA, creating a major pull for agencies to recruit professionals from MICA. However, it started to restrict MICA's identity eventually since MICA sought growth avenues not only as an "advertising school" but as an integrated Marketing Communications School with a scope much broader and larger than advertising.

Brand Differentiation

The differentiation and advantage of brand "MICA" is derived from its processes and systems rather than its product. It starts with the rigorous selection process designed to select the best. The class pedagogy allows for discussions and generation of new ideas. Industry professionals are often invited to take courses in their fields of specialization and the instructors are encouraged to bring new knowledge and insights into the class. The faculty adds to the knowledge bank by writing books and papers, contributing to journals, consultancy projects. The programme ends with a thesis submission by each student leading to creation of new knowledge and insights. It also leads to the end of the programme on a note of inquest. *MICA therefore creates insights for informed choices.*

MICA also offers the industry consultancy and Knowledge Exchange and Information Centre (KEIC) services apart from creating a renewable talent bank for the industry. Its Knowledge and Education Information Centre, KEIC, is one of the most qualified libraries in the area of Marketing Communications. MICA also has the ability to harness youthful energy and add to the productivity of the Institute through live projects for the industry (MICA MINDS) and consultancy projects. MICA has had a strong symbiotic relationship with the communications industry and has developed into a niche brand.

Current Brand Identity

Brand Personality

As per Aaker's five strongest traits of brand personality, traits that are clearly associated with MICA are that of Excitement and Competence. Excitement stems from the fact that MICA is spirited and up-to-date.

Spirited: Spirit of Creativity and providing complete communication solutions. Up-to-date: Contemporary—continues to change and evolve as and when it perceives the need to do so.

Product Attributes

Competence is driven by factors such as reliability, intelligence and success. Reliable: Students joining MICA are sure of a future in marketing communications as MICA has a track record of 100% placements. Industrial stakeholders are assured quality "products" starting with a rigorous selection process to meet the minimum level of aptitude and intelligence. Thereafter, the education programme pedagogy ensures sharpening of intellect through the rigour of debate, discussion and enquiry besides shared experience with professionals from the Integrated Marketing Communications industry. Infrastructure and resources in MICA help students develop and sharpen their intelligence further. Successful: MICA is the leader in the field of marketing communications education and 2664 alumni till date in the industry, is testimony to its leadership.

Target Audience

The target audience for MICA is at two levels:
* The student applicants to the MICA programmes
* The industry as recruiters of the programme graduates

MICA has no problem attracting the students because it is "the place" to study in for the field of marketing communications with a proven placement record to match. The students land up investing close to Rs 3.5 lakh on education, accommodation, etc. during the two years of the PGPC programme. Hence, the student aims for return on investment through the on-campus placement leading to demand for healthy pay packages.

Marketing Environment

The communications industry has evolved from being mass communications based to include below the line communications as a driving force. The market is getting fragmented; and niche segments in the market have emerged with newer means of communication like event management, direct marketing, public relations, etc. MICA has to evolve and grow a step ahead of the customer and industry expectations. *One of MICA's strengths is its flexibility and agility to change and respond to the changes in the environment and the flexibility of the MICAN to adapt and learn led by the spirit of inquiry that MICA inculcates.* That is the most important benefit that MICA offers. Hence, MICA has extended itself to start programme like:

- Post Graduate Certificate Programme in Public Relations and Event Management
- Post Graduate Certificate Programme in Broadcasting Management
- Post Graduate Certificate Programme in Design Management

Besides, the on-going Certificate programme in Crafting Creative Communications develops "ideators" for the advertising industry. This is also an endeavour to shift from the image of an Advertising School to being recognized as an Integrated Marketing Communications Management School and strengthen MICA's position of being the only Institute with an entire range of offerings in the field of integrated marketing communications. MICA started out in 1991 as a product brand offering short-term courses, and then moved to being a service brand, evolving and adapting itself to the emerging requirements and extending its product offerings. Each of these offerings are distinctly different to deliver specific value propositions to different target audiences (stakeholders).

Brand Identity Revised

MICA is not a unidirectional entity but a multifaceted multidirectional organizational entity; a multifaceted multidirectional organization that is dynamic and is growing. This requires a strong corporate identity for itself, which could be distinct from its offerings, since each product can have a distinct position, attributes, benefits and values, targeting a different target audience. Whereas, MICA the corporate brand epitomizes quality education in communications management, dynamism and drive to create and add to new knowledge in the field, MICA PGPC is the contemporary, integrated, customer centric post graduate course in integrated marketing communications management.

MICA: DESIRED POSITIONING

MICA, the service brand, stands for contemporary quality education, in every field that is a touch point with the consumer, offered to the best of students inculcating in them a spirit of inquiry, flexibility and lateral thinking to offer holistic communications strategies for communication-driven businesses.

Issues

Is MICA correct in offering different value propositions instead of just one programme? Will it create confusion in the minds of the stakeholders? How should this be tackled? Is MICA doing the right thing by foraying deeply into the area of marketing communications management, or should it diversify into other related areas like an education in just marketing, or extend to offer an education in general management?

Is MICA's intent to reposition itself, and modify its identity and image from being an "advertising school" to offering a series of service products representing MICA's leadership as an "integrated marketing communications management" institute, the correct brand strategy?

MICA Brand Profile

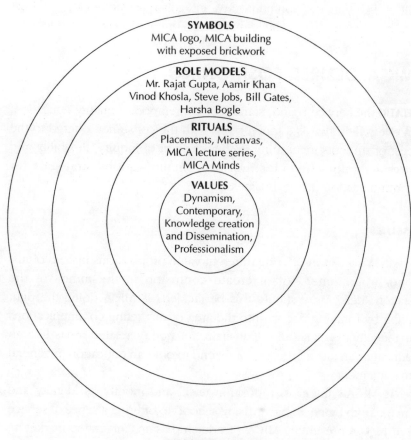

SYMBOLS
MICA logo, MICA building
with exposed brickwork

ROLE MODELS
Mr. Rajat Gupta, Aamir Khan
Vinod Khosla, Steve Jobs, Bill Gates,
Harsha Bogle

RITUALS
Placements, Micanvas,
MICA lecture series,
MICA Minds

VALUES
Dynamism,
Contemporary,
Knowledge creation
and Dissemination,
Professionalism

HOFESTEDE MODEL

Figure 9.6

MICA Brand Profile

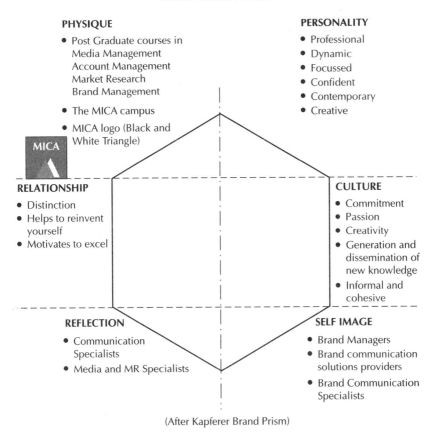

PHYSIQUE
- Post Graduate courses in
  Media Management
  Account Management
  Market Research
  Brand Management
- The MICA campus
- MICA logo (Black and
  White Triangle)

PERSONALITY
- Professional
- Dynamic
- Focussed
- Confident
- Contemporary
- Creative

RELATIONSHIP
- Distinction
- Helps to reinvent
  yourself
- Motivates to excel

CULTURE
- Commitment
- Passion
- Creativity
- Generation and
  dissemination of
  new knowledge
- Informal and
  cohesive

REFLECTION
- Communication
  Specialists
- Media and MR Specialists

SELF IMAGE
- Brand Managers
- Brand communication
  solutions providers
- Brand Communication
  Specialists

(After Kapferer Brand Prism)

Figure 9.7

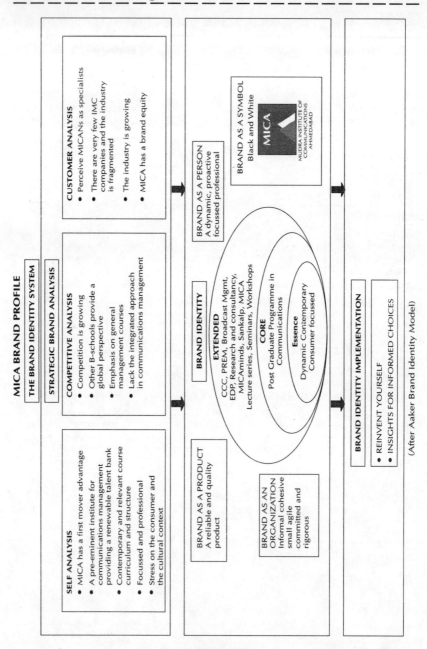

MICA BRAND PROFILE

THE BRAND IDENTITY SYSTEM

STRATEGIC BRAND ANALYSIS

SELF ANALYSIS
• MICA has a first mover advantage
• A pre-eminent institute for communications management providing a renewable talent bank
• Contemporary and relevant course curriculum and structure
• Focussed and professional
• Stress on the consumer and the cultural context

COMPETITIVE ANALYSIS
• Competition is growing
• Other B-schools provide a global perspective
• Emphasis on general management courses
• Lack the integrated approach in communications management

CUSTOMER ANALYSIS
• Perceive MICANs as specialists
• There are very few IMC companies and the industry is fragmented
• The industry is growing
• MICA has a brand equity

BRAND AS A PRODUCT
A reliable and quality product

BRAND AS AN ORGANIZATION
Informal cohesive small agile committed and rigorous

BRAND IDENTITY

EXTENDED
CCC, PREM, Broadcast Mgmt, EDP, Research and consultancy, MICAminds, Sankalp, MICA Lecture series, Seminars, Workshops

CORE
Post Graduate Programme in Communications

Essence
Dynamic Contemporary Consumer focussed

BRAND AS A PERSON
A dynamic, proactive focussed professional

BRAND AS A SYMBOL
Black and White

MICA
MUDRA INSTITUTE OF COMMUNICATIONS AHMEDABAD

BRAND IDENTITY IMPLEMENTATION
• REINVENT YOURSELF
• INSIGHTS FOR INFORMED CHOICES

(After Aaker Brand Identity Model)

Figure 9.8

CASE STUDY ON HIMANI
SONA CHANDI CHYAVANPRASH

Emami is associated with Ayurvedic products in the personal care category since its inception. In the year 1999, Emami had taken a decision to enter into the Ayurvedic OTC health care market. Management was ready to expand the portfolio of products, increase the revenue and establish the company as a major player in Ayurvedic industry. The problem was, how? Management entrusted the job to two budding Directors, Mr Aditya Agarwal and Mr Manish Goenka.

Mr Agarwal and Mr Goenka were wondering how to go ahead, numerous brainstorming sessions were held and ways started to open up. Reviewing the market information and its own strength the duo decided to foray into the Chyavanprash market.

Since time immemorial, Chyavanprash has been the magic potion of life, an elixir of vitality and vigour. For this first time in 20th century, some entrepreneurial enthusiasts made it in factories and marketed for the masses as per the norms and enlightenment of modern science.

A spoonful of Chyavanprash twice a day, is consumed today in households across India (mainly in the Northern and Western part) as an essential tonic in winter. It is an essential fortification for all for building immunity, protection from cough and cold, activating digestion system and boosting energy and vitality, more so for the children and elderly. An age-old belief in the goodness of Chyavanprash has been carried forward by generations.

Emami had a dual challenge, creating the image of the company in Ayurvedic market on one side and fighting the big established brands in the market on the other. The first objective of the company was to make a Chyavanprash, which would be suitable for today's life which is full of stress, polluted environment and hectic lifestyle. After several years of research, Padmashree Dr. Suresh Chaturvedi, Dr H.S. Sharma and some other eminent Ayurvedic experts of India in Himani Ayurvedic Science Foundation created a unique Chyavanprash, which is softer, tastier and as per Ayurvedic treatise well differentiated with Gold and Silver as prime ingredients. The genius of Sona Chandi was born.

The market was already crowded with brands like Dabur, Baidyanath, Zandu and many other regional players. Emami had taken up a tough job to give a unique brand name to its Chyavanprash in this generic product market. A simple brand name, easy to remember and pronounce, "Sona Chandi" won the race among many as it brings upfront the unique difference between itself and other brands for the consumer. It also creates a mystic and premium feel about the product. A unique square shaped gold coloured packaging with gold foil label gave it a premium and distinct look from the other brands. Sona Chandi Chyavanprash was ready for the race. But the task was merely half done. The battle for the space in the market and the consumer's mind was about to begin.

Dabur had the largest market share—60% of the 8500 Ton Chyavanprash market (150 crore) followed by Baidyanath (15%) and Zandu (10%) (ORG 200 U+R) (Annexure 1). Dabur was very aggressive in the media with a strong positioning of immunity, protection from cough and cold for the family. Baidyanath and Zandu were long time players with a loyal consumer base.

The challenge for Sona Chandi was to crack this loyal category. The advertising agency (Ambience) and the brand team agreed not to communicate anything very generic for the category—instead, energy, strength, vigour and sharp mind. Thus the tag line based on key ingredients became 'Sona De Surakshit Tan, Chandi De Tej Dimag'. Strong visuals with Kallaripet (traditional material art of Kerala) fight with sword and shield were made. The brand was test marketed in 1999 and rolled out nationally in the year 2000.

Consumer Research had shown that the consumers of all these brands specially Dabur were very much satisfied with the performance of the brand, in terms of its taste, benefit, price, etc. The market share was steady and the entire category was almost stagnant.

Sona Chandi brought a new refreshing idea in this traditional product category. The brand imageries, communication and the benefits were quite unique. It got tremendous response from the market, from trade and consumers both. Sona Chandi started grabbing market share from other players specially from Zandu and Baidyanath in the very first year of its launch.

The brand faced aggressive retaliation from category leader, Dabur. Not only in terms of increased media presence but a little shift in the positioning was also observed, from protection from cough and cold to an immunity platform in general.

The Brand Directors of Sona Chandi knew very well that it would not be possible for them to compete with the leader in terms of media spend. They opted for the celebrity route to break the media clutter and catch the consumer's attention. The sponsorship of Cricket Association of Bengal presented them a golden chance to associate the brand with the captain of the Indian Cricket Team, Saurav Ganguly.

The progress of Sona Chandi has become a phenomenon of its own. It has given a new meaning and a fresh perspective to the category, which is very much evident from the market facts. Sona Chandi established itself as a very strong brand leaving behind Baidyanath and Zandu (Annexure 2). It is even giving Dabur a strong fight in states like M.P. Sona Chandi has snatched market share not only from Baidyanath and Zandu but also from Dabur.

It has earned the confidence of the consumers in the very beginning itself. In fact, it has found a very innovative way to earn the consumer's confidence with its money back offer. The consumer can get his money back if he/she is unsatisfied with the quality of the product, probably the first Chyavanprash brand to exude such a confidence about its quality in the FMCG market of India.

Sona Chandi got phenomenal response from the market since the beginning, but it has its own problem also. Chyavanprash is normally consumed in 4–5 winter months (approx. 65%). But for Sona Chandi the seasonal skew is almost 100%, which means there is hardly any off-season sale. The Brand Directors sat together to analyse the reasons and its possible solution(s). Looking at the trend of ORG data, primary sales and consumer information, they understood that the chunk of the Sona Chandi franchisees are primarily winter consumers of Chyavanprash. Most of the franchisees are in early adoption phase, it would take a long time to win the loyal die-hard year round consumers of other brands. In order to stride faster, the importance of sales in off-season was easily understood, but the question was how?

They were looking into the reports of the consumer research and various market feedback. A big idea came out from the consumer's behaviour. There is a common belief among consumers that Chyavanprash produces heat in the body and it is being consumed in winter by most people. People don't prefer to have Chyavanprash in other seasons, as it is very sticky and heats up the body. But a need for immunity, energy and stamina exists in summer also, perhaps even more than winter. A need-gap scenario came up in the forefront, as there was no product available to fill up this gap.

The brand team started thinking to develop a product, which will give the immunity benefit of Chyavanprash without generating heat and will have cooling effect on the body system. Himani Ayurveda Science Foundation, again delivered a marvellous brand: Sona Chandi Amritprash, has seen the light of day in the summer of 2002. The first of its kind, full of the goodness of Chyavanprash but with cooling herbs to prevent the various summer ailments and to provide energy, stamina besides the benefits of Gold and Silver. It has got encouraging response from the market. Sona Chandi as a brand got a chance to be even closer to the consumers and give them healthy body, active mind for the full year. To create awareness about Amritprash, sampling through magazines, various BTL activities like window display, door-to-door etc. played a vital role. Emami is confident that Amritprash will grow even faster in years to come and will establish itself as a product category by itself.

Consumer study had shown a weakness of Sona Chandi Chyavanprash, in that users of other brands have low confidence in Sona Chandi for its real gold content. The Brand Directors wanted to win the confidence of other brand users. An innovative gold challenge offer was formulated: who ever proves that Sona Chandi does not contain Gold, will be given 1 kg of pure gold. The challenge was communicated through TV and Press. Emami is hopeful that it will help to gain the confidence of other brand users and help to encourage brand switching.

Sona Chandi still has a long way to go, but the Company is confident that Sona Chandi will cross all the hurdles on its way. Only time holds the answer.

Annexure 1

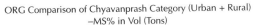

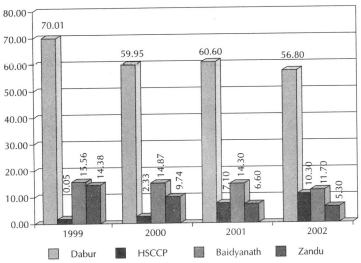

ORG Comparison of Chyavanprash Category (Urban + Rural)
–MS% in Vol (Tons)

	Dabur	HSCCP	Baidyanath	Zandu
1999	70.01	0.05	15.56	14.38
2000	59.95	2.33	14.87	9.74
2001	60.60	7.10	14.30	6.60
2002	56.80	10.30	11.70	5.30

Annexure 2

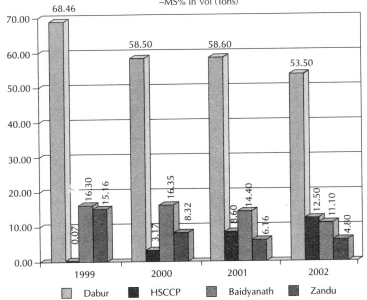

ORG Comparison of Chyavanprash Category (Urban + Rural)
–MS% in Vol (Tons)

	Dabur	HSCCP	Baidyanath	Zandu
1999	68.46	0.07	16.30	15.16
2000	58.50	3.17	16.35	8.32
2001	58.60	8.60	14.40	6.16
2002	53.50	12.50	11.10	4.80

Chapter 10

Stretch Your Brand – but Watch its Limits

RULES AND RISKS OF BRAND EXTENSION

Why does Coca Cola lend its name to a range of clothes? Why does the name of the world's most famous cigarette also adorn sports garments? Why does Dettol—the household name for antiseptic liquids—become a bath soap as well? And whoever would have thought of Cadbury mashed potatoes?

To those of us who have been brought up on a diet of the 'distinct brand identity', on the philosophy of 'one product, one brand name', of a brand being a 'single, indivisible, unique entity'—to us this habit of slapping on the same brand name to a host of other products is somewhat disturbing. And yet this trend is accelerating.

Earlier Pattern

Earlier, we were familiar—and comfortable—with a corporate name doing duty for several brands: Bajaj scooters, Bajaj mixies and Bajaj water heaters, for example. We were also familiar with the same brand name being used for closely related products—Colgate toothpaste and toothbrushes.

But what is happening today seems to upset all our earlier notions of the sanctity and uniqueness of a brand name. There were some companies which resolutely stuck to the philosophy so 'one product, one brand name'. Although Swastik's Det was both a detergent powder and a detergent bar, Hindustan Lever did not brand its detergent bar as Surf but called it Rin. And when the company launched another cheaper bar they called it Wheel, not Rin Popular or Rin Janata! And the company's low-cost detergent powder is also branded as Wheel.

What are the forces behind this fundamental change in our traditional philosophy of branding? We discussed this phenomenon briefly when we considered the 'Who am I?' aspect of a brand in Chapter 4. But what is the driving force behind this phenomenon?

Brand Equity

So much consumer loyalty and goodwill surrounds a successful brand name that it is seen as the direct source of much of the owner-company's profit.

A spokesman of the Philip Morris Company—which owns the Marlboro brand—was reported as saying, "I would sell my fixed assets at $30 million but I wouldn't sell the Marlboro name for $300 million". This belief that the brand name has a direct financial worth, no less than investment in fixed assets, has given rise to the notion of brand equity: the brand name functions like an asset which has a direct impact on the bottom line. The clearest manifestation is the high value paid for brand names during buy-outs and mergers.

Probably one of the earliest references to the concept of brand equity is to be found in a discussion of 'Brand Extensions' by Gamble. He refers to "brands with well-established equities" being acquired. In a later context, Dr Tauber writes (1988):

> *The brand name suddenly has emerged as the most coveted corporate asset of all. Brands no longer are merely products competing for market share; they're annuities...*[2]

He gives a more precise definition of brand equity. It is not to be confused with brand personality or image. It is:

"The incremental value of a business above the value of its physical assets due to the market position achieved by its brand and the extension potential of the brand."[3]

In a letter to the author (August 10, 1989), Mr Stephen King, then of the WPP Group, UK—the holding company for J Walter Thompson and Ogilvy & Mathers—writes:

> *One of the hot issues in the UK now is that of putting a value on brands in the balance sheet. A rush of take-overs has made people aware that a company's brands are by a long way its greatest assets. Lots of unlikely people, like accountants and chief actuaries and bankers and even chief executives, are beginning to feel that they really ought to know what brands are and how to create really good ones.*

Drawing upon this concept of brand equity, marketers have extended the names of successful brands to several new products in several categories. Tauber says that in the USA almost half of all new products are brand extensions. A new term has arisen: Superbranding—the use of the same name for several brands in many categories and marketed under that brand name in many countries. Alsop and Abrams say:

We anticipate a world of 100 to 200 *superbrands* that have found ways to capitalize on their existing reputations.[4]

Does this sound somewhat extreme to Indian ears?

From Promotion to Licensing

In the past, we have seen the extension of brand names, usually to related products, as a means of creating wider exposure to the brand name. The Sun Lager name was printed on beer glasses, for instance, and given away by the company. There were Bournvita and Nescafe mugs. Soon, however, the manufacturer of such items found that he could use a popular brand name to market his product.

Thus was born the business of licensing which has become a major activity in developed markets like the USA. As an example, the New York Simplicity Pattern Company's name "commands such power in the home sewing and crafts field that through licensing, the company can bring consumers Simplicity brand sewing machines, scissors, kraft kits and about 1,200 other related products".[5]

In licensing a brand name for use on products made by others, the owner of the brand name takes care to ensure a level of quality, consistent with the image of his brand. He also ensures a degree of compatibility with the licensed product which will carry his brand name. The Marlboro name may be used for sports clothing but one can hardly imagine its use for lipstick.

In this form of brand extension, the licencee relieves the owner of the brand name—the licensor—from many headaches by taking on the functions of making, selling and advertising the product. In return, the licensor rents out his trade marks and logos and receives royalties.

Although this form of licensing is big business in the West, it is not yet very visible in India. What we have at this time is the use of famous characters like Mickey Mouse, against payment of a licence fee, as a promotional aid to sell products like toys or ice-cream. There is considerable potential for the licensing business in India. "The party has just begun", comments *Business India.*[5]

Franchising

A somewhat close cousin of licensing is the system of franchising which is catching on in India. The owner of the brand name (which may refer to a product or a service) awards a franchise to another party which runs the business—either an outlet, a producer or service outfit—and the franchisee pays a fee or royalty to the franchisor. Thus, Tata's Titan are appointing franchised outlets for sales and service of their watches. Soft drinks are generally franchised. The owner of the brand name appoints bottlers, supplies them with the concentrate and backs them with national advertising for the brand. Mothercare India which operates a chain of stores for children's requirements, is setting up franchised outlets under the name of Little Kingdom. This is somewhat similar to exclusive dealer outlets (not permitted by the MRTP Act) which operate under the same brand name and only stock products bearing one brand name or family of brand names.

Neither licensing nor franchising should be confused with the act of using an outside manufacturer's skills and resources to have the item produced and then branding it with the name of the company's own product. Thus, Bata buys out T-shirts, kit bags and various sports accessories from third parties, brands them with the Power name and logo and sells them through its own outlets. Similarly for shirts bearing another Bata brand name—Ambassador. This practice has long been in vogue and extends all the way from industrial products to consumer durables and packaged products. This is, in effect, marrying the power (no pun!) of the brand name to the production efficiency of an outside supplier. Quite often, however, the company may decide to manufacture the brand extension in-house.

Brand Extension

A successful brand is like a powerhouse containing enough energy to illuminate distant territories. Such a brand name holds enormous appeal for consumers. It has stood the test of time and competition. This is the driving force behind brand extensions—this huge accumulation of consumer-pulling power which can be harnessed beyond the brand's traditional market boundaries.

This is what explains the extension from Ivory soap to Ivory shampoo, from Dettol antiseptic to Dettol soap, from Pond's Dreamflower talc to Pond's Dreamflower soap, from North Star shoes to North Star apparel. Some of these have faded away.

The other driving force is the present-day high cost of launching an altogether new brand. With increasingly competitive markets and escalating media costs, it makes sound financial and marketing sense to spin out the inner force of a respected brand for new incarnations.

Paradoxically, we find examples of such new incarnations with brands that are in the declining phase of their life cycle as well as those in the prime of life.

In Sickness and in Health

The story of Gold Flake is a good illustration of taking over a strong brand name from a category which is static or declining—like plain cigarettes—to a market all set for growth like King-sized filters. A very successful brand was the result: Gold Flake Filter Kings.

Charminar, once the largest-selling cigarette brand in India, belongs unfortunately to a declining category: dark, strong tobacco in a plain (non-filter) cigarette. And yet the name holds magic. It cannot be allowed to go to waste. Hence the spawning of numerous offshoots— Charms, Charminar Gold, Charminar Virginia Filter (Exhibit 10.2, Plate 23).

Forhan's Regular, in spite of its undoubted goodness for the gums, is in decline because it simply cannot satisfy the younger toothpaste-user of today who demands taste and foam. Hence its offshoot— Foaming Forhan's with fluoride. The brand name Forhan's is too valuable to be allowed to wither away.

Keo Karpin is a buoyant and growing light hair oil. The brand name has been extended to launch a skin ointment and a baby oil. And the most vigorous of the new brand names in India—Nirma has been extended to launch other successful products: Nirma detergent bar and Nirma toilet soap.

Beware of the Trap

Trout and Ries are dead against such extensions—they call it the line extension trap. They give two arguments.

First, they say, a highly successful brand almost *owns* the category. The sign of its success is that consumers begin to think of the brand name as generic. "This is the essence of positioning. To make your brand name stand for the generic. So the prospect freely uses the brand name for the generic."[7] Like "Hand me a Bayer", meaning an aspirin tablet. This advantage, they think, is lost if the brand name is extended to other categories, say Bayer decongestants.

Second, when a brand has etched a clear position in the prospect's mind, extension of the brand name to some other product dilutes that position. Like extending the Bayer name to non-aspirin tablets.

We do not agree with the first argument but we do, conditionally, agree with the second.

Nirma, you might argue, means detergent powder, so how can it also be a detergent bar? The consumer has no such problem. He has taken happily to both. Trout and Ries describe the prospect's way of looking at products as the 'outside–in' view. Well, here is the 'outside–in' view of the prospect in relation to Nirma: 60% market share for the powder, Nirma detergent bar gained 33.4% market share.

A brand extension should be 'No–go', however, if it does indeed conflict with or dilute the sharply focussed position of the mother brand in the prospect's mind. Does Dettol soap for a 100% bath dilute or conflict with the clear, sharp position of the original, viz. Dettol antiseptic liquid? We do not think so and neither does the consumer. Would a Dettol deodorant stick or spray conflict with that original position—the foundation of Dettol's success? Perhaps not. Would a Dettol prickly heat powder hurt that position? Possibly not. But a Dettol perfume probably would.

Apart from obvious dangers in such brand extension, there is also the high risk that the failure of a brand extension would injure the reputation of the original. Pre-testing consumer acceptance becomes even more critical with a brand extension because several reputations are at stake.

Line Extension versus Brand Extension

But before we take up this issue of fit or compatibility for a brand extension, let us clear up a semantic problem.

Line extension and *brand extension* are often used interchangeably. This would not be right. *Line extensions* should refer only to additions to an existing product line of a company in a given category—to 'fill out' the line. Thus, Marvel was an addition to the Godrej toilet soap line which already included Cinthol and Fresca. Wheel was a line extension to Hindustan Lever's line of detergent bars which already had Rin.

Use of the same brand name for a line extension can be tricky. Can you imagine the present Cinthol, a Cinthol Shikakai soap and a Cinthol with its own beauty cream—all fighting for a place in the consumer's mind? The one situation where it might work (we say *might*) is in the form of extra strength—like Clinic Shampoo and Clinic Plus; or Vicks VapoRub and Vicks VapoRub Plus. But there too, the dangers of cannibalization are high.

By contrast, brand extension refers to using an existing brand name to enter another product market (category) altogether. We saw several examples earlier, like Dettol antiseptic liquid and Dettol soap.

A High-Risk Game

But beware!

According to an Ernst & Young survey in 1998, fully 72% of brand extensions flop. The explanation seems to be that the extension did not add anything new or better to attract consumers. As the *Harvard Business Review* had pointed out, extensions are more a sign of the marketer's desperation than inventiveness.

If you have a promising product idea should it carry the mother brand's name or a new one? Trout quotes a telling example from Levis.

In an attempt to attack the dress-up market. Levis Strauss and Co introduced Levis Pantela Sportswear, Levis Tailored Classics and Levis Action Slacks and Suits.

Apparently, confusion reigned! Levis then developed a new brand called 'Dockers', targeted at 25–45 year old Baby Boomers. With an up-scale image and a non-denim brand name, Dockers is "the number one selling pant in America... and is a multi-billion dollar global business."

One way to tackle this question is to test the 'elasticity' of your brand name, to which we turn later.

Brand Positioning

It is my belief that mothers of young babies are concerned overwhelmingly with their health and all-round growth.

I found this when we were-launching Farex. We positioned it as "Baby's first solid food for all-round growth". Sales increased spectacularly. We realised (through focus groups and larger research) that at this stage mothers looked out anxiously for the signs of baby's healthy growth, e.g. the stages of crawling, walking and speaking at the right time as advised by their paediatrician.

I would suggest that the Positioning statement for the new brand should be on the following lines:

"This (Brand name) is a pure, ayurvedic, all-natural oil that has ingredients which make it more beneficial for your baby's health than any other baby oil."

Reason—Why

This Positioning should be supported by reference to the expertise of Pt. Shastri, Padma Bhushan. He would talk about these beneficial effects in consumer language. This is an oil that will stimulate the baby's health and growth and has much more value than cosmetic properties as in other oils.

In other words, re-position Johnson's as a "Cosmetic" baby oil. Its superiority to Dabur must also be implied.

Brand Name

This should reflect the Positioning strategy. As a crude attempt, I would name it:

Active & Healthy

1-2-3

Ayurvedic Baby Oil

Criteria for Brand Extension

When we do undertake a brand extension we must give special attention to three critical criteria. You will note that all three are closely interrelated.

(i) *The "Fit"*

First, the category chosen for the brand extension must be seen as compatible with the nature of the parent brand and the expertise it represents. There must be a *fit*. Management judgement acts as the first screen. Will Nirma be acceptable as a scourer, a dish-washing liquid, a wax polish, a toilet cleaner? Will it be equally acceptable as cooking oil, as branded spice, as sauce, ketchup and noodles? What do consumers think?

Gamble, to whom we referred earlier, gives examples of consumer research in the sixties to test the *fit* between the Pet Milk Company and the extensions being considered under the Pet name. Thus, "baby foods were perceived as being close to the Pet image...Pickles were regarded as distant and inconsistent". In the context of brand extension, says Gamble, "the concept of constellations of related products comes into the picture".[9]

More recently, Professors Aaker and Keller made a study to find out how far a brand name could be stretched. They checked consumer perceptions to aid management judgement. What they did was to slap on some well-known brand names on a variety of different products and check consumer response. These were some of their findings:[10]

- McDonald's reputation for fast, efficient service did not carry over to photo-processing services.
- Heinken wine won't work. People would expect it to taste like beer.
- Heinken popcorn was not seen as needing Heinken's know-how.

C. Merle Crawford describes how a consumer research technique called *brand elasticity analysis* can measure the elasticity of a brand— its ability to stretch to other product categories and still carry its consumer franchise. Crawford also reports a hypothetical elasticity profile for the well-known Minute Maid brand of orange juice. Thus, it would be most elastic, i.e. there would be a good *fit* of the Minute Maid brand name with jellies soups, even dinner rolls; but it was least elastic with packaged meats, ice-cream and peanut butter. Cakes were a borderline case.[11]

A company in India, very successful in beverages, undertook a study to measure how well consumers would accept the corporate name (which also served as the umbrella brand name for their beverages), when applied to a range of other products being considered for diversification. The findings were revealing.

The sample was drawn from housewives in all the four metros in the Rs 1,500 + household income group, in the age-group of 25 to 45, and at least matriculates. A score of 3 indicated 'perfectly natural', i.e. a good fit between the corporate name and the new product category; 2 indicated 'not surprising'; a score of 1 meant 'surprising'. These were some of the stores:

Another beverage	2.9
Biscuits	2.2
Milk	2.0
Bread	1.9
Soft drink	1.9
Fruit juice	1.9
Butter	1.9
Noodles	1.8
Chutney	1.6
Detergent	1.4
Pressure cooker	1.2
Bulbs	1.2

The company further analysed these responses and divided them into two groups:

(a) product categories for which 25% or more consumers said 'perfectly natural' and less than 25% said 'surprising', and

(b) categories for which over 50% said 'surprising' and less than 10% said 'perfectly natural'. This helped to distinguish more clearly the reasonably good fit categories (a), from those that were not (b). The two groups were:

(a)	(b)
Another beverage, biscuits, fruit juice, bread, milk	Bulb, pressure cooker, typewriter, detergent, meat/fish, noodles, *gulab jamun* mix, chutney

Soft drink had a mixed reception being classified under (a) in Mumbai and Chennai, and under (b) in Kolkata.

You can see that it is safer not to make snap judgements, except in the most obvious cases and that executive judgement should be checked with consumer perceptions.

(ii) *The Value Perception*

The second criterion for successful brand extension is to ensure that there is consistency in the value perception of the brand in the new category as compared to its parent brand.

We have to ask ourselves, what does the brand name represent? What is its essential value in the eyes of the consumer? ITC believes that the name Gold Flake represents 'exclusiveness' and 'consistent high quality'. These are the essential 'Gold Flake Values: Although Gold Flake Filter Kings and Gold Flake plain are categories apart, they are both linked by these common values. Thus, the brand extension does not hurt the essential position of either brand.

Dettol represents trusted, hygienic household and personal care. That is the essence of the brand name, its perceived value. To slap it on a beauty cream would be entirely out of character. That is not the distinguishing value of the brand name. That is not the 'Dettol position'.

Bic stands for low cost, utility and disposability. One finds the brand name extending from disposable ball point pens to disposable lighters and razors. Can you imagine the Bic brand name on a handsome, presentation electric shaver?

Nirma represents above all the *value-for-money* position: good quality at a low price. This character, or value, should permeate all its incarnations which, indeed, has happened so far. But, please, not a Nirma Deluxe positioned against Lux International.

In this sense, Trout and Ries are right when they talk of the extension 'trap'. It is, indeed, a trap if the extension is out of line with the basic position which the parent brand occupies in the consumer's mind. Sometimes, we can be taken by surprise by consumers' judgements. Raymond's is the brand name for an expensive, highly regarded, prestigious suiting fabric. What could be more logical than to extend this brand name to ready-to-wear trousers? Good 'inside–out' thinking, as Trout and Ries would say.

Raymond's trousers, branded as Raymond's Double Barrels, promised 'no hassles with tailors' and 'great fit'—a highly desirable benefit in readymades. Consumer response was lukewarm.

When Lintas took over the account, they found that while consumers were perfectly happy with Indian-made fabrics—and Raymond's occupied a lofty place—they associated good fit with foreign brands like Levi's or Wrangler. What Lintas contributed was a re-branding exercise. Re-launch Raymond's ready-to-wear trousers with a brand name that stood for sophistication, class and a hint of the foreign expertise that went with good readymades. The brand name chosen was Park Avenue. Raymond's perceived value was 'great fabric', not 'great fit'. So, the Raymond brand extension didn't work. A new brand name that helped to credibly convey the value of 'great fit'—Park Avenue—did work. "From a fledgling loss-making division in 1983, sales moved up to over Rs 10 crore in 1986 and further doubled by 1988".[12]

The newly branded Park Avenue-initially trousers, shirts and suits—has extended itself to a range of Park Avenue men's toiletries: shaving cream, after-shave, talcum powder and the like.

A successful brand extension must, therefore, have a good fit with the new category and its value perception must match the needs of the target consumer. In the case of Raymond's, as we saw, there was a good fit between the brand name and high quality ready-to-wear trousers but its value perception did not match what the buyer was looking for—'great fit'.

(iii) *The Edge*

The third criterion for a successful brand extension, closely allied to value perception, is the competitive edge. Marketers have found to their cost that this is not automatic. A great brand name in one category is no automatic assurance that it can offer a competitive and persuasive difference over established brands in the new category. Even if the value perception is favourable, consumers will expect to derive some advantage, some new benefit before they switch. The extended brand needs to measure itself against each strong competitor which it will face.

Satisfying this third criterion means that the extended brand must have some inherent quality perception which gives it an edge in the new category. This might be the case with Dettol shaving cream, for instance, or Complan nourishing, tasty biscuit for the school kid's lunch box. Shaving does lead to nicks and cuts. Dettol antiseptic shaving cream would approach the consumer with a built-in edge. The Complan-aware mother, asked to choose between established biscuit brands and the new Complan biscuit, would probably perceive Complan to have an edge in terms of greater nourishment. It was lack of such an edge which caused Glaxo talcum powder for babies to fumble.

Better for Babies?

Logically, what could be a better *fit* than for Glaxo—trusted by mothers for baby foods—to offer those mothers a talcum powder for babies?

This was the reasoning that prompted Glaxo to launch a talcum powder positioned against the overwhelming market leader, Johnson's Baby Powder. The value perception, too, seemed just right: Glaxo understands what is good for babies and that goes for babies' tender skins as well. Thus was launched Glaxo Tender Talc. A good brand name. A good pack. A good product.

Good, but not better in any way than Johnson's—also a trusted name when it comes to the baby's outside. It was judged that the edge would come from the Glaxo name itself. But this name conveyed no inherent advantage to the mother over the baby powder which she had used for years. The brand extension didn't work.

Johnson & Johnson are masters of brand extension when it comes to baby care products. Their corporate brand name has supported each of their extensions, from baby powder to baby soap, shampoo, oil, lotion and cream. The theme in their advertising is:

> *For a hundred years now, we at Johnson & Johnson have been caring for baby-skin...That is why you cannot entrust the care of his skin to just anyone.*

It will require more than a facile brand extension to dislodge Johnson's.

We will look briefly at one other brand extension which have majored on a perceived edge communicated by the brand name itself.

Hair Oil to Skin Cream

Keo-Karpin is an undoubted success in the hair oil business. It dominates the position of 'a light, non-sticky hair oil'; it has acquired value perceptions of making a woman look well-groomed and captivating, and of modernity (see Chapter 2).

When the Keo-Karpin brand ventured into the antiseptic skin cream business in competition with the market leader Boroline, Keo-Karpin cream did not at first use the advantage inherent in the name, viz.

lightness and non-stickiness. Later, the brand extension strategy was modified to bring out the edge inherent in the name (see Exhibit 10.5).

"At last you skin can breath", said the later advertising.

> *Have you noticed how your current brand of antiseptic cream leaves a sticky film behind? And how it blocks up your pores?.. Keo-Karpin is a non-sticky antiseptic cream...so that your skin can breathe....*

The market share of the brand is reported to have moved up to 10%.

Exhibit 10.5 *Keo-Karpin antiseptic cream made progress when it adopted the strong point of the parent brand, Keo-Karpin hair oil, viz. non-sticky, thus allowing your skin to breathe. (Agency: TSA)*

North Star Extension (Exhibits 10.1, 10.3 and 10.4 Plates 23–24)

We look now at one of the best tailored examples of brand extension in India-from North Star shoes to North Star apparel.* Launched in

---

* The author is indebted to Mr D.P. Ghosh of Clarion for providing much of the information on the North Star extension.

Plate 23

Exhibit 10.2 *The name Charminar has wide acceptance and has spawned many extensions. (Courtesy: VST)*

Exhibit 10.1 *A poster for North Star denim jackets and jeans. (Agency: Clarion)*

Plate 24

Exhibit 10.4 *The North Star Spring Collection designed by Murjani of New York. (Agency: Clarion)*

Exhibit 10.3 *A Common Value Perception for North Star shoes and extension into apparel. (Agency: Clarion)*

1978, Bata's North Star brand of footwear was selling one million pairs a year by the early eighties. It had become the symbol of the easy-going, free-spirited way of life. Targeted at young, or at least young-minded, modern consumers receptive to trends from the West, North Star footwear advertising aimed to create the response:

North Star is classy, trendy, casual, vibrant and young. It is now really me.

Taking stock of international fashion trends and the unique, unchallenged position occupied by North Star shoes, casual wear favoured by the young seemed a most natural brand extension. The *fit* was apparent.

The range of apparel was designed with emphasis on denim—universal symbol of the young and free spirited. Murjani—one of the best known international names in contemporary fashion—was chosen as collaborated for the designs. In the USA, Murjani is almost synonymous with Gloria Vanderbilt jeans—with the promise of fashion and fit. The North Star range of apparel has taken advantage of Murjani's careful attention to design, fit, colour and fabric. To mix metaphors a little, one might say that for this brand extension Murjani added the cutting edge. The North Star apparel range has been positioned as:

Contemporary, distinctive, youthful, often daring, always original.

It has been divided into two categories: the core line consisting of classic designs in jeans and jackets which would remain unchanged for some time, and the fashion line garments to be made in limited volume for one season only (See Exhibit 10.4, Plate 15, and Exhibit 10.5, Plate 16).

New North Star shoes have been designed to strengthen a common value perception of comfortable fit, style, youthfulness and 'freedom'. The brand extension has been so managed as to forge an integrated whole in which shoes and apparel complement one another (Exhibit 10.6, Plate 16).

The brand extension also embraces North Star accessories which reflect the target consumer's lifestyle—belts, socks, backpacks, watches, Walkman type music systems.

The retail network has been expanded beyond Bata stores. Specially designed North Star outlets, where the mood and decor will match the North Star spirit, are being opened in all major cities.

The goal: To make North Star apparel the top-selling brand in the market for casual, trendy clothing.

Although not a major brand any longer, we have included this extension in the new edition because of its exemplary value.

Successful Extensions

The reader is urged to study the discussion on brand extensions in all excellent book entitled "The Brand Gym" by David Taylor.

Taylor points to two important considerations when exploring opportunities for brand extensions. He refers to the "Functional Stretch" and the "Emotional Stretch". The former asks if the brand has the 'competence' to offer a certain product or service. Would you expect Tesco, the highly respected supermarket chain in the U.K., to offer financial services? Apparently they did so with great success.

The second is "Emotional Stretch". Would the emotional and personality associations of the brand make the extension credible? Referring to Tesco again, noted for its good-value associations, would Tesco be successful if they ventured into diamond jewellery?

Study also Prof. Kevin Lane Keller's seminal book entitled "Strategic Brand Management" (1998) where he includes a very thorough discussion on this subject in Chapter 12.

There are many useful ideas in "Brand Asset Management" by Scott M. Devis (2002). For example, to minimise cannibalisation of your existing brand, an innovative extension should have premium pricing. And always make sure that the extension never dilutes what the parent brand stands for and make sure that consumers understand the differential value offered by the extension.

The Tylenol extensions examined in his book are revealing as for example, Tylenol PM. It began to be used by consumers, not so much for pain relief but as a sleeping pill, bolstered by the consumers' confidence in the Tylenol name. Apparently, it became a "huge business".

The book also gives the example of the Marriott Hotel brand which extends down from 'Marriott Vacation', its highest price point, to 'Fairfield Inn', its lowest, each catering to a different segment. There are six such Marriott offerings.

The Emami group in India has several strong brands and is considering viable options for extending its highly successful Navaratna Hair Oil brand and Boroplus antiseptic ointment, the market leader. Launched a few years ago, the Group's "Sona Chandi Chayavanprash" has emerged as a 'Star' in its Brand Portfolio. Encouraged by this success, the Group wishes to extend this brand to a baby oil. Their first thought has been to launch this new product branded as:

"Sona Chandi

&

Fair & Healthy Baby Oil"

The reason being that gold is believed to make the skin fair and which mother (in India!) wouldn't wish her baby to be fair? Another approach to this extension has been put forward by one member of the team:

This sense should be reflected in a better sounding brand name. The 1–2–3 will be somewhat intriguing. It signifies the oil is for babies from day 1 to 3 years.

Parentage

'Sona Chandi' is not yet a volume seller.

I would prefer: 'From Emami'

Packaging

Should suggest modernity coupled with Ayurvedic herbal goodness. Make the pack novel and striking (like the Madhuri Talc package). It should suggest: 'For Baby'.

Brand Persona

Modern, knowledgeable and confident about Ayurvedic goodness and purity.

Marketing Plan

(a) There must be adequate consumer testing of the *Product as it will be marketed,* i.e. in the appropriate package and with an accompanying concept card or leaflet. Alternative prices can be checked among matched samples.

(b) As soon as we are confident about the functional performance of the product, we should begin detailing with paediatricians and nursing homes.

(c) For this purpose we should recruit or re-train 3 to 4 sales reps to work the Kolkata market where, I suggest, we should test-market the product.

(d) Chemists will form an important part of our distribution chain.

Below the Line

(a) As part of the marketing plan, we should consider value added services like setting up 'Active & Healthy Baby Clinics', where mothers can phone (or visit) at any time for expert advice on baby emergencies like wailing with a stomachache in the middle of the night.

(b) These clinics will be manned by medical students specialising in Paediatrics, with a Doctor—on call. (Will their college accept this as part of their clinical training?).

(c) The Clinics would also give advice to mothers on other baby-related problems.

(d) In course of time Emami can design and own an *Event* like, for example:

"*Active & Healthy Baby Contents*".

(e) Sales Promotion schemes could be planned which would help mothers to feel more confident about nurturing their babies. ("What should be the proper height and weight of your baby when it is 6 months?". "What toys are most suitable when your baby is one year old?", etc). These should be related to a booklet on "How to make your baby Active & Healthy: A Guide for Mothers".

SUMMING UP

In India, and much more so abroad, we see a growing trend towards brand extension, that is, using a successful brand name in one category to enter other categories.

There are two forces driving this trend. First is the concept of *brand equity*, the realization that a successful brand name is the most coveted corporate asset, which has the power to generate profit both in its existing market and in extended markets because of the enormous goodwill which it commands. Second is the high cost of introducing an altogether new brand against established competitors.

Licensing a well-known brand to manufacturers of other products—like Coca Cola clothes—is one form of extension. The more important form is for the manufacturer of the brand to extend its name to products in other categories which it markets through its own system: Dettol antiseptic liquid to Dettol soap, for instance. It is estimated that in the USA, almost half of all the new packaged goods are brand extensions.

Trout and Ries warn against the line extension trap. They believe it weakens the generic association of the parent brand and dilutes its position.

The author's opinion is that extensions need not be a trap. They can be effectively managed by matching three criteria.

The first is *fit*. The extended brand must *fit* the new category. Management judgement should be supplemented by the study of consumer perceptions. Some findings of such research are discussed.

The second is *value perception*; it must be consistent with all the categories where the brand is extended. For example, the essential value of Gold Flake is exclusiveness, together with consistent quality, and all Gold Flake extensions represent this.

The third is *competitive edge*: the brand name should have some in-built advantage that gives it competitive strength against established brands in the new categories. Some failures are discussed.

A good example of brand extension in India—North Star shoes to North Star apparel—is discussed in some detail.

'Functional Stretch' and 'Emotional Stretch' must both be considered.

REFERENCES

1. Gamble, Theodore R., "Brand Extension", *Plotting Market Strategy*, Lee Adler (Ed.) (Simon and Schuster, 1967).
2. Tauber, Edward M., "Brand Leverage: Strategy for Growth in a Cost-control World", *Journal of Advertising Research*, August–September 1988.
3. Tauber, op. cit.
4. Alsop, Ronald and Bill Abrams, "Hitchhiking on Proven Brand Names", *The Wall Street Journal on Marketing* (Dow Jones-Irwin, 1986).
5. Kesler, Lori, "Extensions Leave Brand in New Areas", Special Report on Licensing, *Advertising Age,* (June 1, 1987).
6. Taneja, Shiv, "Franchising Mickey Mouse: The Party has Just Begun", *Business India*, (October 31–November 13, 1988).
7. Ries, Al and Jack Trout, *Positioning: The Battle for your Mind* (Warner Books by arrangement with McGraw-Hill, 1986), Chapters 12 & 13.
8. Murphy, John, "What is Branding?", *Branding—A Key Marketing Tool,* (McGraw-Hill, by arrangement with the Macmillan Press Ltd, 1987), Chapter 1.
9. Murphy, op. cit.
10. Aaker, David A. and S. Keller, *Adweek's Marketing Week,* (August 8, 1988), p. 18.
11. Crawford, Merle C., *New Products Management* (Irwin, 1987), pp 146–148.
12. Chandwani, Ajay, "Readymade Success", *A&M: Advertising and Marketing,* (May 1989).

FURTHER READING

- Green, Paul A. and Kreiger, "A Consumer Based Approach to Designing Product Line Extensions", *Journal of Product Innovation Management*, March 1987, pp 21–32.
- Kane, Chester L., "How to Increase the Odds for Successful Brand Extension", *Journal of Product Innovation Management*, September 1987, pp 199–203.
- Tauber, Edward M., "Brand Franchise Extension: New Product Benefits from Existing Brand Names", *Business Horizons*, March–April 1981, pp 36–41.

Appendix

Positioning: Definitions and Observations

Alpert, Lewis and Ronald Gatty
"The differentiation of brands by studying the ways in which their consumers differ as well as how consumer perceptions of various brands differ is termed 'product positioning'."
("Product Positioning by Behavioural Lifestyles", *Journal of Marketing*, April, 1969)

Ayer's Dictionary of Advertising Terms
Positioning:
"The art and science of fitting the product or service to one or more segments of the broad market in such a way as to set it meaningfully apart from competition."

(Philadelphia: Ayer Press, 1976)

Beckman, Kurtz, Boone
"Product positioning refers to the consumer's perception of a product's attributes, use, quality and advantages and disadvantages in relation to competing brands."

(*Foundations of Marketing*, Holt, Rinehart, 1986)

Berkowitz, Kerin, Rudelius
"Product positioning refers to the place an offering occupies in the consumer's mind on important attributes relative to competitive offerings."

(*Marketing*, Times Mirror Mosby Publishing Co., 1986)

Cravens, David W and Charles W Lamb
"We shall use the term Position to indicate how our marketing programme is perceived by the buyer relative to the programmes of our key competitors."

(*Strategic Marketing: Cases and Applications*, Irwin, 1986)

Crawford, Merle C
"Once a target market has been selected, the new product marketers must differentiate their item from products already offered to that

target group. This differentiating is called positioning the product and is now in wide spread use."

(New Products Management, Irwin, 1987)

Cundiff, Edward W, Richard R Still, Norman A P Govoni

"Positioning is significant to consumers in that it provides a basis for comparing alternative choices in the marketplace. The marketer can guide the consumer by furnishing clues to help position the product in relationship to others..."

(Fundamentals of Modern Marketing, Prentice-Hall, 1985)

Day, George S

"_Product positioning_ refers to the customer's perceptions of the place a product or brand occupies in a given market."

(Strategic Management Journal, July–September, 1981)

Ennis, F Beaven

The theory of positioning is...

"the identification of an exclusive niche in the market or the creation of a unique perception of the product that satisfies an unfulfilled consumer need and that serves to distinguish the product from competing alternatives"

(Handbook of Modern Marketing, Victor P Buell (Ed.),
McGraw-Hill, 1986)

Green, Paul E and Donald S Tull

"Brand positioning and market segmentation appear to be the hallmarks of today's marketing research. _Brand (or service) positioning_ deals with measuring the perception that buyers hold about alternative marketplace offerings."

(Research for Marketing Decisions, Prentice-Hall of India, 1986)

Hardy, Kenneth G

"Very simply, positioning is defining the package of Benefits relative to competition that will be offered to particular target segments."

(Business Quarterly, November, 1986)

Harrison, Tony

"The 'position' a product or service is said to occupy is the extremely simplified persona that the product represents in the mind of a typical consumer. It is the sum of those attributes normally ascribed to it by consumers..."

(*A Handbook of Advertising Techniques*, Kogan page, 1987)

Hehman, Raymond D

"Positioning is your product as the consumer thinks of it. Since the consumer is the ultimate user of the product, the consumer's perception of your product is what your product really is."

(*Product Management*, Dow Jones Irwin, 1984)

Holmes, John H

"... a definition of a product's position would be the perceived image consumers have of one product in relation to their perceived image of

(1) Similar products marketed by competing firms, and

(2) Kindred brands which might be offered by the innovating firm."

("Profitable Product Positioning", *MSU Business Topics*, Spring, 1973)

Kotler, Philip

Market positioning is "arranging for a product to occupy a clear, distinctive and desirable place in the market and in the minds of target consumers."

(*Marketing Essentials*, Prentice-Hall, 1984)

Macmillan's Dictionary of Marketing and Advertising

The dictionary first quotes Alpert and Gatty and then adds:

"Product positioning consists of defining end consumer needs and then developing differentiated products and services which match precisely these pre-identified requirements so that the supplier is able to focus specifically upon selected market segments."

Brand Positioning is "the policy used to ensure that the brand has a distinctive position in the marketplace, identifiable by the consuming public ... Brand Positioning (has) to ensure the brand a distinct niche in the market."

Michael J Baker (Ed.), Macmillan, 1984)

Mittelstadt, Charles A

"Positioning refers to how you want your brand 'thought about' in connection with competitors in its product category. Positioning needs to be specific to *your* brand aimed at a specific target audience."

(*Marketing Basics*, Centre for Advertising Services,
Interpublic Group, 1986)

O'Shaughnessy, John

ᵉ"The words 'Position' and 'Positioning' can often be confusing. They are used in many different ways. We define positioning as fitting the product to the segment where product performance and appeal most correspond".

(Competitive Marketing: A Strategic Approach,
George, Allen, Unwin, 1984)

Reibstein, David J

"Positioning is the activity of trying to get customers to perceive a company's product differently from the way they perceive what competitors are offering. The customer's viewpoint is the crucial aspect of product positioning."

(Marketing: Concepts, Strategies and Decisions, Prentice-Hall, 1985)

Rothschild, Michael

"Positioning refers to the place a brand occupies in the mind in relation to a given product class. This place was originally a product-related concept... concerning market structure... The concept now refers to the place that the brand holds in the consumer's mind relative to perceptions and preferences."

(Marketing Communications: From Fundamentals to Strategies,
Heath, 1987)

Ward, John

Fundamentally, a positioning is an *identity*... Every year, the competition for identity and raison d'etre hots up, rendering certain procedures mandatory... Visibility, realism and consistency in the advertising behind such a positioning are... crucial... And disciplined identification of the niche or segment likely to be turned on to the positioning is equally important.

(Chapter on 'Brand Positioning' in *How to Plan Advertising*,
Don Cowley (Ed.), Cassel, London, 1987)

Wind, Yoram, J

"... The product (brand) positioning should be assessed by measuring consumers' or organisational buyer's *perceptions* and *preference* for the product in relation to its competitors (both branded and generic).

(Product Policy: Concepts, Methods and Strategy,
Addison-Wesley Publishing Co., 1982)